D0065151

LARRY McREYNOLDS THE BIG PICTURE

Larry McReynolds
The Big Picture

My Life from Pit Road to the Broadcast Booth

By Larry McReynolds with Bob Zeller

 DAVID BULL PUBLISHING

Library of Congress Control Number: 2002109554.

ISBN: 1 893618 21 8

David Bull Publishing, logo, and colophon are trademarks of
David Bull Publishing, Inc.

Book and cover design: Tom Morgan, Blue Design, Portland, Maine

Printed in the United States

10 9 8 7 6 5 4 3

David Bull Publishing
4250 East Camelback Road
Suite K150
Phoenix, AZ 85018

602-852-9500
602-852-9503 (fax)

www.bullpublishing.com

Acknowledgments

My wife of 19 years, Linda, who told a lot of stories in the book, but mostly who has stood behind me and supported me for most of my career through many good, but a whole lot of tough times, and who during our entire marriage has made many sacrifices, but has never complained.

My three children: Brooke, Brandon, and Kendall, who for their entire lives, have spent many days and nights without their dad, who was off chasing his dream and doing what he so much enjoyed doing.

Bob Zeller and David Bull, who without their dedication and commitment, this book would never have happened. Mostly, I'm thankful for the friendship of these two guys. I'd also like to thank Steve Waid, Deb Williams, Tom Morgan, Anna Gilbert, and James Penhune for their contributions to the project.

Neil Goldberg, who has taught me so much about the broadcast field, who was good enough to let Bob Zeller take a close look behind the scenes of a race broadcast on FOX, and who I always hope I'll be working with.

Pam Miller, who stuck her neck out in 1995 and recommended the people of TNN and World Sports use me part time as a pit reporter for some of the race broadcasts. I will always be so thankful for the gamble she took on me.

David Hill, Ed Goren, Bill Brown, and Larry Jones of FOX Sports, who gave me the opportunity of a lifetime at the beginning of 2001 to stay involved with this sport and do a job that I look forward to each and every day.

Three owners in Winston Cup that I've worked for as a crew chief; Kenny Bernstein, Robert Yates, and Richard Childress, who taught me so much about winning and losing, about people, about business, and about life in general. I will always treasure their friendship, and the opportunities they gave me.

The race fans, who without their continued support, none of us would ever be able to do our job in the sport that we love and enjoy so much.

Larry McReynolds
Mooresville, N.C.
August, 2002

CONTENTS

Prologue

We were seven seconds away from having a great day on Sunday, February 18, 2001. For three hours and five minutes, the finest racers in the world, the drivers in the NASCAR Winston Cup series, had raced in a tight, frenzied pack. They had made 199 trips around the massive two-and-a-half-mile oval of Daytona International Speedway. And the week that marked my debut as a FOX network broadcaster had gone without a hitch.

But on the last lap, in the last turn, in a sudden, terrible crash about seven seconds from the finish, we had lost Dale Earnhardt, NASCAR's greatest driver. The outpouring of grief in the following days was unlike anything I had ever seen. It went far beyond our world of stock-car racing. Dale's death was national news, and his picture appeared on the cover of *Time* magazine.

I knew Dale better than most people knew him, even most of his fellow racers. For 18 of the most incredible and most difficult months of my life, I had worked with him as his crew chief. I was the man who decided how to set up his race car, the guy who made the calls on his pit stops.

Dale was a legend long before I joined him. He already had his seven Winston Cup championships when he began pestering me to come work with him for the 1997 season. By then, I had been a crew chief in NASCAR's top series for more than a decade, and I had achieved super-star status among wrench turners.

I had been Davey Allison's crew chief during his greatest days driving the famous No. 28 Texaco Havoline Ford owned by Robert Yates Racing. In the wake of Davey's tragic death in 1993, I had helped guide Ernie Irvan to some of his greatest moments before—and after—the crash that nearly killed him.

Dale and his car owner, Richard Childress, had picked me to lift their team out of the doldrums. I'd won 22 career Winston Cup races, including two Daytona 500s. Dale had only won two races in 1996 and finished in fourth place for the Winston Cup championship.

You could describe my 18 months as the crew chief of the famous black No. 3 Goodwrench Chevrolet as 'bittersweet', but that word doesn't come close to expressing all of the highs and lows. With Larry McReynolds as his crew chief in 1997, Dale ran worse than he had *ever* run in the Winston Cup series, even as a rookie. Here we thought we were going to waltz together to a record-setting eighth Winston Cup championship, and we couldn't win a single race. Yet, in 1998, Dale triumphed over his 20-year jinx to win his first and only Daytona 500.

During the lowest of the low points of that 1997 season with Dale, I began to consider a career change. Even before joining forces with Dale, I'd experimented with a different line of work in racing. In 1995, I had worked as a pit reporter on a TNN television broadcast of a Busch series race. I had a blast. And people liked the passion and the enthusiasm and the insights that I brought to my television work.

By the end of 2000, long after I'd left Dale's team, I was ready to make the switch. I joined the legendary Darrell Waltrip as a booth analyst for the FOX NASCAR racing broadcasts.

And now, the first race in my new career—my first Daytona 500 as a broadcaster—had ended in unthinkable tragedy. My first was Dale Earnhardt's last race. On the last lap. In the last turn.

I was thinking about all of this and more during the two hours I sat in the massive Calvary Church in Charlotte, waiting for Dale Earnhardt's memorial service to begin. It was Thursday, February 22, four days after the race.

The day before, Dale's wife, Teresa, and their 12-year-old daughter, Taylor Nicole, and his other children and the rest of the immediate families had said good-bye at a small, private funeral in Mooresville, where he was buried. Teresa had arranged for this larger service for Dale's friends and all of the racing fraternity. There are two balconies and 5,200 seats in Calvary Church, so even as large as the immediate NASCAR family is, all of us who came didn't come close to filling the place.

Teresa had decided to allow the service to be televised, and that had to be a tough decision. I know when my wife, Linda, and I heard about that, we were shocked. My thought was, "You're going to turn a man's funeral into a television show?" But the more I thought about it, the more I understood.

Dale's millions of fans across the country deserved a chance to say good-bye. There were many thousands of Dale Earnhardt fans, and Teresa wanted all of them to be able to see the service, since they were not allowed to attend.

FOX had asked me if I wanted to be a part of the broadcast. I said absolutely not. My broadcasting skills were simply not up to a challenge like that. It was too huge. It was too personal. At that point, all I wanted to do at the service was pay my respects. I didn't want to go on the air.

The day of the service was cold, damp, and overcast. Just to the north of us, it was sleeting and snowing. Because of the weather, Linda and I got an early start from our home on Lake Norman in Mooresville, about 20 miles north of Charlotte, for the trip all the way across the city to south Charlotte. We brought with us our oldest child, Brooke, who was 11.

We got there two hours early. The temperature was just above freezing, and you could see the breaths of the parking attendants. Buses were pulling into the parking lot carrying entire Winston Cup teams. Inside the church, it was like a cavern of quiet. The dull, gray light of the day came through a wall of windows several stories high behind the altar. Hundreds of pipes from the church's pipe organ—one of the world's largest—towered side by side behind the altar. Two huge projection screens hanging down on either side of the altar showed slides of peaceful green meadows, purple mountain ranges, golden sunsets, fast-running streams, and fields of flowers. Below them, and all across the front of the altar, were hundreds of floral arrangements. The most distinctive of them displayed a large black 3 in the center.

I sat in that church pew and just thought about things. Most of the time, I thought about Dale. Those two hours before the service were the most peaceful two hours I'd had for a long, long time.

I remembered how we had flown back to North Carolina together on Dale's jet after the race at Sears Point in Sonoma, California, in 1997. We didn't talk about the car or the race. He talked about his past, and how he had come up in racing, and about his love for his dad. Ralph Earnhardt had been a racer, too, and one of the toughest. Dale loved him, feared him, and idolized him all at the same time. When Ralph was 45, he suffered a heart attack and died in his shop in Mooresville. Dale was 22. I could tell Dale still missed him terribly.

I thought about the 1997 Southern 500 at Darlington and that scary moment when Dale passed out behind the wheel during the first lap. I thought about winning the Daytona 500 in 1998, and how everyone poured out onto pit road to salute Dale on his way to victory lane. That night, he and I did a lot of television interviews on pit road. Dale had a big ol' cigar, and he sat there just puffing away.

I thought about the day before the race, and how Dale had talked to a little girl from the Make-A-Wish Foundation on pit road after the "Happy Hour" final practice. He had stayed for 10 minutes talking to that girl, and she had given him a penny for luck. When he got back to the garage, he was on a mission. Here we were, hashing over a motor that wasn't running quite right, and all Dale cared about was getting that good-luck penny glued to the dashboard.

As I sat there in that huge church, I looked around and saw all of Dale's oldest and toughest rivals sitting with their own thoughts. These guys had had their confrontations with him, but they were truly grieving because they still loved the man and they knew what he meant to the sport.

Dale was to Winston Cup racing what Elvis Presley was to rock and roll. Rock and roll didn't stop when Elvis died, but it damn sure did change. And Winston Cup racing didn't stop when Dale Earnhardt died, but it was damn sure going to be a lot different without that black No. 3 out there with Dale behind the wheel.

I thought about Dale for a long time. Then I thought about the other drivers I had lost, or almost lost. I thought about Butch Lindley, lying there in that hospital bed in a coma, and how night after night I would talk to him, tell him stories, ask him questions, rub his feet. But he never woke up.

I thought about Davey Allison, the most focused man I've ever met. From the smallest to the biggest tasks, Davey was dedicated to everything he did. He had tried and tried to get me to be his crew chief, and I had put him off for more than a year. Then, when we finally joined forces, it was impossible to know we would be together only a little more than two years. And what an incredible time it was! We won the Daytona 500. In 1992, we survived one of the wildest years any driver has ever had in NASCAR, only to lose the Winston Cup championship in the final race because of pure, dumb bad luck. "Oh well," we said, "we'll get 'em in 1993." Then Davey was gone, taken from us in a helicopter crash.

I'd loved Davey like a brother, and after he died, I asked car owner Robert Yates if I could have the helmet Davey wore in the race at New Hampshire the day before he had the helicopter crash. Robert gave it to me, and today it is one of my most cherished possessions.

After Davey left us, God blessed us with Ernie Irvan. Ernie was an incredible driver, and I remembered how he had lifted the spirits of our team with his respect for Davey and the No. 28 car, and with his ability to flat-out drive the wheels off the thing.

And less than a year after Ernie came to us and we started winning again, we almost lost him, too. I thought about the night before Ernie's crash at Michigan in 1994 and how he'd set up a Monopoly game outside his motorcoach when I stopped by to talk about the plans for that fateful next morning. And I thought about that long, quiet drive to the hospital in Ypsilanti after Ernie crashed.

Thousands of crew chiefs have come and gone in the history of NASCAR, but none of them has a story of triumph and tragedy quite like mine. I couldn't help but wonder how many more times I would have to go to a funeral and sit in a church pew and think about someone else I'd lost. The sadness would come again, yes, but I knew that I would ultimately react as I had to every tragedy I've faced in my 26 years in the sport. I would go on. I would go to the next race and work as hard as I could to do the best job in whatever I was doing, whether it was being a crew chief or a broadcaster.

Week after week, at the great racetracks spread all across our country, the green flag inevitably starts the next race. Lap after lap, week after week, month after month, year after year, the rhythm of the Winston Cup schedule relentlessly moves us forward. You keep going because the schedule keeps going. You never give up. No matter what happens, you know you're not only part of a race team, but you're part of a business. There are mouths to feed and bills to pay. People depend on you for their livelihoods. So even if you suffer the worst tragedy of all, even if you lose your driver, you keep going.

And just as surely as I sat in that church pew that morning, I knew that 24 hours later I would be sitting in the seat of my Chevrolet Suburban, driving once more back to Rockingham for the next race, as I had for more than 20 years.

All of us in the racing fraternity go to the next race with heavy hearts, and we try to get through the weekend as quickly as possible and be done with it. And we do it again the next weekend, except it's a little easier than the one before.

It's the rhythm of racing in the NASCAR Winston Cup series, a sport that has given me all I have, and taken back a good bit of what it gave me. Through it all, I have always tried my hardest. And I never have given up. But that's a trait that harkens back to my first days as a racer back in my hometown of Birmingham, Alabama.

CHAPTER ONE

Racing with Aunt Noreen

A lot has changed since I left Birmingham, Alabama, in 1980 to pursue a career in Winston Cup. But a lot has remained the same. My old house is still there, as well as my grandparents' house, my old schools, and the gas station where my father worked on weekends.

Most of the old shopping center in our neighborhood, Five Points West, is closed. But across the street, my Little League ball field is still there. And behind that, they still race every Friday night in the summer at Birmingham International Raceway.

They were racing at BIR back in 1959, when I was born. I came into the world on January 10, the only child of Mary Crump McReynolds and Lawrence Joseph McReynolds Jr. They named me Lawrence Joseph McReynolds III. I was born at Carraway Medical Center.

My dad, who was always known as "Buck," worked as a crane operator at the U.S. Steel plant in Birmingham. My mother was a housewife, but served as resident manager of the Warrior Terrace apartments in the Five Points West neighborhood, which is on the western edge of Birmingham. Since my mom managed the place, we lived there for free in a tiny one-bedroom apartment at the front of the complex. All it had was a living room, kitchen, bedroom, and bathroom. I shared the bedroom with my parents.

I don't remember a lot about the place. But when I was five or six years old, I got a go-cart for Christmas, and I can remember wearing a big circle into the gravel parking area out behind our apartment, driving that go-cart around and around and around that little lot.

My mom wanted so much to get us out of the little apartment and into a home of our own where I could have my own bedroom. But my dad wouldn't do it. He was very conservative, and he wanted to stay in that apartment because of the deal we got. That was one of the things that led to their divorce.

After being married for 16 years, my mom and dad decided that they simply didn't love each other anymore. They just didn't agree on a lot of things. When I was seven, they divorced. It was tough. I was an only child. It forced me to do a lot of growing up at an early age. Still, they had what you would call a good divorce. They both loved me and continued to be very involved in my life. And my dad would still come over and have dinner with us every once in a while.

My mom had to go out and get a job. She became a telephone operator on the switchboard at Baptist Medical Center in Birmingham. She worked a lot of days and many night shifts. Fairview Elementary, where I went to school, was right behind the home of my maternal grandparents, James and Mary Rogers. So I would stay with Pa-Pa and Na-Na four or five nights a week because it was more convenient for my mother's schedule. They had a little sleeping porch out back that became my room. At eight in the morning, I'd hear the bell for classes and head out the back gate and across the schoolyard. I was a good student—all As and Bs.

My Aunt Noreen also lived there when I was growing up. She's 10 years older than me, so when I was in elementary school, she was a teenager. We were more like brother and sister than nephew and aunt. I could go to her and talk about anything. She was a definite hot-rodder. She had a 1965 or 1966 Malibu Super Sport with a four-speed manual transmission. She stayed in trouble with the police because of that hot rod. When I graduated from elementary school, I stopped staying at my grandparents' house and went back to live with my mother, but I spent nearly as much time with my father. In spite of the divorce, we remained a very close family, even after my dad remarried when I was a junior in high school.

I loved sports and played all of them when I was growing up. I played on the high school golf team. I played Little League baseball and football. I was the catcher on the baseball team and center on the football team. My dad was always a coach, and let me tell you, he made it hard on me. My dad made me live harder than anybody else on the ball team.

I also worked as a kid. My mom and dad both believed in work, and they held two jobs each. My dad worked weekends at the local Gulf station. My mom's second job was at the coat-check room at the Tutweiler Hotel. So I worked, too. I helped my mom at the coat-check room, and during the summer I helped my dad at the Gulf station, pumping gas, cleaning windshields, and checking the oil and tires so he could devote his time to the repair work he was doing.

The Alabama State Fairgrounds is right next to my old Five Points West neighborhood, and its most prominent feature is the Birmingham International Raceway. BIR is a five-eighths-mile asphalt track with a large, enclosed grandstand on the front straight. It looks kind of like a horse track, but there's been auto racing there since the early part of the 20th century. It's a tough circuit—a large, short track, with long, fast straights and long, flat turns. Some drivers, even some more prominent ones, never seemed to get the hang of the place. BIR is where I had my first look at auto racing. I was nine years old.

BIR has always held weekly races during the summer, but my first race was when all the big NASCAR stars came to town for a 100-mile Grand National event on June 8, 1968. Mom and Dad had no interest in racing. But my grandfather enjoyed it and my aunt was a big fan, so they took me with them. The track was about two blocks from Pa-Pa's house, and we walked to the race. More than 5,000 fans crowded into BIR that day.

This was before Grand National became Winston Cup in 1972, and NASCAR's big league still had a 49-race schedule that included many small tracks across the southeast, including Birmingham. Actually, 1968 was the last year the Grand National series came to Birmingham. Richard Petty won the 1968 race, and I can still see him in that blue Plymouth circling the track. He ran away with the race, leading all but one of the 160 laps. Eighteen drivers had started, including Bobby Allison, David Pearson, and Bobby Isaac.

In 1973, Noreen had been dating a man named Butch Mears for about five months, and they decided to get married. Noreen got her own place with Butch, and they continued to come to the local races at BIR on a regular basis with me and my grandfather. My dad also started taking me to Talladega Superspeedway to see the Winston Cup races. I think he came to enjoy it, too, because it was, and still is, such a spectacle. Even if you're not a race fan, Talladega has to be overwhelming when you see it for the first time.

They used to let the fans come down on the track after the races. One time my dad and I went down. We walked down the frontstretch to turn four and in that time-honored tradition of fans, we walked up the 33-degree banking. It took us a couple of minutes, but we made it. My dad couldn't believe how steep it was, and that got him laughing so hard he could barely climb up.

I always encouraged my dad to get seats where we could see the garage. On race morning, I loved to sit and watch guys like Harry Hyde, Leonard Wood, and Junior Johnson prepare their cars. I thought it would be just the greatest thing to be able to work on race cars for a living.

In the spring of 1975, when I was finishing 10th grade at Ensley High School, Butch, Noreen, and I came out for opening day at BIR. The track was starting a new division—street stock hobby. You took a two-door sedan, took all the windows out of it, all the interior out of it, mounted the gas tank in the trunk, did a little work on the motor, put some racing tires on, and you went out and raced.

There were two cars on that first day. One was driven by a man, and the other was driven by a woman. I can still remember their names—Mike Ray and Kathy Speakman. They raced each other. Mike won.

"I can do that," my aunt said. "I want to do that."

"Well," Butch said jokingly, "Go out and get you some sponsors, and we'll build you one."

That was the wrong thing to tell Aunt Noreen. She went out and rounded up more sponsors than she could put on the car. Butch didn't have anyone to help him build that car, except me, and I didn't know anything at all about cars.

But we built one. It was a 1965 or '66 Chevrolet Caprice. We got the car from Charles Finley, who ran an auto salvage yard where my uncle worked. Noreen and Butch lived in Ensley, the town just west of our neighborhood. Their little house was on a steep hill overlooking the steel mills, and the entire bottom floor of the house was a garage with a back entrance. There was room for one car.

We didn't have a lot of tools or equipment. We didn't even have a vise. When Butch and I were installing the roll bar, I was his vise. I'd hold that bar and he'd cover me with a fender cover. Then he'd go to work grinding on that bar. Some nights we'd work late, and sometimes I'd fall sound asleep under that fender cover, holding that roll bar while he was grinding on it.

When we got out to the track and started racing, and then worked on the car after racing it, I was hooked. All I wanted to do was work on that car and race it. My interest in all other sports melted away.

It was during this time that Butch got me a part-time job at the auto salvage yard where he worked. It was in the Hooper City neighborhood of north Birmingham. It's about a 20-minute car ride from the Five Points West neighborhood, so my dad bought me my first car. I had to pay for the gas and insurance. It was a green 1971 Ford Pinto.

That green Pinto was all the car I needed, and it was the only car I ever had in Birmingham. As much as I loved racing, I didn't really care about my own wheels. As much as I wanted to work on race cars, I never had a need to go fast, or even the desire. All I needed was some basic transportation to get back and forth from home to the salvage yard. And believe me, that's all that old Pinto was—basic transportation.

I didn't know a lot about cars when I showed up for work at the salvage yard. The first thing that the owner, Charles Finley, told me to do was go out and pull the brake rotors off a group of cars that had recently arrived. I didn't know what a brake rotor was. I didn't dare ask Charles Finley. I went and asked my uncle, and he got me started pulling the parts.

At first all I had was an old toolbox with a pair of pliers, a screwdriver, and a hammer. But I started buying tools. And every time I'd encounter a part that had to be removed with a special tool, I'd find that tool.

I threw myself into the job like I threw myself into racing. Sometimes I'd work so late there that I'd just spend the night in the mobile home next to the office. I wouldn't go home. And when I went out in that yard, I was on a mission. I would not come back without the part.

I did some pretty crazy stuff to get parts. The gasoline tanks used to be held to the frame by two metal straps. I wouldn't think a thing about lighting a cutting torch and snipping those two gas-tank straps. Charles told me, "Larry, you're going to blow yourself up one of these days."

But I never even had a fire. Whatever it took to pull a part, that's what I did. To the best of my memory, I never came back up to the office and told Charles I couldn't get a part off. Bolts could be rusted and pieces could seem impossible to get to, but I always figured out a way. Charles taught me a lot. He taught me how to deal with people, and how to develop a successful business. He understood how to price parts to maximize sales. By the time I left in 1980, I was all but running that junkyard for Charles.

If we got a little tight on money, we'd load a flatbed tractor-trailer truck with junked cars. It wasn't too far to the scrap metal place, and we'd get pretty good money—$300 to $400—for a load of junked cars. If you stacked them right, you could get seven or eight cars on the trailer.

I got the trailer loaded one day, took a step back, and thought, "Man, I got them things up there pretty high." But then I figured, "Ah, it'll be all right."

Charles came out and said, "Larry, you got them cars stacked pretty high, don't you?"

"Yeah," I said. "Probably a little higher than normal. But I think they'll be OK."

One of my uncles had a tractor-trailer license, and he drove the truck to the scrap metal yard. When he came back, an unmarked police car was following him. My uncle had wiped out every traffic light between the salvage yard and the scrap metal place—probably about a dozen lights. They fined Charles fairly substantially for it, too. But I think

Charles was amused more than anything else. He didn't even reprimand me. Of course, he'd seen the loaded truck, too.

An automobile salvage yard is one hell of a place for your first job. There isn't a hotter place on Earth in the summer, or a colder place in winter. I used to do all kinds of things to stay cool or warm. I had pocket warmers, battery powered heater socks—you name it, I had it.

Halfway through high school, I decided I was not going to go to college. I changed my curriculum so that my classes ended at noon. That way, I could work at the salvage yard and make money in the afternoons. Then, in the evenings, I'd go work on my aunt's race car. I was so fixated on racing that I didn't do much socially. There were four or five guys I'd sometimes hang around with, but only once a month or so on a Friday night.

One of the local sponsors who agreed to help out my aunt was Pepsi. They wanted her to take her race car up to Talladega for the Winston Cup race and drive around the track during the parade lap. Butch drove, and I sat over on the right side floorboard. Noreen was in the back, sitting up through the open back window, wearing her driver's uniform and waving to everyone. We thought we were something.

Before the race started, they let us in the garage and pits. I walked past David Pearson and thought, "There's the Silver Fox. This guy is almost like a god." I can relate to how excited fans get when they see a great race-car driver up close, because I know that's how I felt when I walked a few inches from David Pearson.

We didn't have access to the pits during the race, so we watched from a motorhome owned by friends. It was parked in the infield. And that day was the first time I got a taste of the infamous infield crowd at Talladega. Near the end of the race, I looked down from the motorhome and saw six or eight men *and* women start fighting each other like cats and dogs. It was an all-out brawl. When I say fighting, I mean hitting each other with bottles, pulling hair, throwing stuff, blood flying everywhere. I thought, "My Lord, why did these people even come to the race?"

I went to most of the Talladega races during my racing years in Birmingham, usually with Charles Finley, who had some good friends who parked their motor home outside the track and spent the weekend there.

We'd go up there on Friday afternoon after work. There wasn't enough room in their little Winnebago for me, so I slept in the back of Charles's station wagon. We'd do some pretty heavy drinking Friday, go to the Saturday race, drink some more, and go to the big race on Sunday. Normally on Sunday morning, I wasn't exactly ready to jump right out of the back of that station wagon. Sometimes I wasn't feeling the greatest when I took my seat in the grandstands.

I worked on my aunt's race car during the 1975 and 1976 seasons. But Noreen never really had any great success racing. It wasn't long before I felt like I was spinning my wheels. I needed a bigger challenge than what our little family team could provide.

By the summer of 1976, I was totally hooked on racing. I knew I wanted to work on race cars more than anything else. By then I had even seen my first Daytona 500 in person. If I was going to pursue racing as a career, I needed to do something different than work on my aunt's hobby stock car.

One Saturday afternoon at the salvage yard in the fall of 1976, Charles said, "Larry, I'm going to drive up to Nashville tonight to watch Bobby Ray and them race. Want to go with me?"

"Yeah," I said.

Bobby Ray Jones was a local businessman who owned one of the most competitive race cars that ran at BIR. Charles Finley gave him a little money, and Bobby Ray's car advertised the junkyard. His driver was a local racer named Richard Orton.

We closed the yard at about 2 p.m. that day and off to Nashville we went. The race was at the Fairgrounds Speedway. When we went into the pits, I was mesmerized by everything I saw, but more then anything I wanted to *do* something. I felt awkward at first, but I eased my way in with the team. I'd help push the car or pick up tires—anything to help out. Well, by the time the night ended, I was right in there, digging with them.

Even though I'd worked on my aunt's car, I was still three steps below a rookie. After the race, before they could push the car on the trailer, they had to take off the spoiler underneath the front bumper. I grabbed a wrench and started turning one of the bolts that kept the spoiler attached. The bolt wouldn't turn, but I kept pushing until it broke off. Only then did I realize I had been *tightening* the bolt, not loosening it.

But Bobby Ray saw my enthusiasm and how eager I was to work. After we loaded the car, he turned to me and said, "If you ever get tired helping your aunt, you can come on over and help us out any time you want."

For the next week, all I could think about was Bobby Ray's offer. Finally, I called him.

"We'd love to have you help us," he said, "but what about Noreen?"

"She's probably not going to do much more than what she's doing right now, and I really want to work on a top-notch car that has a chance to win," I said.

"Larry," he said, "All you have to do is come out here. We work almost every night on this thing. But it's going to be just like when you were working for Noreen. I don't pay anybody. I can't afford to. We just barely make it to the track each week."

When I told Noreen what I was going to do, she blew up. She was livid. After all, it was just her and me and Butch. She was very bitter when I left. We didn't speak for almost a year, but we got over it. Noreen went ahead and continued to race for almost 10 years. She even ran in some All-Pro races—a step up from the local weekly events.

Once I began working for Bobby Ray, I really started burning the candle at both ends. My high school grades began to slip, but all I wanted was to do well enough to graduate.

I'd go to school in the morning, then make the 20-minute drive over to the salvage yard and work all afternoon there. Then I'd hop in my Pinto for another 20-minute drive over to Minor, a suburb northwest of Birmingham where Bobby Ray lived and had his shop.

When I started in 1976, Bobby Ray's car was a Pontiac LeMans. Richard Orton won the track championship that year without winning a race. That didn't bother me. I knew I was with a competitive team, and just the opportunity to work at the level was enough for me, at least for starters.

That October, in the second month of my senior year of high school, I drove all the way up to Charlotte Motor Speedway (now Lowe's Motor Speedway). I was still only 17 years old. Richard had landed a ride in a Sportsman's race at Charlotte. He asked me if I wanted to be on his crew.

When I got out of school Friday, I threw my stuff together and lit out of Birmingham in my little Pinto. I finally got up there late Friday night or early Saturday morning. Qualifying was Saturday and Richard missed the show. Richard and his dad decided to head right back to Birmingham. I needed some rest, so they let me have the room.

I was like a lost puppy on an island in Charlotte that Saturday night. I wandered downtown, found a movie theater, and saw *Marathon Man* with Dustin Hoffman. Then I got a good night's rest and drove back to Birmingham on Sunday. I didn't even go to the race.

In 1977, I graduated from high school. The Ensley High School senior prom was on a Thursday night and graduation rehearsal was the next morning. The prom was at the downtown Sheraton Hotel, and I wore a baby blue tuxedo. Not long after the prom got going, I took my date home and went back to the hotel. A group of us guys had rented a room, and we partied and played cards all night long. When it came time for rehearsal, I was still wearing my baby blue tux.

After rehearsal, I drove up to Nashville as quick as I could for Friday night qualifying for a big feature race at the fairgrounds. After the race on Saturday, I turned around and drove back home on Saturday night for my graduation on Sunday. It's only 180 miles from Nashville to Birmingham on Interstate 65, but that was one of the many Saturday nights when it seemed like the longest road in the world.

I had all sorts of tricks to stay awake. I'd take a cooler full of ice and set it on the seat beside me and take ice and rub it on my forehead and face. Or I'd take a broken toothpick and lodge it between two of my teeth to irritate me enough to stay awake.

After I finished high school, I began working full time at the salvage yard. And I spent three or four nights a week working at Bobby Ray's place. Bobby Ray Jones and his wife, Linda, became almost a second mom and dad to me.

We didn't do a whole lot of racing in 1977. But Bobby Ray was doing a lot of work on other team's cars, and I was helping him. I was set on learning as much as I could. Bobby Ray wasn't paying me a dime, of course, and a lot of people thought I was getting ripped off. Charles Finley used to wear me out about it. But the way I looked at it, this was my college. I had a job. And I wasn't looking to make a lot of money.

Money wasn't important to me, as long as I could buy gas, pay my car insurance, and make ends meet.

My hope was that Bobby Ray would take that money he was making from working on other race cars and put it back into racing. And he did. It's just that, in 1977, he didn't feel like he had the best opportunity. And Bobby Ray was one of the most adamant racers about not wanting to race unless he had a chance to win.

In 1978, Bobby Ray decided he wanted to race again. So we started building a Camaro race car. Pretty soon we began hearing who was going to drive it, and that man was one of the greatest drivers NASCAR had ever known.

CHAPTER TWO

They Nicknamed Our Team "Cakewalk"

n the spring of 1978, as we were busy preparing our new Camaro late-model stock car, Bobby Ray Jones made arrangements with Birmingham International Raceway to have Cale Yarborough drive it in one of the major midsummer features.

Cale Yarborough! I could hardly believe I would be working as a crew member for the great Cale Yarborough. In 1978, he was almost unbeatable in the Winston Cup series. He'd won the championship in 1976 and 1977 and was on his way to a third consecutive title.

It was an off weekend for Winston Cup, and Cale was moonlighting with Bobby Ray's one-race deal at Birmingham. I had the feeling he was going to come in there, kick everybody's asses, and take their names.

We painted the car red, and because Cale was driving it, we put the number 11 on it, which was the number of his Winston Cup car at the time. Qualifying was on Saturday and the race was on Sunday. Cale came down, qualified the car, and flew back home. He came back the next day, started the race, and promptly burned the brakes off the car. Sixty laps into the race, we were done.

Cale was friendly, but it didn't bother him very much when the car fell out. And he was out that back gate during the very next caution period. As I watched Cale walk out the back gate and looked at my race car with burned brakes, I thought, "Well, this wasn't such a special deal after all."

We ran a few more races that summer. We hired Neil Bonnett, who was from Hueytown, Alabama, to drive the car in a couple of races. Neil was just entering his prime as Winston Cup driver, and he ran really fast in our car. We thought we had a shot at winning one race, but he got tangled up with another car on the backstretch and wrecked big time. We spent the next few weeks repairing the car, but there was a kink in the left frame rail after that crash. It didn't seem to make much difference—the car was still fast.

Dave Mader III, a local racer whose father was also a well-known local driver, had been roaming around that summer without a ride. So Bobby Ray offered the seat to him, and we began preparing the car for the 125-lap feature on Labor Day night, which ended the racing season at BIR.

We had a choice of tires for that race. We could buy softer tires, which would make us faster, or we could buy harder tires, which were slower but lasted longer. Bobby Ray was pretty conservative and didn't want to spend a lot of money on tires, so we bought the harder ones. Most of the other teams weren't too worried about their tire bill and bought the softer tires.

When the race started, Dave fell back. In 10 or 15 laps, the leaders had put three-quarters of a lap on Dave. It looked bad for us. But slowly he began regaining the lost ground. And by lap 60, the tires on the other cars were worn out, and they were slipping and sliding around the track. Dave took the lead just past lap 100 and went on to win.

I'd been working on race cars for four years, but until then, I'd never won a race. There's just no way to describe how rewarding it was to finally win—and it just made me want to race that much more.

During the remainder of the 1978 season, we went to a number of the big autumn features in the area. We sat on the pole just about everywhere we went. And we damn near won all of the races, too. We won at Opp, Alabama. We won at Montgomery. We won at Mobile. We finished second at Jackson, Mississippi. And we ended the 1978 season with a huge victory in the Snowball Derby in Pensacola, Florida. It's one of the season's biggest races for short-track, late-model sportsmen drivers. Mark Martin, who at that time was competing for (and would win) the American Speed Association championship, pulled in there with his professional truck and trailer. We arrived in a pickup truck with a camper shell, pulling our car on a little trailer.

We didn't have radios, and we didn't want to be at a disadvantage, so we pooled our money, came up with $100, and leased radios for that race—one for the car, one for the pits. We battled Mark tooth and nail during the final 50 laps and beat him.

By then, I was effectively the crew chief of the team, because I was putting so much time into the car. And we were winning so many races that our team was nicknamed "Cakewalk." The pressure was worse than when we were not winning. We dreaded the thought of losing, and wondered when it would happen.

Dave drove for us throughout the 1979 season. We ran at BIR most of the time, but not regularly enough to win the track championship. That didn't matter to me. We had won a championship in 1976 without winning a race. Now all I wanted to do was win races. That was much more rewarding. And we did a lot of winning. We probably won three out of every five races. When we pulled through that gate, you could almost hear them all moan, "Oh man, here's that 11 car. We're in trouble."

Winning that much, of course, makes people angry at you. Fans and competitors start getting on you. Tempers can flare. When we were running with Dave in 1979, he and a Georgia driver named Jody Ridley were the worst of rivals. They hated each other. One weekend in Huntsville in 1979, Dave and Jody started on the front row. Jody was on the pole and had the first pit. Next to him was Don Sprouse, who was running a car owned by a fellow named Bob Rogers out of Greenville, South Carolina. We had the next pit.

Jody and Dave ran the first 50 or 75 laps side by side, beating and banging on each other just about every lap. Well, they finally wrecked. We ended up with the worst of the deal. The toe-out (the small amount the front tires are turned out) was knocked way in. But we fixed the damage and sent Dave back out there.

Biddle Ridley, Jody's brother, thought we were going back out only to wreck Jody. You know what? He was probably right, except something was still wrong with the car. As Dave brought the car back off the track, I looked up and saw Biddle standing there with a ball peen hammer in his hand.

When we saw this, our entire team immediately headed toward the Ridley pits. And they were coming toward us. A huge fight broke out right in the middle of Bob Rogers's pit. Well, we fought and we fought and we fought. We fought so long, we destroyed Bob's pit.

But I'm not much of a fighter. Jody's son, Anthony, had me on the ground, and I thought he was going to kill me. I had a gold chain around my neck, and he was twisting it so hard I knew I was going to suffocate. Finally, the chain broke.

I could hear one of our crewmen, Al Hall, screaming at me, "Bite him! Bite him!" And I thought, "How can I bite him? I can't even breath." As the fighting began to spill onto the racetrack, cops and security guards finally came out of the grandstands. When I heard someone say ""Huntsville Jail," I stopped fighting. So did everyone else. Nobody was really hurt and nobody got arrested, but I doubt Bob Rogers thought too kindly of his neighbors on either side.

I don't think any of us said a word on the drive back to Birmingham. Bobby Ray's wife was with us, and when we pulled into their driveway, she got out of that truck, looked at all of us in disgust, and said, "Let me tell every one of you something. If this is what it's come down to—if this is what it's going to be like at the racetrack—you all will never race another race out of this garage as long as you live." Needless to say, we got her message.

One of the neatest things that happened to me in 1979 came after we won a Sunday afternoon race at BIR. When Dave was in victory lane, someone called me up there to have a picture taken with him. I was as grubby as a crew chief could be. We'd been racing a couple or three days. My hair was kind of long, mostly because I hadn't had time to get a haircut. My white T-shirt was as black as night.

But when they called me up there, I suddenly found myself in the middle of a ceremony. The track was giving me their Jimmy Morris Sportsmanship Award. The award was named for a local driver who had lost his life in a tragic highway accident. Jimmy's son and daughter were there to present it to me. I was really proud to receive it, because some of the racers who had won before me included Bobby Allison, Neil Bonnett, and Red Farmer.

Racing had become my life. During the late seventies, four of us worked on the race car. Me, Bobby Ray, Tommy McCoy, and Al Hall. All that mattered to me back then was the challenge of preparing a piece of equipment to its greatest potential and matching wits with others who were doing the same thing. I became obsessed with trying to outsmart and outwit the other teams, and the one sure way I knew how to do it was to outwork them.

From 1978 until 1980 when I left Birmingham, you could almost set a clock to my schedule. I'd get up and be at the salvage yard at eight o'clock. I'd work until five. Then I'd head straight over to Bobby Ray's place in Minor, stopping just long enough at a McDonald's or Burger King to grab something to go.

Al Hall says they all knew when I was coming because they could hear that old Pinto puttering up the street. It may have been the butt of a lot of jokes, but Al also said, "We made sure we kept that little old car running."

One or two nights a week, I would work all night long on that race car and quit just in time to go home, clean up, shower, and get back to the salvage yard by 8 a.m.

I came up with a little trick, especially during the summer, to get some rest during those long, hot days at the salvage yard. I'd go out there and get underneath one of the old, wrecked cars, where it was nice and cool in the shade. I'd take two shop towels and tie them around my wrists. Then I'd put my hands above the driveshaft and tie the towels together so my hands were supported up there. If somebody looked out, they could see me under the car with my hands up there as if I was working. But I'd be taking a hell of a good power nap. That's all I needed—20 or 30 minutes—just a little something to restore my energy.

I didn't do much of anything other than race and work. I didn't date. From the time I became old enough to date until I left Birmingham, the number of dates I had you could count on both hands and still have a few fingers left over. It wasn't that I didn't like girls. I just loved racing.

In 1980, Dave decided to leave us. He had been offered a new ride by these folks out of Jackson, Mississippi, who owned a cattle company. They offered him not only a race car to drive, but also a full-time job maintaining the car and a percentage of the winnings. It was an offer he couldn't refuse.

Dave tried to get me to go with him. But even though I was young and eager, I just didn't have a good feeling about the whole deal. And I couldn't see picking up and moving to Jackson. My instincts told me not to go, so I didn't. Dave's deal came apart about halfway through the season.

About the time Dave left, a Tennessee driver named Mike Alexander called up Bobby Ray. Mike was struggling to run his own deal out of Franklin, but he had a sponsor, Century Construction. So Bobby Ray gave him the ride.

For me, the hardest thing about the transition was repainting the race car. We had won so many races with that little red No. 11 Camaro. We called it "The Red Bird." Now we had to paint it white and change the number to 84—Mike's number. The Red Bird was our baby, and it liked to have killed us to change it. We had the painter paint "In Memory of The Red Bird" in little bitty words on the back.

Mike put the "new" car on the pole in its first race on a Sunday afternoon. Dave sat on the outside pole in his new ride. I prepared myself for the worst. I had always thought that Dave was the reason we were winning so much. I was so disappointed when he left. And I didn't have much confidence in Mike because he seemed almost too nice. I was afraid he wouldn't be aggressive enough on the track. He was a small guy, and we called him "Little Mike."

Mike proved me wrong right away. There was nothing little about him when he was driving a race car. He went out there and won that race. Dave didn't even finish second. I realized that maybe it was more the car than the driver. It gave me a lot of confidence in what I was doing. And it gave me a lot of confidence in Mike Alexander.

With the sponsorship that Mike brought with him, we could race more during 1980 than we ever had before. So we raced all over the Southeast. If we raced at Birmingham on Friday night, we'd go up to Nashville for the Saturday races there. Or if we went to Pensacola for the Friday night show, we drove over to Mobile or Jackson, Mississippi, for the Saturday night shows there. And it didn't matter whether it was at BIR, Nashville, Pensacola, Mobile, or Jackson, we usually won.

We had a crew cab dually with a trailer, and we'd often stuff seven people in that truck. Bobby Ray would get us a hotel room, but usually just one. We'd make sure we got two double beds. That way, we could drag the mattresses off the box springs and actually have four beds. And we'd put as many people in that room as we could fit. We'd much rather buy a set of new tires for our race car than have two nice hotel rooms.

We did the craziest things to race. One weekend in May 1980, we went up to Nashville for a Friday night feature. Little Mike also had another ride. He had been hired in a one-race deal to drive D. K. Ulrich's car in the Winston Cup race at Nashville that day—his first Winston Cup race.

We were standing in the pits before the race in Nashville when a guy who worked for Junie Donlavey in Richmond came up to Bobby Ray. Junie's guy said, "Hey, I just talked to Paul Sawyer in Richmond and he's running a big race there tomorrow and he's only got 11 cars. He wanted to know if you guys could come up there and help him out. He said he'd pay some of your tire bill and some of your expenses."

I looked at Bobby Ray and Bobby Ray looked at me and I said, "Heck, what have we got to lose but a little sleep?" Mike qualified 12th for the Winston Cup race and ran pretty well to finish 10th. Afterward, we loaded him in our truck and off to Richmond we went. It was well after midnight before we left. Well, you can't hardly get to Richmond from Nashville. It's more than 600 miles and all the way across the Appalachian Mountains. We finally got to Richmond about 11 or 12 on Sunday morning. They were running a Goody's Dash race, so the gates were closed to the infield.

None of us had ever been to the Richmond track, which back then was called Richmond Fairgrounds Raceway and was an old half-mile track. So we sat there at the back gate looking over the fence, and just by eyeballing the track we had to *guess* at what gear we needed to run. I actually changed the gear while the car was on the trailer, as we waited at the gate.

Paul Sawyer only managed to get 11 other cars, but my oh my, the 11 he had were driven by some of the finest short-track drivers in the country: Bob Senneker, Ed Howe, Jody Ridley, Butch Lindley, Mark Martin. We finished about sixth that day. Neil Bonnett won. Everybody was tearing up tires as fast as the crews could put them on the cars. Nobody could make their tires last.

About 100 laps into the race, we had one brand of tire on one side and a different brand on the other side. We'd already torn up four sets. After the race was over, we all piled into the truck and drove back to Birmingham. You can get to Birmingham from Richmond. But this time, the trip was *705* miles.

We drove through the night Sunday. And when we got back to Birmingham, I drove the truck and trailer straight to the junkyard and went to work. I had not been in a bed since I got up Saturday morning. I'm sure I spent part of that Monday underneath a car with my hands tied to the driveshaft.

This kind of flat-out pace was routine. And I still wasn't making any money from racing. It always *cost* me money to race when I was in Birmingham. I bought my gas. I bought my own food. During the six years I was racing in Birmingham, I never made one penny working on a race car.

I had reached a point where I needed to figure out how to make a living at racing. My lifestyle was killing me. I was only 21 years old, and I weighed about 155 pounds and stayed sick all the time. By that time I was living on my own, sharing a rented apartment with my cousin and his wife, who were six or seven years older than me. I was shortcutting work at the salvage yard. I took a lot of Fridays off so we could make the four-hour drive down to Pensacola and race there on Friday night. And I would often work all night Thursday getting the car ready.

"How long can a person do this?" I wondered. I knew I wanted to work on race cars more than anything else, so I needed to figure out how to make a living doing it. And my dream was to make it into the Winston Cup series.

In May of 1980, we went to Charlotte to run our car in a Busch series race. Darrell Waltrip, who was racing in the 600, wandered by our pits and put the radio headset on for a few moments and talked to Little Mike. I tried hard to impress Darrell and show him what a good mechanic I was and how organized I was. I wanted so badly to break into Winston Cup racing—to get someone to notice me.

That spring, Charles Finley and I had begun having disagreements over how to run the salvage yard. The biggest problem was that I'm the type of guy who wants to finish something when I start it. Charles was the type of guy who focused on whatever would make him the most money the fastest.

One day, it all came to a head. I had probably been working on the race car throughout the previous night. And the argument had to have been over a trivial matter. More than likely, I was trying to get a $75 fender delivered to someone by noon as promised, and Charles wanted me to drop that and get a $650 motor delivered.

I was all but running the yard by then, but Charles made sure I knew who was the boss. I decided I wasn't going to take it anymore. I walked out, and I remember screaming at him as I left. I was probably telling him where he could stick his junkyard.

The owner of another junkyard—A & S Auto Parts—down in Bessemer, just a few miles west of Birmingham, heard I'd left Finley. He called me up and said, "Why don't you come on down here and go to work for me?" So I went to work for him.

One day I was in a rush to check something, and I ran through the back door going about 100 mph and ran smack into the blades of a fork-lift that had been carelessly parked right outside the door. Next thing I knew, I was on the ground with blood pouring out of my forehead. I mean, one of those forks just gashed my forehead right open. It took eight or nine stitches to close the cut.

The doctor told me to stay home and take it easy, so I sat around the house for a week in late June. I watched every soap opera I could watch and read every magazine I could read. NASCAR used to put out a small newsletter, so I sat on the couch and read that, too. I got to the last page and at the bottom were four or five little advertisements. One of those ads caught my eye.

HELP WANTED – New racing team looking for young ener-getic second-in-command to become crew chief. Plan to run for Rookie-of-the-Year in 1981. Contact Dana Williamson, Rogers Racing Team, Greenville, S. C.

I called and talked with Dana, whose father, Bob Rogers, owned the team. We'd raced against him a little bit. And, unfortunately, that big fight we'd had with Jody Ridley's team happened right in the middle of his pit. I hung up the phone thinking I was probably just one of 10 million mechanics trying to get the job. And even if I wasn't one of 10 million, I figured I had no chance after getting into that fight. I didn't hear anything for a few weeks. But one day in late July or early August, Dana called back and told me they were planning to run a car in the season finale at BIR — a Monday night race on Labor Day weekend.

"How about if we get up with you then?" she asked. "And you can just come back to Greenville with us. We're going to run in two or three more Winston Cup races this season with Don Sprouse as our driver. You can come work with us for a few weeks. We'll see if we like you and you can see if you like us, and we'll go from there."

I worked on Little Mike's car at Bobby Ray's place all day and night Saturday, all day and all night Sunday, and on Monday morning before we went out to the track. It was hard to leave Bobby Ray and the guys. But when Bob Rogers and his team came through that gate with the No. 37 car, I shook Bobby Ray's hand, said good-bye to Little Mike and the crew, and started working on Bob Rogers's car.

Little Mike sat on the pole and won the race. And it's the only time in my career when I was working on one race car but really pulling for another car to win. That night, I rode back to Greenville with Bob Rogers. I alternated staying with the Rogers and the Sprouses for the next couple of weeks while I worked at the shop. Pretty soon, Bob said, "Boy, Larry, we'd love for you to commit to us and move up here."

So when we got a little break, I flew back home, got my Pinto, rented a U-Haul, loaded my stuff, and went back to Greenville. I was scared to death when I left Birmingham. My mom and dad and all of my family were there. But I would be racing for a living. I wanted to find out if I was doing the right thing, and I wanted to ask someone whose opinion would not be biased in any way. So just before I went to Greenville, I visited Donnie Allison over at the Allison shop in Hueytown.

When I got there, Donnie was working on this little All-Pro car. Donnie is as hard-core as they come, and the whole time we talked, he never quit working on that race car. I told him about the opportunity I had with Rogers.

Donnie paused for a second, looked me straight in the eye, pointed his finger at me and said: "I'm going to tell you two things, boy. You just *think* you've worked hard on those cars for Bobby Ray Jones. Boy, you don't know what hard work is yet. And another thing. You know that race you guys won out there at BIR with Little Mike a few weeks ago? Well, you'd better find that checkered flag and hold onto it tight, because it's going to be a long damn time before you ever see another one!"

CHAPTER THREE

Some Doors Open, More Doors Close

You remember a lot of things about your career, like your first win and your first pole. But my first Winston Cup race is one that I will always remember, too—it was the Capital City 400 on September 7, 1980. It was great to walk in that Winston Cup garage at Richmond and know that I worked there.

This was my bread and butter—what I did for a living. I had worked so hard for so many years and never made a dime in racing, but now it was different. I was making $350 a week as a mechanic. Our team was small—just four of us including the crew chief. In those days no one had titles or areas of specialization like they do today. Back then we all did it all.

Don Sprouse had a decent qualifying run and started 10th in the 29-car field. But we didn't do that well in the race and finished 15th, 22 laps down. Our share of the purse was $940. Our next race was at Martinsville at the end of September. Don started 14th in one of those big ol' Chevy Impalas we had before NASCAR downsized the cars.

Bob had a "weekend warrior" pit crew to help us, and a guy named Charlie out of a tire service store in Greenville was changing tires for us that day. During a pit stop, Charlie didn't get the lug nuts tight on the right front wheel. When Don went down the frontstretch into turn one, the right front wheel came off. He went straight into the outside wall. He wasn't hurt, but that Impala was destroyed. We had planned to run at Charlotte and Atlanta, but that was our only car, so we just stopped racing and concentrated on building the new down-sized car for the upcoming season.

My first full year in the NASCAR Winston Cup series was 1981. The first race of the year was actually the road-course race at Riverside, California. The three of us—Raymond Kelly, Bill Miller, and me—drove the truck with the car in it to Riverside. And we attempted both of the two qualifying sessions, and at the end of the second qualifying session we were one car behind the last car to make the field on time. Because we were a new team we didn't have a provisional to fall back on. Even though it was very devastating to miss the show, I'm very proud today to say that in my 21 years of being in Winston Cup racing that it's the only event I went to that the team I worked with had to load up and come home.

We went on to the second race of the year, the Daytona 500. It had been five years since my first visit to Daytona as a spectator, and now I was returning as part of the show. I was going over the wall on pit road as the jack man for the No. 37 Rogers Leasing Oldsmobile. But ours was a rookie team with a rookie driver, and Don crashed halfway through the Twin 125 qualifying race. The car wasn't badly damaged, so we were able to repair it. Not that we had much choice—we didn't have a backup car. We made it into the Daytona 500 on our qualifying time. We started 39th in a 42-car field.

Don wasn't used to running 500-mile races. It wasn't long into the race before he was plumb worn out. Kyle Petty had already fallen out, so we put him in our car to relieve Don and we finished 20th. Today, a 20th place finish is not bad. You're often on the lead lap. But back in 1981 a 20th place finish wasn't good. We were 19 laps down.

But it was cool to be at my first Daytona 500 as a mechanic and to jack a car driven by a Petty. And while Kyle was helping us out, his daddy was winning the race. Richard Petty won his seventh Daytona 500 in 1981, outfoxing the field with a fuel-only pit stop late in the race.

At Richmond a week later, Don finished 11 laps down and Bob Rogers replaced him with my good friend and former driver, Mike Alexander. I was not involved in the decision, but I was delighted when I heard the news. My friendship with Mike had been one of the reasons my decision to leave Birmingham was so difficult. Although Don Sprouse really wasn't a Winston Cup–level driver, he was not happy about getting fired. Don and Bob had raced together for a long time and were friends, but it was many years before they spoke to each other again.

With Mike behind the wheel, the team continued to struggle. But a ray of hope came shining through at Martinsville Speedway in April. We had a fast car in practice for the Virginia 500, but we lost an engine, which prevented us from qualifying on pole day. We changed the engine and ran fast in Saturday morning practice. Then we set a new track record at 89.094 mph in the second round of qualifying. We were faster than Ricky Rudd, who'd won the pole the day before.

The jubilation we felt was tempered by the fact that NASCAR inspectors were all over that race car when Mike brought it to the garage. A low-budget rookie team with a rookie driver was not supposed to break the track record. Art Krebs, the NASCAR official who checked carburetors and engines, was so far underneath that hood and down that intake, I thought his two feet were going to be all anyone could see. But he didn't find anything. And neither did anyone else, because the car was absolutely straight. They finally concluded, "Them old boys musta just got a good lap in. So be it."

We finished 14 laps down in the race, but back then you could still finish pretty high in the standings that far behind, and we crossed the finish line in 10th place. It was our first top 10.

The next weekend, we headed home to Alabama for my first Winston Cup race at Talladega. Once again, Mike was strong in qualifying—we were third fastest. But we blew an engine on lap 136. We were making really good power, running good, and qualifying good, but we just couldn't figure out how to make those motors last.

We went to Nashville after Talladega, and once again Mike was a rocket and was second fastest in qualifying. But he spun three times during the race and finished 10 laps down. We blew an engine at Dover and blew another one in the World 600. We skipped Texas and Riverside, but went to Michigan, where we blew yet another motor.

The Pepsi 400 at Daytona in July was a high point in a summer that was otherwise pretty dismal. Mike started 15th, but we managed to finish seventh, our best ever. We were the last car on the lead lap, and to finish on the same lap as the winner was a first, too.

In July 1981, we drove up to Pocono Raceway. In those days we drove to all the tracks. We took only one car, one extra motor, and a few spare parts. We hauled it on a single-axle truck. Bob Rogers owned an auto leasing company, so we'd also take a rental car. Most of the team would ride in the car, but a couple of us would be in the truck.

Mike started 17th and finished 17th, five laps down. We packed up the truck and headed home. I was driving the car. Dana Williamson was in the passenger seat, and Mike Alexander was in the rear seat. Behind us, crewman Bill Miller was driving the truck and our crew chief, Raymond Kelly, was riding with him.

We got about 20 or 30 miles from the track, and all of a sudden, where the Interstate ended, traffic was bumper to bumper as everyone squeezed into one lane. As I slowed, I thought about the truck behind us and looked in the rearview mirror. All I could see was the grille of the truck as it bore down on us. It looked like it was running about 80 mph. It hit us in the back and knocked us for what felt like 1,000 yards. Actually, it was probably only about 100 feet. We hit another car and came to a stop.

I took a quick look at Dana to make sure she was OK. I looked in the rearview mirror at Mike. He looked OK. Fortunately, all of us had been wearing our seat belts. I went to open my door. It wouldn't open. I looked in the rearview mirror again, and all I could see was fire.

I was able to bail out of the passenger door. I took Dana with me. Mike got out on his own. That rental car burned up, with all of our stuff in the trunk, right there in the middle of that Pennsylvania highway. After the fire was put out, we rummaged through what was left of the trunk. There wasn't anything worth salvaging.

The truck was hardly damaged. The front bumper was bent back a few inches. So after we took care of the police reports and had the wreckage towed to a salvage yard, all five of us piled into the cab of that truck and off to Greenville we went. We were all so relieved to have survived the crash without a scratch that there were no hard feelings toward the crewman who had been driving the truck.

In August we drove up to Michigan, where Mike finished 10th. But he tore down a piece of the fence at Bristol. And at Richmond, we never finished a lap and were scored last. After the race, Bob fired Mike. It was another tough decision, but Mike was tearing up a lot of equipment, mostly, I think, from the pressure to succeed. He was trying too hard.

Also, I think we were hurt by the truth in that old racing axiom: You can take a rookie driver and put him with a veteran team and be OK. And you can take a veteran driver and put him with a rookie team and be OK. But if you take a rookie driver and put him with a rookie team, you have a recipe for a very low level of success.

Bob went out and hired another rookie. But 26-year-old Tim Richmond was not your average rookie. He had finished ninth in the 1980 Indianapolis 500 and was named rookie of the year at the Brickyard. Tim had switched to NASCAR in 1981, and I was sure the minute I saw him on the track in our car that he had special talents.

All of a sudden, we looked like we knew what we were doing. Tim drove every lap as hard as you could ever ask anybody to drive a race car. He had great feel for a car, even if he couldn't really tell you what was happening. Tim would use his hands and his head and his hips to try to tell you what the car was doing. And then you still had to do a lot of guesswork to figure out what it was *really* doing.

But you know what? All you had to do was get that race car *close* to good, and Tim would figure out how to do the rest. In our first race together, Tim finished ninth at Dover.

The National 500 at Charlotte Motor Speedway was Tim's fourth race for Rogers leasing. We had not tested, but we carried a car there that Tim liked. Early in the race, Tim complained that the throttle was hanging on him. We lifted the hood during an early caution and discovered that something had chewed the air cleaner almost in two.

We couldn't figure out what it was, but some of the throttle return springs had been knocked off, so we put them back on and sent Tim on his way. With about 30 laps to go, we were third. Darrell Waltrip was leading, Bobby Allison was second, and we were next. Darrell and Bobby still had to make one more pit stop. We did not have to stop again. I thought we had the race in the bag.

Then Tim lost oil pressure, and the motor blew up with 17 laps to go. We brought out the caution that Darrell and Bobby needed. They finished one-two. It was not until after that race that we figured out what had destroyed that air cleaner and ultimately the engine. The head of the bolt that holds the oil pump belt pulley on the end of the crankshaft had broken off and come up and flown around the air cleaner, tearing it up. For most of the rest of the race, that pulley had stayed on, but when that pulley came off, the oil pump belt came off, and the engine blew. We were on track to win that race and $40,000. Bob Rogers put that broken bolt in a frame and put a caption below it that said, "$40,000."

Before the start of the 1982 season, Tim Richmond took another ride, probably for more money, with a new team out of Richmond, Virginia. It hurt our feelings because of how well we'd run. Ironically, that season Tim didn't even make the Daytona 500.

We had secured sponsorship for 1982 from Simoniz car polish. Indy car driver Tom Sneva was part of the deal. But he was primarily driving Indy cars, so he couldn't run all the NASCAR races. So we got Donnie Allison and Neil Bonnett involved.

Tom ran for us at Daytona, Richmond, and Atlanta. Neil was in the car at Bristol, North Wilkesboro, and Nashville, and Donnie drove at Darlington, Martinsville, Talladega, and Dover. The arrangement with Tom didn't go at all well. At Richmond he was like a fish out of water, and the arrangement was pretty complicated, with him trying to drive in both series. Somehow, Bob got out of the deal with Tom. Looking back with the benefit of experience, I think Tom was thrown a curve having to get into a car with a feel that's so different, because there's so much less horsepower and downforce compared to an Indy car. Our team was trying its best, but we didn't have the size and experience to provide him with the best equipment.

With Donnie, we finished ninth at Darlington in the spring, and it was a hard-earned finish. Darlington is a tough track, and back then the spring race was 500 miles long. Well, Donnie started giving out. His brother Bobby had already dropped out with a blown engine, so we put Bobby in the car to relieve Donnie. Drivers didn't have cool air blowing into their helmets like they do today. You just went out there and did your job.

Here we were, just a second-year team, and the great Bobby Allison was behind the wheel of our car. I thought that was pretty cool. Considering the finish, it was obvious Bobby ran well. Afterward, he told us, "You know, this car maybe drove as good as my car." That made our little crew of four feel pretty good.

In May, we started to pick up some momentum. Donnie finished sixth at Talladega. Six days later, Neil was fifth at Nashville. Donnie was back in the car at Dover and finished eighth. But the sponsorship with Simoniz was for only the first 10 races. It ended after Charlotte, where Donnie blew an engine early in the World 600.

By that time Bob Rogers had been running the race team mostly out of his own pocket for a year and a half, and he decided to quit. He held an auction to sell the race equipment in the summer of 1982. One of those who came to the auction was Jackie Martin, Mark Martin's mother. Mark was running his own team that year, and she was managing it. She knew of me from racing against Mark on short tracks when I was with Bobby Ray, and she had seen me around the Winston Cup garage in 1982 because both our teams were running all the races that year.

"What are you going to do now, Larry?" she asked.

"I'm not real sure what to do, Mrs. Martin," I said. I didn't really know Mark's mom then. She straightened me out real quick about her name.

"Call me Jackie, not Mrs. Martin," she said. "Anyhow, we'd like to talk to you about coming to work with us on Mark's team." This was very flattering, and I was shocked by her offer. I took the job and moved to Charlotte. I was excited to move there because that's where most of the teams are based—it's the center of Winston Cup racing. There was only one team in Greenville, South Carolina, and it had just closed its doors on me.

Mark had a very small team in one of the little shops at the northeast corner of Morehead Road and U.S. 29 next to Charlotte Motor Speedway. I was probably making a little more than I'd made with Rogers—maybe $400 a week—but I didn't care about the money. All I cared about was being able to race. There were seven or eight guys working for Mark, and we were all in our early to mid 20s. We would go out and eat together, spend the off weekends together. It was nothing for all of us to load up the van and head for the beach for a weekend.

The Southern 500 used to be held on Labor Day at Darlington Raceway, and they had a unique format for the weekend. Pole qualifying was Thursday, second round qualifying Friday, and final practice Saturday. The racetrack was closed on Sunday, so you'd leave the track Saturday evening and not return until Monday morning. This opened the possibilities of getting into all sorts of trouble.

We stayed at the Thunderbird Motor Inn in Florence, a few miles from the track. A lot of the teams stayed there. Somehow, I got hooked up with Ronnie Childress, Richard Childress's brother. He and I got some moonshine and drank it there by the pool. We drank and drank and we drank until we didn't know what world we were in.

Next thing I knew, we were throwing all the pool furniture into the pool, jumping in ourselves and floating around on it. Finally I became coherent enough to get out of there, head back to the room, and go to bed. When I woke up the next morning, all the furniture was still floating in the pool. I slunk out of there with a terrible hangover that lasted until about Tuesday. I didn't really want to be tied to this episode. We worked very hard, but we played even harder—sometimes too hard.

Mark didn't have much success with his race team. He only had one top-10 finish when I was with him, and that came at Riverside in the team's last race. At the end of the season, Mark disbanded the team and held his own auction. It seemed like every race team I'd worked for had closed its doors. Maybe Donnie Allison was right about the hard knocks I'd experience in Winston Cup. I even thought about going back to Birmingham and working for Charles Finley in the salvage yard again.

Not a lot was happening in my racing career at this time, but things were looking much better in the dating department. One of the guys on Mark's team had a girlfriend named Linda. They were both from Indiana. When Mark closed down his shop in Indiana and moved to North Carolina to start in Winston Cup, they had moved as well.

Before I went to work for Mark, the truck driver at Rogers Racing had preceded me. He was telling me about Mark's team and he said, "This one guy on the team, his girlfriend, I'm telling you, we're talking about some kind of pair of legs." Needless to say, that piqued my interest. Since we all spent so much time together, I got to know Linda. We became friends and liked each other a lot. Later, Linda broke up with her boyfriend, and he left the team. We began dating in January 1983. Until then, I hadn't had too many thoughts about too many women because I had such a one-track mind about race cars. I was always insecure about girls and dating, and I almost couldn't picture myself with Linda.

On our first date, I took her to this pizza place in Charlotte. It was icy out, so I was trying to impress her and do the right thing. I was holding onto her so she wouldn't slip on the ice. Of course, I was the one who slipped and fell on the ice. I was so embarrassed. But she just laughed and thought it was cute.

Back in racing I had several options for the 1983 season. I had decided that from this point forward I'd only work for a top team that had the finances to keep racing. I had talked to Richard Childress. I'd driven up to Level Cross, outside Greensboro, and talked to the Pettys. But Tim Richmond had called and told me about a new team he was driving for—Blue Max Racing. It was owned by drag racer Raymond Beadle. They had landed sponsorship from Old Milwaukee Beer.

I took the job as their truck driver and tire specialist. It was my first job with a major team. Beadle had hired a lot of heavy hitters for the crew. Tim Brewer, who had spent years with Junior Johnson, was the crew chief. Other former Johnson employees on the team were Harold Elliott, the engine builder, and Bobby Jones, another crewman.

But it was a terrible situation. There was a lot of infighting and power struggles. Far worse than that, paychecks were bouncing right from the start. When we went to Daytona, we hadn't been paid in a month. Nobody had any expense account money. Tim Brewer had to go into his personal account to keep us fed. We got to Darlington, the fifth race of the season, and I carried my wheels down to the tire building to get tires mounted. The dealer, Thurman Huggins, was standing there.

"You might as well take them wheels back to your truck," he said. "We are not mounting any tires for you guys. Not a single tire bill has been paid this year."

I went back to Brewer. "Man, we got problems," I said. "Goodyear ain't mounting us any tires."

Tim went down there and wrote a personal check to pay for part of the bill. Goodyear mounted tires for us. Then Richmond went out and not only won the pole at 157.818 mph, he blew the rest of the field away. On Sunday, as he was speeding down the backstretch on the first lap, the engine blew up, he spun, and took out about a third of the field. There was a lot of finger-pointing when we got back to the shop. I decided the big time wasn't for me. I was much happier working with the smaller teams. Then I got a call from Bob Rogers.

"I want you to come back and work for me," he said. "I want you to be the crew chief this time. I'm not going to try Winston Cup. I'm just going to do this Busch Grand National car with Butch Lindley." I was going to be able to go back to Greenville, South Carolina, which I loved, and I would be in charge. I could do what I thought needed to be done without answering to anyone but Bob. It would be my own deal.

Right after the fiasco at Darlington, I told Tim Brewer I was leaving. He did not object. He knew the score. So the biggest dilemma I faced was with Linda. We'd only been dating four or five months, but I'd fallen in love with her and I was pretty sure she had fallen for me. But she had a job in Charlotte as an orthodontist's assistant. And now it looked like I was moving back to Greenville.

I thought a lot about how to handle it, and finally I decided just to come right out and say what was on my mind. I told her what Bob had offered. I said I wanted to move back to Greenville. She looked pretty hard at me and listened closely.

"You know, I got something else I'd like to ask you," I said. "Would you move to Greenville with me and would you marry me?"

"Yes."

Her answer almost surprised me. Even though we'd only been dating for a few months, there was no question in my mind that I wanted her to be my wife. I don't know what I would have done if she had said no. I really wanted to go to Greenville, but I didn't want to lose her. It turned out I had nothing to worry about. Linda was so in love with me, she said she would have gone anywhere with me. We set our wedding date for October 29.

In May 1983, we moved to Greenville. I rented an apartment. Linda stayed there, and I stayed with one of the guys on the race team. At least that's what we told our parents. Most of the time, I stayed there with Linda.

She found a job right away with a local orthodontist. I started putting cars together for Butch. We didn't have a lot of luck in the first four or five races, and we tore up a lot of equipment. This meant we had to rush to build a new short-track car to bring to a race at Langley Speedway in Hampton, Virginia, in early July.

I had just two full-time employees besides myself. We built that car in a week and a half. I did not go to bed for a week. I took naps at the shop, but I had not been in bed at all. The car wasn't really even finished when we left that Saturday morning for Virginia. When we got there, Robert Black, NASCAR's top official at the race, just shook his head when he saw our car. We just had open holes under the windshield where the aluminum closeouts (which cover the open area where the windshield wipers would ordinarily be) were supposed to go. I taped cardboard over the holes.

The car was still bare sheet metal. I took a bottle of shoe polish and wrote a number on each side and Butch's name on the top. Even then, the car just wasn't ready, and we missed half of practice trying to pacify Black. He wanted us to run, but his attitude was, "Man, why did you guys bring *this* race car?"

"It's all we got, Robert," I said. "And I've been friggin' working on it all week right up till we left for here."

In qualifying, Tommy Ellis sat on the pole with a new track record. Butch also broke the old record in our sheet-metal gray Pontiac and won the second starting spot. It was a 200-lap race, and when they started it, I was so tired I just sat down in a chair in the pits. I was hardly able to pay any attention to some of the best racing you'll ever see.

For the first 50 or 60 laps, Tommy and Butch ran side by side. Tommy would just barely lead a lap, then Butch would just barely lead one. They ran just like they'd started, lap after lap after lap.

At Langley, when you came off pit road, you came out almost right dead in the middle of turn one. As Glenn Jarrett was exiting pit road, he accidentally drove into Tommy. Tommy got into Butch. And the last I saw of Butch and our brand new, almost-finished race car was watching it go wheels up completely out of the racetrack.

When we got back to South Carolina, Bob Rogers had bad news. He was quitting. The Busch deal had cost him more than he had expected, and we'd torn up a lot of cars without having a sponsor. We'd run only three races, and Bob Rogers had closed the doors on me again. We had some pretty heated words, and we didn't speak to each other for quite a while. I was mad, I was hurt, I was bitter, I was lost—you name it. What was I going to tell Linda?

Linda's response was typical of her: "You know, Larry, as long as we've got each other, that's all that really counts. It'll work out. You'll see."

But it was tough when that paycheck stopped coming. I can remember sitting at the kitchen table with my head in my hands, walking through all our troubles in my mind, wondering how we'd get through it. We'd often take advantage of the "buy one, get one free" offer at the local Little Caesar's. We'd eat one for dinner and save the other for the next day.

Word of my plight got around Greenville, and just about the time I started wondering real hard to figure out what I was going to do, a big fellow named Bill Terry, who owns some clubs in the area, called me and offered me a job.

"We're running an All-Pro/Grand American car up at Greenville-Pickens Speedway every Saturday night," he said. "I tell you what. You come out here every Monday and work on these race cars for me. And you work through to Saturday. And every Saturday night I'll pay you in cash, and you can tell me whether you want to work another week or not."

I was getting married in three months. My career was on hold. But Bill Terry was like a savior. I had a lot of fun working on his All-Pro team. It wasn't what I wanted to do, but I had Sundays off in the late summer of 1983 and plenty of time to spend with Linda while we were planning our wedding. So it was a pretty cool deal.

One Saturday night in August we were out at Greenville-Pickens with our local driver, Donnie Bishop, when I noticed a fellow hanging around our trailer. After the race, he came up to me and shoved a card in my hand. "Don't say anything now," he said. "Call me next week."

A few moments after he walked away, I looked at the name on the card. It read "Bobby Hawkins." I didn't know Bobby, but I knew he was a Winston Cup car owner. He had the Chattanooga Chew car, and his driver was David Pearson. I called him.

"Larry, I don't know what your plans are," he said. "But we need some help. Would you be interested in going to work for us?" The team was running out of Pearson's shop in Whitney, a little suburb of Spartanburg, South Carolina. So in late August of 1983, I went to work up there. I think that Bobby noticed how hard I worked and how dedicated and focused I was. He saw I wasn't afraid to tackle any job.

My first race with Bobby Hawkins was the Southern 500 at Darlington. One weekend, I'm tuning a Grand American car for a guy named Donnie Bishop at Greenville-Pickens. The next weekend, I'm headed to the Southern 500 with the Silver Fox.

Pearson was the master of Darlington. He'd won 10 500-mile races there. But in the practice before qualifying, we weren't very good. I was about to panic. I went to the crew chief, who was David's son, Ricky.

"What's the deal?" I asked. "We're here at Darlington with David Pearson, and we're running terrible. What's the matter?"

"Don't worry, we'll be fine," he said.

I even went up to David.

"What's the problem, David?" I said.

David chewed on that gum of his. He blinked his eyes and said, "We'll be all right."

Sure enough, after running about 25th fastest in practice, David went out there and qualified fifth. He knew what he was talking about. In the race itself, David led 18 laps and we finished 10th.

We raced once more in 1983. David finished 39th in a 40-car field when we lost a valve about a third of the way into the race at Charlotte in early October.

A few weeks later, on October 29, Linda and I were married at Aldersgate Baptist Church in Greenville. Linda was Catholic and I had been raised in the Church of Christ, which was about as different from Catholic as you can get. So we decided to have the service in a Baptist church.

It was a fairly small wedding. Our families were there, and all three of the Pearson brothers—Ricky, Larry, and Eddie. That night we drove up to Charlotte and stayed at the Marriott SouthPark Hotel. A few weeks later, we went on our honeymoon to Paradise Island in the Bahamas. We couldn't really afford it, but we did it anyway. We ended up having to put our port charges and duty taxes on our credit card because we didn't have enough cash to cover it.

CHAPTER FOUR

Racing with the Silver Fox

n 1984, I started my first full season with Bobby Hawkins. We had sponsorship from Chattanooga Chew and were still working out of David Pearson's shop in Whitney. We ran a limited schedule—just 11 races—and we didn't do that well. We had only three top-10 finishes. David finished ninth in the World 600 and ninth at Michigan, but that was about it.

That limited schedule was really all David wanted to run. And that's all that Chattanooga Chew wanted to sponsor. When you're running that infrequently, it's hard to keep up with what's going on. Our cars were a little off in their bodies and chassis. And I'm not sure David really had his heart in it.

Up at David's shop, the pace of work was more than comfortable. We'd start work at 9 a.m.—and not a minute before. When the clock struck 12, we'd go eat lunch. At five o'clock, the day was done. We'd never work a minute past five. It was the first time in many a year I'd worked a regular schedule.

The Pearsons were great, and I enjoyed my time at the shop. It was a little awkward because I was the only guy in the shop whose last name wasn't Pearson. Once every three or four weeks, David would come in and say, "Let's go play golf," so me and all the Pearsons would close the doors and go play golf. I really had no say in this. I never even owned a key to the shop. And Bobby Hawkins never messed with us at all.

I was a little disappointed with the way we ran, but what a great time to be a newlywed. Linda and I had two or three weekends a month we could call our own. We'd usually watch the Winston Cup race on television Sunday, and we had plenty of time to go out to dinner, go to the beach, or go out with friends on Friday and Saturday night. I was living like a normal human being for the first time in my adult life.

I can't say I learned a lot during this time, but I enjoyed working with Jake Elder, who came to help the team in the latter part of 1983. Jake was one of my heroes—one of the crew chiefs I had watched through my binoculars while sitting in the Talladega grandstands. When Jake said something, I listened. I tried to be a sponge when he was around.

At the end of the 1984 season, David took the Chattanooga Chew sponsorship to car owner Hoss Ellington and closed the doors in Whitney. We hauled everything out of David's shop near Spartanburg and moved it back to Traveler's Rest, outside Greenville, to a shop Bobby Hawkins already had. I spent most of the early winter getting everything organized and cleaned up. But after that, we didn't really have any plan and nothing much to do. By this time there were only one or two other employees besides me, and we did not have a car, a driver, or a racing program.

In early 1985, Bobby asked me what I wanted to do. "I want to race," I told him. We borrowed a Winston Cup car from "Big Daddy" Terry and put Butch Lindley in it for the Winston Cup race at Richmond. We fell out after 352 laps with a broken lug stud and finished 19th. But it wasn't a bad effort. It looked like we might have something promising.

I came up with a suggestion: Why don't we all build a really good double-throwdown short-track car for Butch? So Mike Laughlin, a race car chassis builder in the Greenville area, built us a chassis, and we hung a Chevy body on it.

Butch Lindley was one of the greatest short-track drivers ever. He had finished second at Martinsville in 1982 in one of his first Winston Cup races. He was also a two-time NASCAR late-model sportsman champion. He turned 37 years old as we made the final preparations on his new car.

Butch was also one of the most meticulous race car drivers I ever met, and probably one of the smartest in terms of taking care of his equipment and knowing what he wanted in a race car. When we were building that car for him, he was very adamant about various things he wanted, particularly brakes. By then I knew Butch well enough to know that the best thing we could do was give him exactly what he asked for.

He never really worked on the car himself, and it would half drive me crazy because he'd come to the shop and sit for hours on this little old stepladder we had and watch us work. We also spent a lot of time talking on the telephone. I'd work at the shop for 10 or 11 hours, get home, grab dinner, and then the phone would ring. It would be Butch, and he'd keep me on the phone for a couple of hours, thinking out loud about what we might do to make the car better: "What do you think about how we have that quarter panel?" or "Think we've got that fan shroud built right?"

We planned to run Butch in our new short-track car at North Wilkesboro in mid-April. And if everything went well there, we were going to run at Martinsville the weekend after that. About a week and a half before the North Wilkesboro race, I called Butch and told him to come by the shop so we could mount his seat and get the pedals fitted. "Well, I'm running an All-Pro race this weekend in Bradenton [Florida] for a guy out of Birmingham," he said. "We'll be driving down on Friday morning, so when I head out, I'll come by the shop and we can get that stuff done."

Butch came by, and we fitted everything for the next weekend at North Wilkesboro. Early that Saturday morning, probably at one or two o'clock, the phone rang at our apartment. It was my Aunt Noreen from Birmingham. She said she had heard that Butch had been killed at Bradenton. I just dropped the phone.

I was in shock, but I had to know what happened, so I started making phone calls. My aunt didn't have the story exactly right, but she was not far off. Butch had suffered a severe head injury and was in a coma.

He had been driving a red and white Camaro owned by Frankie Grille of Birmingham, Alabama. He had been in front, and the advertised 125 laps had been run. The race should have been over. But they had a rule that said the last 10 laps had to be run under a green flag, so the cars were still running. Butch was leading the way when the trailing arm pulled apart on his Camaro. It sent him into a spin, and he slammed hard into the third turn wall with the driver's side of the car. They said his head might have hit the wall.

They moved Butch from Florida to a Virginia hospital that had a head injury specialist. But there was not really much anyone could do for him. Finally, they moved him back to Greenville and put him in a hospital there. Eventually, his wife Joan had to put him in a nursing home. He had to be watched 24 hours a day.

Joan had no insurance to pay for special care, so while he was still in the hospital in Greenville, we signed up to sit with Butch and relieve the family. We'd sit with him for two nights a week from 6 to

10 p.m. We did this for two or three months, before he was moved to the nursing home.

I would talk to him, read to him, ask him questions, even yell at him, hoping that something would bring him out of the coma. Every time I went to visit, I had faith that this would be the time he would answer me. I figured that one day he'd wake up, look at us, and say, "What in the world happened?" But unfortunately he never did.

You have to give a fair amount of care to a person in a vegetative state. I would massage Butch's feet and do exercises for him so he didn't draw up. He could easily choke, so I'd have to suction out his tracheotomy from time to time to keep his breathing passage clear.

Sometimes I'd be late, and Linda would go over there ahead of me. Butch would make noises, and that scared her a little bit, so she always insisted that the door be kept open and tried not to let anyone know how scared it made her.

Once Butch was moved to a nursing home, Joan didn't need us to volunteer anymore. Linda went and visited him, but I never did. I guess I had just lost faith that he would ever come around, and I didn't want to see him lying there as a vegetable anymore. Butch died on June 6, 1990, a little over five years after his accident. He was the first driver I had ever been involved with who had been hurt.

The day after Butch's accident, I was still more or less in a state of shock. I spent the day at our apartment, talking to this person and that. Bobby Hawkins called and asked me to meet him at the shop. I walked out of the apartment and didn't even tell Linda I was leaving. It was almost like I was walking around in a trance.

Bobby wanted to talk about where we went from there and what we needed to do, but I wasn't really ready yet to help make those decisions. Butch's injury even had me second-guessing my choice of careers. I really felt lost. We had a small race team, yes, but we had a good budget. Most importantly, we had had a plan and a driver. But now I had no idea what was going to happen to Butch, and our plan was gone.

My racing career, which had seemed like a really good deal five years earlier, now didn't seem so great. Time after time it seemed like everything would almost become good, then it would go bad. With Bob Rogers, we got ourselves a great race car driver in Tim Richmond. But then the sponsorship ended and Bob closed his doors. I went to Mark Martin's shop and then he closed his doors. We ran well at my first major team, Blue Max, but the situation was intolerable. I went back to Bob Rogers, and he closed up on me again. Finally, just as I was getting some momentum with Butch, this horrible thing had happened.

But I knew deep down that we couldn't just roll over. Out of respect to Butch, Bobby and I decided not to race at North Wilkesboro. But we decided to go to Martinsville, and we needed a driver.

"Why don't we call Morgan Shepherd and see if he is interested?" I said. Morgan was very interested. He was a 44-year-old journeyman driver out of Conover, North Carolina. He had won as a rookie in 1981 at Martinsville, but he didn't have a full-time ride in 1985. We managed to test for a day at Martinsville and qualified third for the race.

Geoff Bodine took the lead early in the race, but Morgan worked his way into second and was all over Bodine's bumper. Then on lap 140, he blew a tire and spun. Martinsville used to have a little two-foot gap in the frontstretch wall so people could walk from the grandstands to the track when no one was racing, and as Morgan spun down the frontstretch, he caught that opening. The collision destroyed our new short-track car. I had never seen a car torn up that badly at little ol' Martinsville. Once again, I had gotten pumped up only to be smashed down. At least we had done well until the crash. I couldn't help but feel a little bit good about it. As a part-time team, we had qualified third with a new car and a substitute driver, and then we had run well in the race.

We didn't run all through the summer, but somehow Bobby struck a deal with Junior Johnson, who already had two cars, to put David Pearson in a third car for the July race at Talladega. Junior was running Chevrolets, but they built a Ford Thunderbird for David.

Ricky Pearson and I went up to Ingle Hollow to help Junior's boys finish the car before leaving for Talladega. We worked around the clock for about three days, then left Junior's shop about six or seven on the night before we had to be at Talladega. I was driving the truck because Ricky didn't drive tractor-trailers. But I was dog tired. We stopped in Spartanburg and Ricky got his stuff at his house. I already had my clothes with me. Then we drove down that road toward Alabama. I don't think I have ever been more tired trying to drive. Finally, just outside of Atlanta, I had to stop. Ricky was so tired, I could hardly wake him up to tell him I had to sleep.

"I know that racetrack is going to open up at seven with or without us, but I can't hold my head up any longer," I said.

I laid my head on the steering wheel and catnapped for about an hour and a half. Then we got back on the road. I was so relieved to see Talladega. We were a couple of hours late, but we were lucky to even be there. We qualified third, then dropped out after only 54 laps and finished 35th.

It's not like I wasn't used to putting out that kind of effort. In fact, I had really stepped up the hours and effort at Bobby's shop, even if we weren't running many races. No more David Pearson hours for me. By the summer of 1985, I was working almost all of the time.

By then, I had been married two years, and Linda and I were running over some pretty bumpy roads. Our problems were my fault because I had let racing take over my life. I had put Linda second and was taking her for granted. I had gone from working 35 hours a week and being home most nights to working night and day. It had really started when we built the short-track car for Butch, and it continued through the year. Since there were only three of us working, it took a lot longer to get stuff done.

But in all honesty, I became a workaholic again. I worked many nights at the shop when I didn't need to work. I was totally focused on getting every *i* dotted and *t* crossed. I thought we could be successful and win some races. And that's what I wanted more than anything.

Linda tried to adapt, but it was tough. We weren't hanging out with Bob Rogers and our old Greenville friends anymore. She had her work as a dental hygienist, but most of her colleagues were married. She'd hang out with them sometimes, yet always felt like the third wheel. She did a lot of shopping and watched a lot of TV.

We did OK for three or four months, but as summer came and I started building another race car, the problem got a lot worse. She'd call me at the shop and say, "Hi Larry, when are you going to be home for dinner?"

"Oh, six or so." I'd tell her what she wanted to hear. Well, along about nine or 10, here I'd come. By then, she had already reheated supper three or four times and finally eaten by herself—again.

Some mornings I would come in at two o'clock and she'd be getting up only a few hours later to get ready for work. She wanted to get out of our apartment and move into a house. She wanted to talk about having a family. I wasn't ready for kids and didn't care about having a house.

One night we went out with friends to the club at the local Holiday Inn. About 10 o'clock I told Linda I was ready to go. She thought I wanted to go home. I took her home and went back to the shop. After having it so smooth for almost two years, she was faced with this regimen. She wasn't seeking any special attention—just *something*.

Linda was telling me these things, but I wasn't listening. It just kept on and on. She began to go to church and pray about it—sometimes daily—because she thought if she prayed hard enough, it would make everything right. I guess you could say the prayers eventually did work. But at the time, she was just getting sadder and more depressed each day.

She reached a point where she didn't want it anymore. And then she reached a point where she couldn't take it anymore.

One summer night in 1985 I came home fairly late, walked in the front door, and she wasn't there. It didn't take me long to realize that she wasn't the only thing that wasn't there. She had taken most of her stuff, too. I had no idea where to find her. I tried to go to bed that night, didn't sleep, and finally met her when she arrived the next morning at the orthodontist's office.

She said she had moved into an apartment a couple of blocks away. "I can't live this way," she said. "I'm going to get a life for myself, and you go ahead and race."

I can be a pretty overbearing person, and I simply could not accept this. I insisted that she come home. I wouldn't leave her alone. I called her morning, noon, and night. Suddenly I didn't care about work at all anymore. I didn't care about the cars, and I didn't care about the races. I continued working, but I just didn't care.

Our team returned to the track for the Southern 500 at Darlington on Labor Day weekend. Morgan Shepherd qualified 15th, but the engine blew after only 22 laps. I was *relieved* to drop out early. All I could think about was trying to get Linda back. I was driving the truck, so I could not leave until the race was over. I can still see Joe Gazaway, a NASCAR official, raising hell with me for moving our truck and trailer around in the garage before the race was over. I was just trying to be first in line at the gate.

And when the race ended, I was first out of that gate. I left Darlington like I was shot out of a cannon. I'm not sure how fast I drove home, but at that point, I didn't care if I went to jail or got in a wreck. I didn't much care about anything except Linda.

Of course, I was smothering her, and that was just making her angrier and angrier. I wasn't smart enough to realize all I was doing was shoving her farther and farther away. I was treating her like a race car and was going to fix our problems my way and fix them today.

After about a month of putting myself through living hell—I wasn't eating, I wasn't sleeping—I got the message. It was delivered to me by Dana Williamson, who sat me down at her house and told me to leave Linda alone.

"You're not going to fix this problem," she said. "You've got to back off. If you do that, you'll probably be amazed at what happens."

I was tired, frustrated, hurt, mad, aggravated—all those things. "Fine," I said angrily. "I'm done."

Dana explained the problem to me. She said Linda wanted just one night a week to call our own. And she wanted me to be reliable about coming home. But Dana said I'd pushed it too far at that point, and Linda wasn't ready to even talk about it. I had no one to blame but myself. I couldn't believe what I had been doing. Linda wanted a house. I'd said no. That was one of the things that had pulled my mom and dad apart. And damned if I wasn't letting the same thing pull us apart, too.

I backed off, and was totally miserable. I worked a lot during those days. I spent a lot of time with Dana and her husband. I stayed away from our apartment as much as possible. I only went there to sleep.

About a week went by, and I had just gone to bed when I heard the front door unlock. Linda walked in. I got up, and we sat down together. "Larry, I don't want to live without you," she said. "I want to live *with* you. But there's some things we've got to fix. When you tell me you're coming home at a certain time, I want to be able to know that you will be home then. And I want to have some time for us. And I don't want to live in this apartment anymore. I want a house. And I want to think about having a family."

By then, I was ready to *really* listen and ready to take this problem *really* seriously. And I took it a step farther. My mother was a member of the Church of Christ. My dad was a Catholic. Because of that, my mom, my dad, and me had never stepped through the door of a church together as a family.

I didn't want that. And when we had a family, I didn't want to put my kids through that. So I told Linda, "There's another thing I can do. I want to join the Catholic Church." She was pretty shocked by that. But I saw it through. And it was a lot of work—classes and study, and you have to have a sponsor. There's a lot to it. It took me five or six months. But I did it.

It's tough fitting church into the schedule of a racer, but Linda and I always have tried to go to church every chance we get. One of the good things about being a Catholic is that the churches have a lot of services, including Saturday night. When we were at the racetrack, we usually went to Saturday evening mass. That's how we got to know Davey and Liz Allison, and Alan Kulwicki, when they started racing in the Winston Cup series.

Another thing that brought Linda and me closer together was that I made her part of the team. She became the team's scorer in the pits. She began coming with me to every race.

By the fall of 1985, everything was coming back together. But it was also one of the busiest times of my life. We bought a house in Greenville and began to move in. I was studying to become a Catholic. We were racing again, too, and our season ended on a positive note, when Morgan finished seventh at Charlotte and fifth at Atlanta.

In November, Bobby Hawkins sold half of the team to Kenny Bernstein, the NHRA (National Hot Rod Association) drag racer. The

R. J. Reynolds Tobacco Company and the folks at Winston helped set the deal up. They were already tight with Kenny because of their drag-racing sponsorship.

Kenny had made a name for himself in NHRA by winning the 1985 Funny Car championship. But he wanted to get into stock-car racing, too. He had a driver, Joe Ruttman; a manufacturer, Buick; and most importantly, he had a sponsor, Quaker State Motor Oil.

Kenny had everything but a race team. And Bobby Hawkins had a race team but almost nothing else. But after a few weeks of the half-and-half ownership, it was obvious that Kenny's regimented style did not fit with Bobby's seat-of-the-pants approach, and Kenny bought the team outright.

With all the elements in place, Kenny planned to run the full Winston Cup schedule in 1986. We had to take a part-time team and hire people and build cars and make it a full-time team. The task was almost overwhelming, but I kept my priorities in order. I reserved one night a week for Linda. I'd go home early, and we would go out to dinner. If I told her I was going to do something, I'd do it. And I stuck with my plan to become a Catholic. During those evenings I was at the shop, she was busy decorating our brand-new house.

When Kenny bought the team, Bobby had a couple of stipulations. And one was that Kenny had to keep me and one other guy, Clyde Brookshire, our team manager, for at least one year. In December of 1985, I could tell something was going on. I finally cornered Clyde at lunch one day.

"Something's going on with Kenny. What is it, Clyde?" I asked.

Clyde said, "Man, I hate to tell you this, Larry, but Kenny's trying to hire Gary Nelson to replace you as crew chief."

"What's so bad about that?" I said. "If they hire Gary Nelson, you know who's going to benefit from that more than anyone? Me! I mean, you could put all of my crew chief experience in a salad bowl and still have room left over. Clyde, it's crazy that they would want to hide that from me. How stupid would I be to object to that?"

So I waited for the news to come down, but it never did. In late December, Kenny came into the shop and told me, "I couldn't make it happen with Gary. He wouldn't move down here to Traveler's Rest. Would you be my crew chief?"

It had taken me five full years, but I finally had the job I really wanted in the NASCAR Winston Cup series. Now I would be in charge of the shop. I'd be in charge of setting up the cars. And I was the guy who would be making the calls in the pits. I couldn't wait to get back to Daytona.

CHAPTER FIVE

Breaking Rules and Breaking into Victory Lane

My first driver as a Winston Cup crew chief was Joe Ruttman, a 41-year-old native of Southern California with a famous last name in auto racing. Joe's older brother, Troy, won the 1952 Indianapolis 500 at 22—the youngest 500 winner ever. Joe was seven at the time. Joe got into stock-car racing through the United States Auto Club, the former sanctioning body for the Indy 500, and had been a regular in the Winston Cup series since 1981.

As much as I looked forward to going back to Daytona, we didn't run well and left with a DNF (did not finish). Joe went head-on into the outside wall while trying to avoid Neil Bonnett, who had broken a wheel. A bunch of other cars crashed, too.

We went to Richmond, and as usual, the weather was bad. Qualifying was rained out. We were a new team, and I wasn't even sure we would make the show. But the rules were a little bit different in those days.

NASCAR lined the cars up according to the way they finished in the Daytona 500. Not only did we make the race, we started 17th.

We gave Joe a stout car and he drove to the front. The track was slippery, and it was a wild day with a lot of wrecks. He took the lead on lap 323 and was in front for 21 laps. In the final laps, Joe was fourth, trailing Dale Earnhardt, Darrell Waltrip, and Geoff Bodine. With three laps to go, Waltrip got past Earnhardt in turns one and two. As they reached turn three, Earnhardt hooked Waltrip's right rear quarter panel, and they both crashed. Bodine crashed into them, and as Joe tried to snake by, he crashed, too.

Kyle Petty, who had been running fifth, made it through the mess and won the race—his first career Winston Cup victory. Meanwhile, our spotter was screaming, "Get going, get going!" Joe managed to get our wrecked Buick LeSabre going again and crossed the line second.

We were a rookie Winston Cup team in our first full season, and we had finished second in our second race. I thought, "Gosh, maybe this deal isn't that hard after all." Then we began having motor problems, and I changed my mind. We had three DNFs in the next four races.

Our season improved once we got back to the short tracks. Joe finished fifth at North Wilkesboro. And at Martinsville, he was the runner-up behind Ricky Rudd. We had a flat tire about halfway through that race, and the sway bar arm rubbed on the asphalt when the tire went down. The front sway bar arm rubbed apart and finally snapped in two, and Joe had to adjust his driving style to compensate for a car that was as loose as a goose. We made adjustments to help him, and Joe actually started running pretty good and finished second without a front sway bar.

You have to be prepared for the unexpected, both on and off the track. The June race at Pocono was a good example of that. Joe qualified 10th, and we were running pretty well when the bottom fell out of the sky around lap 92. It was raining so hard you couldn't see from one end of the frontstretch to the other.

NASCAR was trying feverishly to get the race to the halfway point at lap 100, when it would be official. The field ran six or seven laps under caution in a monsoon. A couple of cars, including the one driven by Bobby Allison, hydroplaned on the water and crashed. Joe called on the radio: "Larry, I can't see."

"Joe, we're in the top 10. You've got to run those last laps to the red," I replied. I finally had him lower the window net, loosen his belts, and steer with his head hanging out the window. By this time, lightning was striking all around. I was hooked by my radio to a nearby antenna. A lightning bolt struck close by. I looked down at my radio and it was almost glowing it was so hot. I cued the mike and said, "Joe, you're on your own till the red flag." I unhooked from that radio and found myself some shelter. I've never seen a storm disappear so quickly. The sun came back out, and we were soon racing again. Joe finished seventh.

We had a nice stretch in June and July, with four top-10 finishes in five races, then we struggled through August. But when we got back to the short tracks in September, we started rolling again. We finished sixth at Richmond and led a bunch of laps, sixth at Dover, fifth at Martinsville, and sixth at North Wilkesboro.

Back in those days, the NASCAR inspections were nowhere near as rigorous as they are now, and a lot of teams, including ours, were willing to try just about anything they thought they could get away with.

NASCAR had a rule that said the two lower control arms in the front end could be no more than a half-inch different in length. For passenger cars, the control arms are the same length. In racing, especially at the short tracks, it's better to have the left control arm shorter than the right arm, because that puts more left offset in the car, which puts more weight on the left side and sets the car up to go faster through those left turns. At a place like Martinsville, you make 1,000 sharp left turns in a race.

So what we did was use a right lower control arm that was about three-fourths to seven-eighths of an inch longer, which was too much offset to pass inspection. To disguise that offset we had a guy design us some bolts that had offset heads, so it looked as though the arms were attached to the frame in the location specified by the rules.

At the time, they measured the arms only during the inspection before the first practice. After inspection, we'd pull those fake bolts out (which were really just studs to hold the arm in place; you couldn't race the car with them) and put the real bolts in, and, *voila,* we'd have our seven-eighths of an inch offset.

At Martinsville in September, someone must have ratted us out. When Tim Earp, the NASCAR inspector, got underneath the car, the first thing he did was take out his pocketknife and just pop those fake bolts out. He crawled back out and said, "I want these bolts and I want that lower control arm that is too long."

Well, obviously we were caught dead. But all they did was take the unauthorized control arms. We didn't get fined. Back in those days, you didn't get fined unless you had a really major infraction, such as a big motor or softened tires. So we had to put approved control arms on the car, and that threw off all of the geometry on the car. We did not run well in practice and we qualified 17th.

The sun hadn't come up when the track opened at 6 a.m. on race morning. By then, I had made up my mind that the first thing I was going to do, while it was dark, was to take that half-inch offset lower control arm off and put another one on that was too long. I was just going to take my chances. Since I had already been caught, I knew that if I was caught again, I would probably be suspended or heavily fined.

But I took the gamble, and we had a different race car that day. Joe Ruttman drove it to a fifth-place finish. And we never got caught. Back then, they didn't check that area of the car in post-race inspection.

In 1987, Kenny Bernstein replaced Joe Ruttman with Morgan Shepherd. Kenny and Joe did not see eye to eye. Kenny was a driver himself. He had a strong personality and was stubborn about the way he wanted things done. That ended up being the problem with Kenny and a lot of his drivers. His drivers could be stubborn, too.

Morgan and I had run only a few races with each other in 1985, and Kenny thought we had done well enough together to seriously consider Morgan our permanent driver. He thought it would help the team if we just went back and got the guy we were running pretty well with before we'd had Joe.

But Morgan is the classic journeyman driver. He seems to work best under temporary circumstances, when you're racing week to week or month to month. When Morgan becomes a permanent fixture, he can get pretty demanding. Even before the 1987 season started, Morgan wanted to change the whole program. We were at the annual awards banquet at the Waldorf-Astoria in New York, and Morgan started telling Kenny that he wanted to take some cars up to his house in Conover and work on them there. I was opposed to that. And Morgan wanted to change the way we were cooling the gears. I wasn't comfortable with that. I thought we would end up sacrificing durability. I didn't want to fix one problem and create two. I fought Morgan tooth and nail on his changes, and so we really didn't get along very well. I agreed that we needed to get better, but I said we couldn't just turn everything upside down. Not that I wasn't willing to do everything I could to go faster. I'd get away with anything I thought I could get away with.

I wanted to take as much weight out of the cars as I could, so we drilled the whole right side frame rail full of holes. Our chassis was black, and we took black duct tape and filled the holes. We painted it, which made the tape stiff. And it actually bonded pretty well with the metal.

But during inspection at the race at Atlanta in March, Tim Earp started looking down inside our right front door. Then he reached down in there and began feeling the frame rail. You couldn't really see anything by looking, but you could feel it if you got your hand down there.

The next thing I know, Tim was pulling one piece of tape after another out of there. He made us weld a plate over it. Obviously, in hindsight, what I did was stupid. It weakened the chassis and wasn't very safe. If I had been caught like that in 1997 instead of 1987, NASCAR undoubtedly would have suspended me and fined me heavily.

Another neat innovation I figured out around that time was how to seal the air induction at the back of the hood to make more power. The closer you could get the cowl to the air cleaner the better the power, because you get more air into the engine. We made a false side to it that the driver operated with a rod under the dash to seal the area and make it almost like a cold air box. It worked great, but I got cold feet and never used it. I was afraid the driver would slide it out on the track but not be able to get it back in place, out of sight, when he came back in. And even in those days it would have been pretty big if we got caught.

I didn't try to pull very many stunts in the 1990s, after Gary Nelson joined NASCAR and took over as Winston Cup technical director. He knew every trick in the book, because he'd tried most of them himself when he was a crew chief.

In 1987, we again had our best runs at tiny Martinsville Speedway, which was always one of my best tracks. When we arrived for the April race, we knew we had a fast car. We were in the middle of the lineup for qualifying runs, and Morgan went out and set a new track record at a speed of 92.355 mph in the Quaker State Buick.

We were on pins and needles as driver after driver went out and tried to knock us out of the top starting spot. When it was over, we were still on top. It was Morgan's fourth pole position. But it was my first. And it was a great feeling to know that on that day, we were the best—better than Dale Earnhardt, Bobby Allison, Neil Bonnett, Darrell Waltrip, Richard Petty, Harry Gant, and all the rest. And we held that track record for two solid years until Geoff Bodine came along in 1989 and went 93 mph. During the race, we had transmission trouble and broke a timing chain and finished 18th. But that didn't spoil the thrill of winning my first pole position.

A month later, we were at Charlotte Motor Speedway for the World 600. Although we only qualified 20th, we ran well in the race, and a lot of cars had problems. It was very hot that day, and Morgan needed a relief driver, so we asked Sterling Marlin to take the wheel for a while. But Morgan definitely wanted to get back in his car, and did. Sterling had run well, and Morgan built on that and managed to finish second to Kyle Petty, who lapped the field.

That gave our team a boost. Any time you are struggling, one good run gives everybody confidence. Everything that you have been questioning gets answered, at least for a day, and you can use that to build momentum. And we did. We had five more races with top-five finishes during the second half of the season.

The July race at Talladega was not one of them. We weren't running well there, and Morgan wasn't feeling well. The day before the race, he woke up with food poisoning. He ran a little bit in the morning practice, but was one hurting puppy. The stifling July heat in Alabama only made things worse.

Kenny Bernstein's business partner, John Dangler, said, "Look, Joe Ruttman is not doing anything. Why don't we bring him down here to help Morgan?"

We called Joe. "Sure," he said. John sent the team plane to Tennessee to pick him up. NASCAR said he could drive for us Sunday as long as he made some laps in Saturday's final practice. I went over to the Talladega airport, which is right next to the speedway, to wait for Joe to arrive.

While I waited, the ARCA race was being run. It was a 113-lap race. I could see the scoreboard click off the laps—60, 70, 80, 90. Finally, just before 100 laps, I saw the plane coming in. We hustled back over to the track, threw Joe in the car and got him fitted for the final practice.

I just wanted Joe to take it easy and feel the car out. But in the first lap of Happy Hour, Joe came flying down the front straight three-wide in the middle of a bunch of good race cars. It scared the heck out of me. But Joe was tickled to death about the way that race car was driving. Morgan, however, wasn't happy. He didn't want anyone else in his car.

The plan was for Morgan to start the car and Joe to take over during the first caution period. But only 10 laps into the race, the engine blew. I have to admit that a part of me still thinks Morgan did something to that engine to damage it. He knew he couldn't finish the race, but he still didn't want Ruttman behind the wheel. You hate to think a driver would do that, but that's the way I felt, and most of our team thought the same thing, too. I never asked him about it. You just don't ask some things.

We struggled with Morgan for the most part, but we finished third at Michigan in August. I don't remember ever being so excited about finishing third. But it was one of those days where we ran up front all day long with a good, strong race car. Everything clicked. The pit stops were clean and fast.

We managed to pick up three more top-five finishes that season, but we crashed a few more times and continued our up-and-down season until Atlanta in November, where we blew an engine only 49 laps into the event. Morgan finished the year 17th in the Winston Cup points standings. We had won a pole position and finished in the top five seven times, but we had 13 DNFs.

The year before, Morgan had bounced around among five different car owners, missing two races in the process, and had still finished 18th in points and won a race. With us, he ran *every* race in 1987 and still only improved one position in the points. It was time for a driver change.

For the 1988 season, Kenny Bernstein hired a proven winner, Ricky Rudd. Ricky was just 31, but had been a regular in the Winston Cup series since 1977. He had won races in the five previous seasons and had finished in the top 10 in points for eight consecutive years. I was excited about working with all of the promise *and* experience that Ricky had. And we got along pretty well.

During the first part of the season, we were fast but inconsistent. We finished second to Neil Bonnett at Richmond, yet followed with three straight DNFs. We blew engines at Atlanta and Darlington and crashed at Bristol. Then we finished second again at North Wilkesboro and headed to Martinsville.

I felt pretty confident going to Martinsville with Ricky. A driver needs to finesse the track at Martinsville, and Ricky was certainly one of the best at that. We won the pole and led the first 37 laps, but another engine failure put us out with about 50 laps to go. We blew yet another engine at Talladega.

Ricky wrecked in The Winston and hurt his leg. Then, during mid-week practice for the Coca-Cola 600, he blew another engine and nearly hit the wall.

I'd finally reached my breaking point. It was hard enough dealing with the tracks where we weren't running well, which of course put everyone on edge. To be blowing engines right and left, just about every other week, was too much.

I found a phone and called our engine builder, Ron Armstrong, at the shop and just reamed him. Ron was a great guy—one of the most dedicated racers you'd ever find. He was giving us motors with plenty of power, but they weren't holding up. When confronted, Ron always gave the type of answer you didn't want to hear: "Larry, I just don't know what happened to that motor."

Ricky's leg was still hurting him pretty bad the next week, so we had Mike Alexander standing by. Mike got in the car to finish the race and that left Ricky in the pits with us. Ricky was telling us everything we needed to be doing and everything we were doing wrong. He was just a frustrated driver who wanted to help. But after a while, I was thinking, "Man, could you please get back in that race car. You're driving me crazy."

As the season progressed we had some good finishes, but we continued to blow engines. We lost another motor at Pocono in June. At Talladega in July, we tried a little trick I had figured out for qualifying. Any time you can block up the left window, the car will run faster, because less air is getting inside it. We closed the window by snapping a sheet of clear plastic into place behind the regulation window net. I had Ricky pull the plastic off after qualifying so no one would see it when he came into the garage. About the only time we took a chance of having it seen was when we snapped the window net into place on pit road before he drove off to qualify. How much it helped us, I don't know. But it couldn't have hurt. Ricky qualified ninth, but we were packing up the transporter before lap 50 after blowing the engine.

Right before we left for the race at Watkins Glen, Linda and I learned that she was pregnant with our first child, Brooke. This was incredible news, because we had been trying for four years. We were already talking about the possibility of adoption and considering other options. Actually, Linda was pregnant with twins, but we lost one.

So my spirits were soaring when we got to the road course in upstate New York. Not only were Linda and I going to start a family, we were at a racetrack where we had the highest of hopes. Ricky was a great road racer and had been very competitive at the road race at Riverside in June, where he sat on the pole. We took the same car Ricky drove at Riverside to Watkins Glen. He qualified sixth.

On race morning, Ricky's wife, Linda, was standing in the lounge of the transporter. I was telling her about my Linda's pregnancy. I had always admired a diamond "tennis" bracelet Linda Rudd wore, and I commented on it again.

"You know," I said, "if we can win this race today, the first thing I'm going to do when I get home is go and buy a tennis bracelet like that for Linda."

We had our problems early in the race and made an unscheduled pit stop on lap 20 to replace two tires. We fell back to 38th place, but there were eight caution periods and we used them to help get back to the front.

We took the lead, with four laps to go, when Darrell Waltrip had problems and fell back. Linda Rudd was scoring in the pits for the team. After Ricky took the lead, she poked me in the side and pointed to her tennis bracelet.

Rusty Wallace caught Ricky on the final lap, and it was a dogfight to the checkered flag. We just got to see the end of it. As both cars came flying off that final turn, they were sideways. Ricky put Rusty into the dirt to stay ahead. Ricky crossed the finish line about a car length and a half ahead.

We all came over the pit wall and celebrated on pit road like a team always does. There's something really special about the first victory. It was like the weight of the world had been lifted off my shoulders. For eight years, since I had left Birmingham, a little voice had haunted me daily, asking me when I was going to win, reminding me I still hadn't gone to victory lane yet.

Now that I was finally there, I couldn't help but think back to 1980 when I went to Hueytown and visited Donnie Allison, and how he had told me it was "going to be a long damn time" before I ever saw another checkered flag. I reminded Donnie about that conversation the next chance I got.

We were finally getting our act together and were running well in a lot of places. Bob Riley of Riley & Scott, a well-known racing engineering firm out of Indianapolis, was helping us with our chassis development and had been riding Kenny pretty hard about the engine problems. As well he should have.

At Michigan, the very next race, we went back to our old form. Ricky qualified 10th and ran well all day, but with two laps to go, his engine blew. We finished 16th. We had another good run going at Bristol and even led a few laps. But with 49 laps to go, we blew another engine.

At Richmond we ran well on the new, expanded track and qualified 12th. With 55 laps to go, we were in the lead. Three laps later, the engine let go on us. After we loaded the car, I went looking for Bob Riley, and I had trouble finding him. I finally noticed him standing next to an infield concession stand that served beer. Bob was as red as a beet. He had the biggest beer you could buy, and I think he was just drinking his frustrations away.

"We're going to be OK, Bob," I told him. "We just have to ride out this wave. Kenny's going to take care of this problem." I knew that Kenny was as concerned as we were about the problem. The trouble was, we didn't have a lot of options in Greenville for other engine builders.

Things didn't improve. At Martinsville, we qualified 14th and charged to the front once the race started. Ricky took the lead on lap 153, and we dominated most of the rest of the race. By lap 420, Ricky had led for 237 laps. We only had 40 miles to go. I didn't think anything could keep us from winning that race. Suddenly, a plume of smoke erupted from our Buick.

Ricky drove straight into the garage, and I walked back down to the trailer and just sat on the back end, trying to keep my composure. Ricky had finished in the top 10 in points for eight consecutive seasons, but in 1988, because of all of our engine failures, he slipped to 11th.

We had failed to finish 11 races, and 10 of those were because of blown engines. Our sponsor, Quaker State, started taking a lot of heat about its oil and our engines blowing up on race cars.

Nobody was working harder than Ron Armstrong to perfect our engines. The man worked day and night. You'd leave at nine or 10 at night and come back the next morning at seven or eight and Ron would still be working. Toward the end of the season we weren't blowing up as often, but Kenny knew we had to make a change. The pressure from Quaker State to get our engine program fixed made that a necessity. The irony is that, at the time we made that change, I believe Ron was finally about to figure it out—to reach that delicate balance between horsepower and durability.

Solving our engine problem was the main reason Kenny decided at the end of 1988 to move our race team from the old Bobby Hawkins shop in Traveler's Rest, South Carolina, to the Charlotte area.

When I had first asked Kenny to consider moving, he was adamant about not moving "to that hornet's nest in Charlotte, where everybody steals everybody else's help."

What changed his mind was the opportunity to hire engine builder Lou LaRosa, who had been with Richard Childress for a number of years. Lou, however, would not move to South Carolina, so we had to move closer to where he lived.

I was all for the move, even though Linda and I loved Greenville. We had just finished off the upstairs of our home, and Linda was several months pregnant when Kenny decided to move the team. But I knew that it was going to make a lot more sense to be in the Charlotte area.

In Charlotte, we would be in the heart of the action. We'd be much more on top of the sport. We had the driver we needed. Our cars were good. And finally, we'd have reliable engines—built by the man who'd been making Dale Earnhardt's cars go fast. As 1989 approached, I felt as if we finally had all the pieces in place.

CHAPTER SIX

"It's His First Win Let Him Enjoy It."

spent almost the whole winter moving our team from Greenville to Charlotte. We only had eight or 10 employees in South Carolina, and some of them weren't moving with us, so not only did we have to move everything, we had to hire new people.

There wasn't a lot of time to prepare race cars. When we left for Daytona, the car we were going to take to Richmond was nothing more than a chassis. I knew the guys who stayed back at the shop would get a lot of work done on it while we were at Daytona, but I also knew we would have a lot left to do in the week between Daytona and Richmond. In Florida we got off to a slow start, finishing 19th.

The day we got back from Daytona, they were already forecasting heavy snow for Richmond later that week. But NASCAR doesn't plan around weather forecasts. So we moved at full speed and prepared the car. After working until late Thursday night, we then drove 11 hours through terrible conditions to Richmond—it's usually a four-and-a-half-hour trip—only to have the race postponed because of the snow.

We finished 32nd at Rockingham after Dale Earnhardt put Ricky into the wall. Then we lost an engine at Atlanta and had our first DNF.

Lou LaRosa, however, fixed our engine problem. His engines didn't make the power of Ron Armstrong's engines, but they were reliable. We went from blowing 11 engines in 1988 to winning the Sears Diehard award in 1989 for completing the most laps and miles.

After Atlanta, we returned to Richmond to run the snowed-out race and finished fourth after our best run yet that season. The sixth race was at Bristol, and we were still behind in preparing cars. The only backup car we had to take with us was our Daytona backup, which is certainly not the best insurance when you're at a short track like Bristol.

A misting rain began to fall during Saturday practice, but NASCAR kept the green flag out, and everybody was still trying to get laps in. I told Ricky to take it easy because the track was damp. I don't know what Ricky was thinking, but to me it looked as if he was trying to win practice in the rain. And he wrecked the car, seemingly beyond repair. But the thought of trying to race that Daytona backup car was even less appealing than trying to repair the car.

Larry McClure, who owned the Kodak Chevrolet, had his shop in Abingdon, Virginia, only about 20 miles north of the track, and he invited us to use his shop to make the repairs. We worked almost all night that night, brought the car back the next morning and checked it in. The car's setup was way off, but we made lots of adjustments and used up 14 or 15 sets of tires—more than I ever used in any other race.

While that weekend taught me the importance of having a good backup car prepared to its fullest, it really taught me the importance of perseverance. We made the best choice we could, stuck with it, and worked our guts out. And despite problems during the race, Ricky finished eighth at Bristol and completed every lap. But overall, we just weren't running that well.

Between the Martinsville and North Wilkesboro race weekend, my first child, Brooke, was born, on April 17, 1989. The doctor agreed to induce labor so that I would be able to be there with Linda for the delivery. I feel very fortunate that I was able to be there because, so often, the demands of our sport don't allow us to be present for important events like this, and the birth of your first child happens only once.

At Talladega, before the season's ninth race, we struggled in practice and qualified a miserable 32nd. We continued to struggle during the final practice.

I kept trying to get input from Ricky, and he just wouldn't give me any. He just wouldn't tell me much about what the car was doing. Ricky was good about giving feedback at most other tracks, but not at Talladega. There, setting up the car for him was almost like throwing darts wearing a blindfold. I don't think he was comfortable at Daytona and Talladega at those speeds.

We were getting more and more frustrated. Then we finally reached our breaking point with each other. The next thing I knew, we were up in the transporter's lounge in the middle of Happy Hour screaming at each other. Then Ricky walked out. "This is great," I said to myself.

I looked at John Dangler, who was Kenny's eyes and ears at the track when Kenny wasn't there, which was most of the time. "John, we need to put somebody in that race car to see if we can figure out what the hell is going on," I said.

Rick Wilson, who had driven for the Morgan-McClure team, always ran well at Daytona and Talladega, so I went and asked him if he would come run our car for a few laps. He ran maybe 10 or 12 laps right in the middle of the pack, came back in and said, "I don't know what to tell you. This thing drives pretty well. Actually, it's a lot better than my car. I feel like I have control of the front wheels in your car. With my car, I don't know which way it's pointed or which way it's going!"

Next thing I knew, Rick was interrogating me about the settings and setup of our car because he wanted to go work on his. But his report made me feel pretty good. It meant even if we didn't have everything perfect, we weren't as far off as we were showing.

Ricky didn't run that well in the race. He was caught up in somebody else's accident on lap 169 and knocked out of the event. We finished 31st.

A month later, we ran the inaugural race at Sears Point International Raceway (which had replaced Riverside in the schedule) located in the heart of California's wine country just outside Sonoma.

A lot of drivers went to Sears Point in the weeks before the race and tested. We didn't. We qualified fourth, and the three guys who were faster than us were three of the guys who tested. But we felt pretty confident. We had the same car that had won at Watkins Glen. Ricky was in his prime as a road racer.

We took the lead for the first time on lap 11 and led eight circuits. Then we barged into the lead again on lap 22 and staked our claim for the race. A yellow flag flew with about 30 laps to go, and I knew we needed to hit pit road for a splash of fuel. We had just pitted about four laps earlier, but we needed a full tank to go 30 laps.

The fuel-only pit stop is designed to last for just a few seconds. I watched the catch-can man and as soon as I saw fuel run out of the overflow into his can, I shouted in the radio, "Go! Go! Go! Go!" Ricky took off. But as he was leaving, Geoff Bodine was coming in. He hit our right front fender. Ricky went all to pieces on the radio: "It's killed my fender! It's killed my fender!"

Our pit stop was so quick, Ricky popped out on the track *ahead* of the pace car. Now two crazy things were happening at the same time. Ricky should have been held by the NASCAR official at the end of pit road, who holds a stop/go paddle that's red on one side and green on the other. But he gave Ricky the green side of the paddle and out we went in front of the pace car. Technically, we now had a lap on the field.

So now I had Ricky screaming in one ear about his fender and a NASCAR official in my other ear, telling me we were going to have to restart the race from the tail end of the field for trying to steal a lap from the competitors!

I totally, absolutely, threw a fit on pit road. The NASCAR official on pit road is no more than a go-between for the NASCAR officials in the tower and the teams. I knew that, but I was all over him anyway, just to make sure my message got delivered.

So while I was screaming at the NASCAR official, ESPN pit road reporter Jack Arute came up and eavesdropped on us. And just about the time he stuck a microphone in the middle of this heated conversation, I shouted, "All you people are trying to do is [expletive] us out of this race!"

Fortunately, NASCAR came to understand that we didn't do anything wrong and that the mistake was made by the stop-and-go man at the end of pit road. So they put us back behind the pace car where we belonged—in first place. I had another driver look closely at Ricky's fender, and he assured us it wasn't rubbing. I had never even noticed Jack Arute or the microphone.

Ricky kept the lead and went on to beat Rusty Wallace, after some good, tough racing during a wild fender-banging last lap. When I got back to my hotel that evening, the message light was flashing. It was my mother in Birmingham. When I called her back, she wanted to know why I had started using bad language on national television. I was shocked. I had no idea that had gone out on the air. Then I got a call from Linda about it. By then, I was pretty upset. But Jack apologized, and so did Neil Goldberg, the producer.

That day, I learned it was up to me to help watch for Ricky when he was leaving pit road. After that race we developed new phrases to communicate the situation in the pit lane. When the jack dropped and there was no traffic, I shouted, "Clear, clear, clear all the way!" If there was traffic in the pit lane, I yelled, "Keep it tight! Keep it tight!" or even "Stop! Stop!"

Ricky was a determined, fiery driver with a stubborn streak, which he demonstrated at Rockingham that fall. We were running pretty respectably, but then Sterling Marlin got into Ricky and wrecked him. I don't think Sterling did it intentionally, but Ricky thought he did.

Ricky brought the car in and we repaired it. It was a pretty major rebuild, but Ricky got back out there. But I had seen something in his eyes before he left. He was going back out there to retaliate. So I did my best to keep them apart. Every time I saw Ricky get close to Sterling or Sterling get close to Ricky, I would radio Ricky to pit. I'd tell him we needed to look at something, or to change something, or we needed tires.

The wreck with Sterling happened early in the race, so I had to do this for several hundred laps. Eventually, I missed Ricky as he came around the track. Sure enough, he caught Sterling somewhere on the backstretch. I couldn't see it, but I did see the caution flag come out.

Ricky came back around the track, and he was OK. But poor ol' Sterling came back around, and his car looked as if it was running on four broken wagon wheels. It was quite a sight. I had been doing such a good job of keeping Ricky away from Sterling, but I missed just once and that's all it took. Ricky got Sterling back. But that was just Ricky. He was determined. Even if he had to ride around there after the race, he was going to get Sterling back.

We didn't win any more races in 1989. Our best results were a pair of third-place finishes, but with our engine failures under control, we were more consistent. Ricky finished eighth in the Winston Cup points, with a victory, seven top-fives, and 15 top-10 finishes.

For the most part Ricky and I got along pretty well. But problems developed between Ricky and Kenny Bernstein. When Kenny hired Ricky in 1988, he loved Ricky Rudd more than anybody on Earth. But by the latter part of 1989, Kenny probably disliked Ricky Rudd more than anybody on Earth. They were both so stubborn, and by then, they pretty much knew they weren't going to continue racing together in 1990.

During an off weekend in the late summer of 1989, Linda and I went to Myrtle Beach, South Carolina, for a quick vacation. Except I spent almost the entire weekend on the phone in the motel room. I talked with Kenny. Then I talked with Ricky. Then 20 minutes with Kenny. Then 10 minutes with Ricky. It went on and on. I spent two solid days on the phone with those two trying to fix the problems they had with each other.

Their main problem was that they didn't easily trust other people. They both thought the world was out to get them, and inevitably they became suspicious of each other. I think 1990 could have been an awesome year with Ricky at King Racing, but Ricky and Kenny just finally decided to go their separate ways.

In the meantime, I had been contemplating a career change of my own with Davey Allison and his car owner Robert Yates. I was beginning to get to know Davey from seeing him at Mass on Saturday evenings in various race cities around the country.

Davey was a proven winner, with six victories in three years, including two of those in his rookie year of 1987. He and Robert felt that their team needed more leadership, and they thought I was the guy to provide it. It sounded like an exciting challenge. I had spoken with Robert several times, and on Saturday during the support race at Phoenix, I met with him in the front of his trailer. We talked some more about the job, and then I said, "Robert, I'll take it." But the second I left that trailer, the gravity of what I had done dawned on me.

"I can't walk out on that 26 car," I said to myself. "I built that team. I've been there since the beginning—even before Kenny bought the team from Bobby Hawkins." I went back to the hotel that night and cried my eyes out. I told Linda I couldn't take that job. But I felt horrible that I had told Robert I would.

"Larry, you need to call Robert and tell him," she said.

But I just couldn't do it the next day. After we flew back to Charlotte, I had to test at Atlanta on Tuesday and Wednesday. And about the middle of the morning Tuesday, when it was pouring down rain, I got in a car and drove across the highway in front of Atlanta Motor Speedway and called Robert on a convenience store pay phone.

"Robert, I know you're probably going to hate me, and I'm not a very big man for doing what I've done, but I just can't leave that 26 team," I said. "I know I told you I was coming to work for you, but I just *can't* leave. I know I may be making the biggest mistake of my life, but I can't do it."

Robert said, "Larry, I know where you're coming from. I've been in that position before myself. Don't think twice about it. We'll find somebody. Yeah, I'm disappointed. But I understand." I think I knew right then that *someday* I'd go to work for that man.

So I stayed at King Racing, and Kenny hired Brett Bodine as our driver for 1990. Brett was the middle brother of the three racing Bodine brothers. He followed his older brother, Geoff, to the south and ran his first full season in 1988, driving Bud Moore's Ford. He had not yet won a race.

When we returned to Daytona for Speedweeks, Linda and I were standing at the front desk of the Pirate's Cove Motel, checking in for our usual week-and-a-half stay. The phone rang behind the desk and the clerk answered it. "Yeah, he's checking in here right now," she said and passed the phone to me.

It was my stepmother. My dad had collapsed and died of a massive heart attack after he got out of the shower at their home in Bessemer. No one can prepare you for the shock of a moment like that. Linda, Brooke (who was 10 months old), and I flew to Birmingham the next morning. He was buried on Saturday, and we flew back to Daytona Beach on Sunday, still reeling from the experience.

The season started out pretty slow with Brett Bodine. We managed to score only two top-10 finishes in the first six races. The seventh race of the season was at North Wilkesboro, and Brett was running quite well there. We made two long runs in Happy Hour and made a major change in shock absorbers between the runs.

To watch our car at North Wilkesboro, I always used to stand on a little rock wall next to the garage area. As I stood there that day, I could see our car had that really good look to it as it turned in the middle of turns one and two. Brett liked the car, but I thought it was even better than he thought. I thought we could win the race. I left the track after the final practice certain that our car was as good as anybody's.

We were a good top-five car during the race. With a little less than 100 laps to go in the 400-lap race, the field was in the middle of a round of green flag pit stops. A yellow flag came out. We had just pitted for four tires and fuel. For some reason, the pace car picked us up as the leader. I'm pretty sure even to this day that the pace car picked us up by mistake. We were not the leader of that race; Darrell Waltrip was. Brett was raising Cain in my ear because he thought NASCAR was putting him on the tail end of the lead lap. He didn't realize what was going on.

"Brett, shut up. They have you as the leader," I said.

NASCAR didn't change anything, and I thought, "Well now, we can do just fine with this. We've got four fresh tires, a full load of fuel, not a lot of laps to go, and NASCAR has put us in front."

Brett stayed in front the rest of the way and won the first and only race of his career to this point. Darrell finished second. It was my third victory, but the first on an oval.

North Wilkesboro had a unique victory lane that sat atop the hot dog building in the infield. They lifted the winning car on an elevator platform and conducted the celebrations on the roof. We had come close to winning there with Ricky, but I had always watched another car take that elevator ride to the roof of the hot dog stand.

After Brett took the checkered flag and our team rolled the car up on the platform, I made sure I was standing right next to it so I could take that elevator ride.

During all the years I raced at North Wilkesboro, with seven different drivers, I think my car finished in the top 10 every time but once or twice. It's a record I'm proud of.

It felt really good to be back in victory lane, but I went there with a vague feeling of uncertainty. Darrell and some of the other drivers, crew chiefs, and car owners were all over NASCAR because of the scoring foul-up. Since I had my own doubts about how we got the lead, I was worried that NASCAR might somehow change the results.

Darrell has since told me how he was just raising hell about it with NASCAR President Bill France Jr.

Finally, Bill looked at Darrell and said, "How many races have you won, Darrell?"

"Oh, I don't know, Bill. Seventy-nine, I think."

"How many more races do you think you'll win?"

"I think I'll win a few more."

France pointed toward victory lane. "Look at that boy," he said to D. W. "It's his first win. Let him enjoy it."

Kenny Bernstein was usually drag racing when we were racing, so he had not seen our first two victories. This day he had run a drag race in Georgia. He'd been knocked out early, and he and his girlfriend listened to the NASCAR race as they drove back to Charlotte. As they got close to Charlotte, we took the lead. So Kenny drove straight through the city and continued on for another 80 miles to the track.

We were tearing the car down in the garage when Kenny finally got there. I was blown away to see him. "I thought you were racing in Commerce," I said.

"I was," Kenny said, telling me the story. It was nice that Kenny could be with us that afternoon after missing the victories at Watkins Glen and Sonoma. Kenny stayed in Winston Cup racing as a car owner through the 1995 season, but North Wilkesboro turned out to be his final victory as an owner.

We had some other good runs with Brett that year, particularly at my best tracks. Brett finished third at Watkins Glen and fourth at Martinsville in September. He was third when we raced at North Wilkesboro again . Perhaps the biggest highlight of the year, other than winning at North Wilkesboro, was when we won the pole for the Mello Yello 500 at Charlotte Motor Speedway in October.

Brett was a good qualifier. At Charlotte, I was on top of the transporter with Ron Puryear, our engine tuner. Ron was clocking segments with a stopwatch. Ron wasn't smiling. Ron never smiled. When Brett got to the end of the backstretch, Ron poked me. He showed me the stopwatch and said, "If he can get through three and four, trust me, we're on the pole."

Sure enough, Brett sat on the pole. It's great to win a pole position anywhere, but at Charlotte there's always more hype and hoopla. We ran well in the race and led a few laps, but we broke a rocker arm. It wasn't enough to knock us out of the race. We even managed to stay on the lead lap, finishing eighth.

But overall, it was another flat season. Brett finished 12th in the Winston Cup championship. Outside of that North Wilkesboro win, we only had eight other top-10 finishes in the 29-race season. It wasn't that we were dropping out a lot. We only had five DNFs. We just weren't that fast. Our engines were durable now, but we'd sacrificed a lot of horsepower.

We had been parked next to Davey Allison and the Robert Yates Racing No. 28 car at Talladega. On our car for qualifying, we'd have the front grille taped up solid, trying to get the best aerodynamics. I'd look at Davey's car, and they'd have a little bit of the grille left open. Even with that added drag to their car, they were still a second faster than we were per lap. That just about killed me. Once again, engines were our problem.

Back in 1989, when Kenny had replaced our engine builder, Ron Armstrong, with Lou LaRosa, I strongly favored the hire and the team's move to Charlotte to accommodate Lou. But as the season progressed, Lou and I came to hate each other's guts. He was the type of guy who only wanted to hear what made his ears feel good, and I was not a yes man.

During the 1990 season, one week we'd have an awesome motor and one week we'd have one that wouldn't run. When we went to Pocono in June, Brett finished fourth. After the race, he told me, "I'll come by the shop tomorrow because I want to make sure to tell Lou that was one of the best motors we've had all year."

When we went back to Pocono five weeks later with the same car and same setup, but a different engine, we ran terribly. This time Brett told me, "You go home and tell Lou that has to be the worst damn motor he's given us." So I went and told Lou. And he told me, "You can't expect to have motors every week like the one you had in June."

Just a couple of weeks before that, Lou and I had clashed over a tire test for Goodyear at Rockingham. Imagine—a tire test at Rockingham in July. When we race there in February it's about 30 or 40 degrees, and in October its about 50 or 60 degrees if we're lucky. That July it must have been about 100 degrees with about 100 percent humidity. At seven in the morning, you were soaked with sweat. You were miserable before you even got to the track. But it was important to me to maintain a good relationship with Goodyear. So after the race at Daytona, Brett and I had driven to Rockingham to test while our wives stayed at the beach in Florida.

By then, I wasn't sure what to expect from Lou. I figured he might dismiss the significance of the test and give us some old motor he had laying in a corner. So I'd really given him a sermon: "Now Lou, this is the first time Goodyear has ever asked this team and Brett to test, so make sure we have a good motor. We need to look good. Let's make sure we don't have a problem with it."

Brett and I got to the end of the first day of the test and, sure enough, I didn't like what I saw on the spark plugs. And what was coming out of the exhaust pipes didn't look right. So I called Lou. He was sarcastic about the whole thing.

The next morning, after the first or second run, water began coming out of the exhaust pipes. Of course, Lou didn't send an engine guy down there with us. I didn't even have a spark plug holder. I had to use a discarded Big Mac box.

So I found a phone booth, and it was so hot inside it that the windows were steaming up. I was in there trying to explain to him what the spark plugs looked like. Lou responded with more sarcastic comments about how we'd blown up his motor. I told him he'd sent us a piece of crap for a motor, and that's why it blew up.

I told him, "Lou, this will never work. This will never work with me and it will never work with Kenny." Before long, Lou and I would hardly speak to one another. Lou had solved our durability problem, but it didn't take me too long to realize that he had taken us only to a point and that's where it stopped.

At first, Kenny was irritated by my problem with Lou, but I think Kenny realized what the score was when he and Lou and I went in for a meeting to try to solve the problem.

"What do you think your weaknesses are, Lou?" Kenny asked.

"I don't have no weaknesses," Lou replied.

I knew right then that he had given Kenny the wrong answer. Lou would never admit a mistake. It was always somebody else's fault. Lou was gone within a couple of months, and Kenny replaced him with Ron Puryear. Late in 1990, I sat down with Kenny and I signed on for another year. He stepped me up a bit more in pay, so I was now earning around $100,000. That made me proud and a little bit amazed, when I thought back to how I had worked for free for so many years in Birmingham.

CHAPTER SEVEN

My First Races with Davey

A month before the start of the 1991 Winston Cup season, more than 100 motorsports media members dropped by our shop to hear us talk about our expectations for 1991. They were on the Charlotte Motor Speedway's annual media tour.

The King Racing shop was located just off exit 23 of Interstate 77 in Huntersville, North Carolina. When the buses pulled in, all of us on the team were there to greet them, wearing our new Quaker State shop shirts.

I tried to put a good face on it that day for the press, but I wasn't really that optimistic about the season ahead. A three-year battle with motor problems, first with reliability and then with power, had worn me out. And I guess I was still a little bit sour over Kenny and Ricky Rudd not working out their business differences. I think I knew in my heart that it just wasn't going to work—that we would never have all the pieces in place to win consistently. Even though my career was about to make a radical change, I can truthfully say that I wasn't thinking about leaving Kenny at that time.

As it turned out, my final race with King Racing was at Atlanta—the fourth event of the 1991 season. We were still fighting motor problems, but darned if Brett didn't win the outside pole. Then we put our race motor in the car, went out to practice, and couldn't run a lick. Brett told me, "Larry, I believe this is the worst motor I've ever had in Atlanta."

Sure enough, we ran terribly in the race. Actually, the race was delayed by rain after just 47 laps, and we had to finish on Monday. We finished 15th, three laps down.

Davey Allison had crashed before the rain delay. His crew chief, Jake Elder, didn't want to fix the car, but Davey and Robert Yates overruled him. So Davey was back out there on Monday, too. One thing both of our teams shared was that we were wracked with internal problems.

After that race, I drove home with Linda, who was pregnant with Brandon, and Brooke, who was two years old. I bet we didn't speak four words all the way home to Charlotte. We weren't mad at each other; I was just frustrated. We had won the outside pole, and then we put in a motor that was so bad that I don't think it would have been fast if it had fallen out of an airplane.

When we got home, I told Linda I didn't care who called, I wasn't talking to anybody. I sure didn't want to hear from Kenny, since I did not want to talk about how the race motor wouldn't run. I decided to call him on Tuesday when I felt a little better.

As I was unloading our van, I heard the phone ring. I didn't answer it, but Linda did. She knew what I had said about no calls, but she came to me anyway and spoke silently with her lips, indicating, "You might want to take this phone call." I glared at her hard, but she'd already painted me in a corner by suggesting I was there. I went in the house and took the call.

It was Robert. He said, "I am going to make a crew chief change in the morning, and I just want to check one final time to see if you are interested in the job."

I said, "Robert, when and where can we meet?" I'd had my fill of fighting engine problems.

I went right out that Monday night and met Robert at a Waffle House on Sunset Boulevard in Charlotte—a place where we didn't think we'd be seen. We sat and talked until 1 a.m., and we hammered out a deal.

I wasn't sure how Kenny would take this, so I worked out a plan. I went to work on Tuesday and acted like it was a normal day. Then I went back to work at about 10 p.m. that night, cleaned out my office, gathered up all my notes and files, rolled my toolbox out, and left my dealership car parked in the lot. Linda picked me up.

The next morning, Wednesday, I called Kenny and told him I needed to talk to him at the shop. "What do you want to talk about?" he asked. I told him I needed to see him in person. Linda drove me back down there. As we got off the exit ramp, I had Linda pull over in a parking lot. "Am I right on this deal?" I asked her.

"Larry, you're in too deep now to turn back," she said. She was right. By then, I didn't need to tell Kenny I was leaving. It was obvious with one look in my office. When we met, he hollered at me. "Larry, I can't believe you'd come in here like that and clean out your stuff," he said. "You know I'd let you take it all with you."

We screamed at each other a little bit, then settled down into a regular conversation. Kenny was pretty disappointed in me. And in all honesty, I was pretty disappointed in myself. I should have known better. What I did was not gentlemanly. Kenny was not going to throw me out or lock me out. I guess I was just scared about all my records. I'm a fanatic about my notes. I could tell you what right front spring I ran at my very first Winston Cup race back in 1980.

I hung my head a little bit with Kenny. But what made me feel good at the end of the meeting was that Kenny and I hugged each other, and we wished each other the best of luck. And Kenny knew I wasn't going to just any team. I was going to Robert Yates Racing. He understood why I had to take that opportunity.

Kenny Bernstein taught me more about business than anyone in my career except perhaps Richard Childress. He could be harsh. On given days, I wished I'd never seen Kenny Bernstein. After we won at Sears Point in 1989, when I talked to Kenny he lit into me about a couple of minor things. He could be that way. But Kenny was a great business-man, and he is the one who made me a good communicator by preaching its importance. I watched him and patterned myself after his communication skills.

Over at Robert Yates Racing, Robert had fired Jake Elder on Tuesday morning, the day after our meeting. Davey, in the meantime, had flown to Pensacola, Florida, for flight certification training. He had plans to be there all week. Davey's pilot, Sam Manze, got wind of the crew chief change on Wednesday and tracked down Davey.

"I don't know what's going on up at the shop, Davey," Sam said, "but they fired Jake Elder yesterday and they've hired a new guy—some guy named Larry McReynolds."

"Yee haw!" shouted Davey.

"Who the hell is Larry McReynolds?" Sam asked. Davey told him about me.

Davey called me that night, and he was like a kid at Christmas. "This is awesome," he said. "We're going to make it happen now. We're going to win races. We're going to win the championship." It was flattering to know that somebody like Davey Allison had that much confidence in me. But I wasn't automatically assuming anything.

The next day, I walked into the Robert Yates Racing shop for the first time. All the guys looked at me, and I think they felt kind of like Sam Manze had felt. They weren't too sure about Larry McReynolds. And I couldn't blame them.

Not a lot of people knew about Larry McReynolds in early 1991. For all intents and purposes, I had remained with the same team—first owned by Bobby Hawkins, then by Kenny Bernstein—since 1983. As they must have seen it, I was a nobody replacing the legendary Jake Elder. He was one of my idols. I couldn't blame them if they were upset, or at least skeptical.

During my first few days, I got all the guys together and talked with them. I laid out my plan. "This ain't about me," I told them. "We're going to do this deal together. We're going to row this boat together—every blooming one of us."

That meeting started us on the road to gaining confidence in each other. They'd never had a crew chief do that before. These guys had never been given direction. They never knew what the crew chief's plan was. They had been expected to be mind readers.

Those were the last of the good old days in the Winston Cup schedule, and we even had *two* off weekends in a row between the Atlanta race and the next event at Darlington. So our first order of business was a test at Darlington before the race there.

The first time Davey went out and ran, he was pretty fast. He came in, and I knelt down by his window and asked him how the car was. I don't remember exactly what he told me, but the way he said it and the look in his eye and the way we communicated was different right from the start. I knew instantly that we had something special.

I couldn't wait to get back to the hotel that evening to call Linda. I said, "Linda, this is going to be the greatest thing that's ever happened to me and to us. Davey and I are already so tight he knows exactly what I am saying and I know what he is saying. And I knew it right away."

Earlier that evening, I had also called the shop foreman, Gil Kerley, to check in. I told him how things were going at the track and asked him how things were at the shop. Gil about went into shock. "We've never had this kind of call before," he said. "No one ever called on race weekends either, so we never knew how we were in practice. And we didn't find out how we qualified until we heard it on the radio."

When we went back to Darlington for the race, we started struggling. We weren't very good at all, and I got paranoid. On Saturday, I looked at Robert at one point and said, "Robert, we shouldn't be struggling like this with the motors we have and with the driver we have. If you think you've made a mistake hiring me as crew chief, I'll totally understand and we can go our separate ways right now."

"No, no," he said. "We'll be fine. Don't worry about it."

That night, back at the hotel, I met with Davey and we decided to make wholesale changes on the car before the race Sunday. The car was much better as the race started, and it continued to get better the longer we ran. Davey led 31 laps late in the race. And we finished second to Ricky Rudd, who beat us by making one less pit stop during the race. It was a huge confidence builder. Davey and I were on the same page right from the start. We had a terrific first race together. I stopped worrying about finding another job.

The next race was at Bristol. During the final Happy Hour practice, Davey made a 75-lap run. Our lap times were looking pretty good. Davey came on the radio and said, "Guys, this thing feels wonderful!" A crew chief doesn't hear that very often, and when he does, it's a great feeling.

During the race, we led a bunch of laps and so did Darrell Waltrip, who has won more races at Bristol—12—than any other driver. Over the years, there had been no love lost between Darrell and Bobby Allison. And on that Sunday, it trickled down to the next generation of Allisons.

On lap 367, Darrell bullied his way past Davey in turn three. Davey stayed right on D. W.'s bumper, and coming out of turn four the next time around, Davey tapped him and sent him spinning down the frontstretch. The yellow flag flew and NASCAR promptly sent Davey to the back of the pack. Davey was hot about the penalty, and he bitched and moaned and went on and on about it until Robert got on the radio and said, "Look, Davey, you've got a good race car. Put it behind you. We can still win this race."

Sure enough, it didn't take Davey long at all to get back in the lead. Then a rain shower passed over, and the race was stopped for more than an hour. During the red flag, they parked the cars down in turns one and two. I walked down there, and the first thing I saw was Darrell and Davey nose to nose, cussing, screaming, and pointing fingers at each other.

I stayed out of that one. It was like the Hatfield-McCoy feud— handed down through generations. I thought Davey's move was questionable, but I had to support him, so I wasn't going to get into it. Any time you see that kind of fire in your driver, it makes you happy. It's much easier to pull a rope than push it. We didn't win at Bristol— we finished third—but it was more confirmation that we had a good thing going.

The next race, a week later at North Wilkesboro, was another slugfest. Davey was involved in three yellow flags. Bill Elliott, Kyle Petty, and Geoff Bodine were all mad at him. NASCAR tossed Bodine out of the race after he rammed Davey's car when they both spun on lap 333. Petty got into Davey's face after the race. Elliott criticized him, too. But through it all, we somehow managed to stay on the lead lap. We finished sixth.

Now it was on to Martinsville. Before we went there, Davey said, "Larry, I'm telling you right up front. I don't run well at Martinsville. I've always struggled there, especially in qualifying."

"Don't worry," I said. "Martinsville is one of my best tracks." It seemed like every track where Davey didn't have a lot of confidence, I had had success.

Davey, however, was right about qualifying. We started 26th in a 32-car field. But once the race got going, he moved right up. By halfway, Davey was battling in the lead pack. And after he took the lead on lap 364, Davey began checking out. With only 50 laps to go, we were a whopping four seconds ahead.

But Davey's biggest problem at Martinsville was using up his brakes. He'd just burn the brakes right off the car. Finally, with about 45 laps to go, Davey's brakes became so hot they melted the bead of the right front tire and the tire blew out.

We managed to lose only one lap, and we still finished eighth. It was our fourth top-10 finish in a row. When I started with the team, Davey was 21st in points. Now we were fifth. I felt pretty good after the race. In fact, I felt *really* good.

Davey, however, was frustrated. When the media gathered around him after the race, he said, "Can you believe our horrible luck? That's four in a row we've had a chance to win and had something happen beyond our control. I was just sitting out there taking it easy and *blistering* those boys."

We went to Talladega with a fast car, and Davey qualified fourth. But it was a bad weekend. On Saturday, ARCA driver Chris Gehrke was fatally injured in an awful crash on the front straight. In the International Race of Champions, sports-car racer Dorsey Schroeder flipped down the backstretch in a multicar crash, but walked away unhurt.

The mayhem continued on Sunday, when Ernie Irvan triggered a 20-car wreck on the backstretch. Davey got caught up in it. He had seen it coming, too. Two laps before the crash, on lap 71, as cars were bobbing and weaving and going three-wide, Davey came on the radio and said, "Oh, boy. I don't like this."

When the crash happened, Mark Martin's car went vertical before slamming back down on its wheels. Kyle Petty was T-boned and suffered a compound fracture of his upper left leg.

A few days after the race, Kyle had been transferred to Carolinas Medical Center in Charlotte. As it happened, Linda was there too. While she was pregnant with Brandon, she had started hemorrhaging. The doctors were afraid she would miscarry, so they put her in the hospital for three weeks of strict bed rest. And just about every day she was there, Kyle would come wheeling down the hall in his wheelchair and visit her.

After Talladega, the Winston Cup series headed for Charlotte for two weeks, so I was able to visit Linda every day, too. But I was having a hard time thinking about anything but racing, because at Charlotte, we were clearly the class of the field.

We won the pole for The Winston all-star race on a hot Saturday afternoon, with the temperature in the 90s. This was the last time the event was held on a Sunday afternoon. A cold front blew through on Saturday night, and on Sunday the temperature had dropped to the 60s.

But the weather change didn't matter. We were unstoppable. Davey led all 70 laps of that race and won by almost three seconds. With only a few laps to go, I went to Robert and said, "We don't need to beat these people *this* bad. We may not get through inspection next week if we do. NASCAR doesn't like people stinkin' up their show."

I tried to slow Davey down. But trying to get Davey Allison to go slower was like trying to keep a pit bull from barking.

"Yee haw! Yeeee hawww!" Davey shouted as he crossed the finish line.

"That was so easy it was scary," Robert said later.

Davey's dominating victory in The Winston in 1991 was our first win together. It was an awesome feeling standing there in victory lane with him at Charlotte Motor Speedway. Our horsepower was the talk of the garage area.

That Sunday night, I was at Carolinas Medical Center celebrating our win with Linda. Two days later, Brandon was born. He came into this world six weeks early and weighed only five pounds. The doctors said he might have to stay in the hospital another three or four weeks.

The day after Brandon was born, Davey qualified 10th for the Coca-Cola 600. This was a big disappointment. We were certain we could win the pole. But there was a reason for the relatively slow qualifying run. Davey's throttle had started hanging. So when he went into the corners, he turned the ignition off for a moment and hit the brakes hard. Even with that handicap, he was still 10th fastest. And in the final practice, Davey had the fastest car.

Back in those days, our team became legendary for doing whatever it took to give our driver the best chance to win. We thought nothing of changing engines the morning of a race. And the morning of the 1991 Coca-Cola 600 was one of those times.

Less than two hours before the start, as gospel songs from the nearby chapel service drifted through the garage, we were hard at work changing the powerplant on Davey's Ford Thunderbird. Robert had found a torn valve seal. At first he figured it would be no problem. But when we cranked the engine, we saw a little more oil smoke than usual. That might be OK for a shorter race. But not for the 600—NASCAR's longest race. We decided we had to switch to a backup engine. We had no time to lose.

By the time we finished, we were really sweating. Everyone on the team was nervous. We had won The Winston with that faulty engine, and it had been our first backup motor, so now we were going to our *second* backup. Would it be as good? Would it even work right? We couldn't test it. All we could do was make the change and wait for the race to start to see what we had. I had never encountered anything like that.

Davey was more used to this routine at Robert Yates Racing. But he had his own problem. It was a sweltering day, and Davey didn't feel at all well before the race. The sun was so brutal on pit road that it faded the hats our team members were wearing.

So Davey took it easy at first. He didn't report any problems. The car was still fast. And on lap 51, he blew by Dale Earnhardt and took the lead for the first time. Davey creamed the field that day, passing high and low as he led 264 of the final 350 laps before taking the checkered flag 1.2 seconds ahead of Ken Schrader.

"I came in this morning and really didn't feel good," Davey said afterward. "And when I walked over to the car and they were taking the engine out, I thought I was going to throw up right on the spot."

There were nine yellow flags during the race, and these gave Davey his only challenges. He lost the lead and slipped back in the pack three different times during yellow flag pit stops. But each time, Davey just carved through the field like a hot knife through butter.

Davey had also won the race at Charlotte in October 1990, before I had joined the team. Now he had three straight in the same car. "We're going to put that car on jack stands until October," he said.

During the last 100 miles of any race, especially the 600, the driver who's leading often starts to hear things. The crew chief gets nervous, too, wondering what's going to go wrong. With just about 30 laps to go, Davey got on the radio and said, "Hey Larry Mac, guess what?"

My heart went to my throat. What was wrong? Had we torn up a gear? Was a tire going down? Had we lost a cylinder? "What is it?" I asked, dreading the answer.

Davey came back on the radio and said, "You know, Larry, every time I come off turn two and go down the backstretch, there's some Earnhardt fan hanging through the fence just as far as he can. And he's giving me the bird!"

I didn't need to hear *that*. But I pressed the button on my radio and said, "I am glad you shared that with me."

This was actually the first points victory of the year, not only for us, but for any Ford Thunderbird. That didn't stop the Chevy camp from griping. "It's tough to outrun an illegal race car like Davey's," Earnhardt said, even though he finished third. He complained that NASCAR had allowed the Fords too much of an advantage in engine and aerodynamic rules.

I thought, "Give me a break." Davey said it best: "Dale needs to read the rule book. There isn't anything on this car that isn't approved. It's kind of hard for him to be upset, considering he's won two races and Ford hasn't won any before now."

I didn't get involved. Robert taught me that when you point your finger at another competitor for cheating, in essence you're pointing your finger at NASCAR and saying they aren't doing their job.

At the hospital, Brandon was doing better than anyone expected. And after the race was over, I went to the hospital, and Linda and I brought our little boy home. It had been the most incredible month of May in my life. In the space of eight days, I had won my first race with Davey Allison, witnessed the birth of my son, won the Coca-Cola 600, and brought my son home. Who could ask for more blessings than that?

The Team to Beat

avey Allison's back-to-back victories in The Winston and the
Coca-Cola 600 in 1991 put us in the spotlight in the Winston
Cup series. All of a sudden, we were the team everybody was
talking about. We were the team to beat.

The next race, at Dover, we looked like we didn't know how to make
a race car go straight. We struggled in practice, qualified 11th, struggled in Happy Hour, and struggled all through the race. We finished
16th, six laps down to winner Ken Schrader. None of the Chevy drivers complained about our car at Dover.

It was the first weekend of struggle we had experienced as a group
since I joined Robert's team. It's easy to be tight-knit when things are
going well and you're winning races. What separates the best teams from
the backmarkers is their ability to stick together when things go bad.
It's all about persistence.

I told our team we weren't giving up no matter how bad we were.
We were going to keep working until the checkered flag flew at

Sunday's race. And we did. Even though we still finished poorly, we all felt good about giving 100 percent.

After a quick turnaround from Dover, we headed west for the road race at Sears Point. Davey dreaded the trip. At Watkins Glen in 1990, he'd put his car on its roof while trying to qualify. Sears Point had 11 turns back then and was trickier and tougher than the Glen.

A month before the race, he told me, "I don't like road courses. I just don't run very well on them."

"Don't worry," I told him. "We'll be just fine out there. I won out there with Ricky Rudd two years ago, so I've done pretty good. I think I've got a good setup for you."

"OK, whatever," Davey replied. He still didn't sound too happy about the race.

On Friday, we qualified 13th—not bad at all. But on Saturday, we struggled all the way through Happy Hour. That evening, I stayed up half the night trying to hash out what we needed to do. Davey and Robert spent most of the evening with me.

Even when we got to the track Sunday morning, I didn't know exactly what to do. I wasn't sure what I was fighting. It was one of the few times in my career when I talked to other crew chiefs and looked at other cars to see what everyone else was doing.

The biggest issue was how teams had set up their rear track bars. It was generally one of two ways, and we were doing it the opposite of most teams. So we changed the track bar and decided to make a bunch of other changes, too.

The changes obviously helped, because Davey moved up and ran in the top five most of the afternoon. Rusty Wallace dominated the race but dropped back with just a few laps to go when his engine went sour. Mark Martin and Tommy Kendall began battling for the lead, but they tangled. Suddenly Davey was leading with just three laps to go, but Ricky Rudd was on his heels.

Davey did a great job of driving, and as the two cars roared around the course and prepared to take the white flag for the final lap, he led by a few car lengths—a pretty good margin. But Dave Marcis, driving a lapped car, held us up through the esses, allowing Ricky to close the gap. Davey was still more than a car length ahead as they raced toward turn 11—the tightest turn on the course. Ricky waited forever before hitting his brakes for that hairpin turn. His car slid hard into the back of our Ford. Davey spun out. Ricky passed him and took the white flag.

Turn 11 is the only corner I could see from the pit box. "That son of a bitch," I thought. I was livid as Ricky roared past under the white flag. NASCAR didn't have a lot of time to react, but well before Ricky came back around, they had decided to call a foul.

I remember looking at Robert, who was monitoring the NASCAR channel. All of a sudden his eyes got real big and he said, "They're going to black flag Ricky!" I immediately relayed the information to Davey, so he wouldn't overdrive his car in a futile effort to catch up to Ricky. "Stay smooth," I said. "Hit your marks. They're going to penalize Ricky."

Sure enough, as Ricky charged across the finish line, the color of the flag he saw was black. Davey managed to hold on to second place despite the spin. He crossed the line four seconds behind Ricky. But Davey was the first driver to get the checkered flag. We could see all this from the pits. We knew we had won. In the space of a few seconds, our emotions were up, then down, then up again as our team exploded across pit wall in celebration.

After he took the checkered flag, Davey knew the controversy would be boiling as soon as Ricky got back around. So he decided he'd better beat Ricky to victory lane. Instead of turning left into turn one and heading back up through the hills on a complete victory lap, Davey drove straight and went up the Sears Point drag strip a short distance.

"Tell me when the last car goes by," he told our spotter. I thought, "What's he doing?" But Davey was always thinking a step ahead. When the last car passed, Davey turned around, drove backwards down the frontstretch and turned into victory lane. By the time Ricky got there, our car was already parked, and the entire team was celebrating like no tomorrow. All Ricky could do was park nearby and fume to the press. Then he and his crew chief, Waddell Wilson, marched into the NASCAR trailer to protest.

While Ricky and Waddell complained, Robert and I watched post-race inspection. Richard Childress walked over and told Robert, "Y'all need to get over there in that NASCAR trailer because right now they're up there, and if you're not careful, they'll screw you out of this race."

I looked at Robert and said, "What do you want to do?"

"We just need to stay calm and do our deal right here," Robert said. "We know who won this race, and we need to act like it. We're not raising any questions about anything." If we got involved, we'd be making a statement that we were raising questions, too, he said.

There was no specific rule covering this sort of thing, but NASCAR decided to penalize Ricky five seconds, which meant he finished second instead of first. I didn't really care where they put him as long as it was behind us.

After a mediocre race at Pocono, where we finished 12th, we headed to Michigan International Speedway for the Miller Genuine Draft 400. We took the same car that Davey had won with at Charlotte. It was Davey's best car even before I started working for Robert. The team had named the Thunderbird "James Bond 007."

We spent hundreds of hours in 1991 working on every aspect of 007 and our speedway cars. And 007 was one cheated-up race car. It wasn't actually a cheater car, but we did take advantage of every gray area in the NASCAR rule book that we could exploit.

One of Ford's automotive engineers, Louis Duncan, started working closely with us. I had a lot of confidence in Louis and listened to what he said. We began working to maximize the rake of our car by dropping the nose and raising the rear. By raising the rear, we could get more airflow on those rear quarter panels, thus increasing rear downforce. That allowed the car to speed through the turns faster. We were one of the first Ford teams to get really aggressive with putting rake in the car.

You could get by with a lot in 1991. It was the year before Gary Nelson, one of the most knowledgeable crew chiefs in the garage, took over as NASCAR technical director. It was not unusual for us to slide our car through inspection an inch lower than it should have been just because of the way NASCAR measured the height. Sometimes they would measure the nose height about eight inches up the hood, but they would go back 12 inches if they needed to in order to get the number they were looking for. All we were doing was taking full advantage of the NASCAR system that existed then.

We qualified fourth at Michigan and basically ran away with the race. On Saturday, my old racing buddy, Dave Mader III, had won the ARCA race. And on Sunday, another Alabama driver, Hut Stricklin, finished second behind Davey driving Bobby Allison's Raybestos Ford. Hut is married to Pam Allison, Donnie's daughter. The Alabama gang invaded the North and took the state by storm.

Bobby and Judy Allison were there watching. They had the choice of rooting for their son or their own car. Judy told reporters afterward, "Of course I was pulling for Hut at the end. That's what pays my bills, not Davey."

Now we were really on a roll. Every day at the shop, I almost had to pinch myself to be certain that everything was truly happening. There's no feeling in the world quite like going to the racetrack knowing that everybody will be watching *your* team, clocking *your* car, and wondering what you were up to.

From May to August of 1991, Larry McReynolds was more talked about than in the past 11 years combined. We were becoming household names in NASCAR. We were killing them with our power, and we were beating them on aerodynamics. It all came together so fast, and made me think back to what Davey had told me again and again: "Larry, if you'll just come on over, we'll kill these guys."

"Now we've got it going in all areas," Robert said after the Michigan victory. "We started off in a hole this year. There were so many Chevrolet teams that were strong and were winning." Unlike at Charlotte, no one complained that we were illegal. They just talked about how fast we were.

In the Pepsi 400 at Daytona in July, we started second and finished third. We were competitive throughout the race. It was the first time at Daytona that I was working with a team that actually had a chance to win there. At the end of July, we finished ninth at Talladega and moved from fourth to third in Winston Cup points. Davey, however, was furious. We had been running second with three laps to go. Davey attempted to pass Dale Earnhardt for the lead, but couldn't make it. Then another Ford driver, Sterling Marlin, jumped behind Earnhardt and shut out Davey. He fell back.

Afterward, Davey could barely contain his fury as he talked with the media. "All we needed were four more inches and we could have moved up in front of Earnhardt and we would have had him," he said. "If you trust another Ford driver . . . and then they leave you hung out to dry, then that's pitiful."

Davey stalked back to the transporter. He was as mad at himself as anyone. When I got back to the truck, he was up in the lounge and some people were hovering around him. Davey was holding his arm.

"What did you do to your arm?" I asked.

Davey just shook his head. He was too embarrassed to say. Finally he told me he was so mad that he had slammed the side of the truck. He hit it so hard, he broke a bone in his right hand.

I was disgusted with him. "Feel better now?" I said. "If you're going to play grab-ass with a transporter, you're going to lose every time. You know, we have to go to Watkins Glen in two weeks, where you have to shift gears. With your right hand! When we get there, I'd better not hear anything about your arm bothering you."

But a part of me had to admire him, too. It was this same intensity that made him such a great race car driver. I looked at Davey and saw a part of me in him. I'd been known to throw stopwatches and smash clipboards on the pavement. Before we went to Watkins Glen, doctors custom-fitted a cast on his hand that allowed him to steer and shift gears. I could tell his hand was still bothering him, but he didn't say anything to me about it. He knew I had no sympathy.

Davey's hand didn't stop him from having a great run at the Glen. He was running third on the last lap when Mark Martin tried to pass leader Ernie Irvan and spun out, taking Davey with him. By the time he recovered, he was 10th. It was another solid finish, but we all left Watkins Glen with heavy hearts. The veteran driver J. D. McDuffie— a throwback to another era—was killed in a crash.

Now it was back to Michigan. Once again, we had our best car. But this time the playing field had changed. By July 1991, cylinder heads had become a hotly debated issue, partly because Robert had made his so good. One of the reasons we beat everybody so badly at Charlotte in May and Michigan in June was because of the cylinder-head development that Robert and his son, Doug, had done.

A V-8 engine has two cylinder heads. They have eight valves each and a maze of ports and channels that flow vaporized fuel into the engine and exhaust gases out. Robert knew better than most how to increase the efficiency of the flow of fuel and exhaust gases to increase horsepower.

When Robert started working on Ford engines in 1986, they generated about 650 horsepower. But he started looking at every nook and cranny and chopped up the standard Ford heads, so he could rearrange the ports and channels, change the valve angles, and a host of other things. And then he welded the heads back together. It took him weeks to make one pair of heads and cost thousands of extra dollars. But it paid off.

When I arrived in 1991, Robert was getting 700 to 710 horsepower from his engines. Teams were running all sorts of different heads, and the cost of cylinder head development was going through the roof. NASCAR, in its ongoing effort to keep costs down and level the playing field, had decided to approve only one cylinder head for each manufacturer.

NASCAR and Ford racing officials had come to us and said they wanted to make our cylinder head design the approved Ford head. That's not what Ford car owners Junior Johnson or Jack Roush wanted, so it was a touchy political deal within Ford. Nonetheless, Robert's cylinder head was the one approved for the Fords.

What could we do? Robert was already afraid that NASCAR would ban his cylinder heads because of the amount of work he had done on them. Once NASCAR and Ford designated our cylinder heads as the approved design, we had no choice. We had to share. But there was an upside for Robert. He ended up selling heads to many of the teams and had the CNC machine in the shop going nearly 24 hours a day to meet the demand. He also received some compensation from Ford for some of the other associated work he was doing. But from a competitive standpoint it was a crushing blow.

When we returned to Michigan for the Champion Spark Plug 400 on August 18, we qualified third and led a good bit of the race, although we were not as dominant as in June. With 12 laps to go, a yellow flag flew because of a piece of tailpipe on the backstretch.

Everyone had to stop for fuel, but tires were another question. We'd been out there for 40 or 45 laps. We had a big debate in the pits about whether to take tires.

I looked at Robert and said, "What do you think we ought to do here?"

Robert looked at me with a glazed look in his eye. Then he looked down at his wristwatch.

"Why the hell are you looking at your watch?" I asked. It must have just been nervous energy. I made the decision. We took four tires. Dale Jarrett, driving the Wood Brothers Ford, took fuel only and got out of the pits in first place.

We charged through the field and challenged Jarrett for the lead. Normally, with new tires we would have blown right by him. But the four new tires were not perfectly matched. Our Ford Thunderbird was far too tight and pushing up the track.

Still, Davey got up next to Dale and put his nose out in front to lead lap 199. They continued around the track side by side, with Davey on the outside. All 90,000 fans were on their feet, screaming. This was NASCAR stock-car racing at its finest.

Davey pulled a few inches ahead as they entered the home stretch. The cars banged together, producing a wisp of tire smoke. But in the final 200 yards, Dale's car edged ahead again. He regained the lead in the final second of the race and won by eight inches. It was his first career victory.

Davey went down to victory lane and raised Dale's arm in triumph. But we still felt hollow, especially knowing that Dale had beaten us with our own cylinder heads. I don't think I or any of the crewmen said a word in the pits after the race. And at some point during the race, Davey had come on the radio and sarcastically cracked, "Maybe we need to give them something else to outrun us."

We moved into third position in Winston Cup points after Michigan, trailing Dale Earnhardt by only 137 points. Two weeks later, Davey won the pole position for the Southern 500. It was our first pole position together in a points race.

After we clinched the top spot, Robert recalled that one of his greatest moments at Darlington was back in 1972, when Bobby Allison had won the Southern 500 pole and then had gone out and won the race. Robert said when the cars came off turn four at the end of the first lap, Bobby was about 30 car lengths ahead of the rest of the field.

Three days later, at the end of the first lap, Davey came barreling off turn four in the lead. And the rest of the field was about 30 car lengths behind him.

"Look at that! Look at that right there!" Robert shouted. "That's what I'm talking about! Isn't that awesome?"

It truly was awesome. Unfortunately, we didn't finish that way. We had engine problems and ended up 12th, four laps down. That was the month Harry Gant became "Mr. September," winning at Darlington, then Richmond, Dover, and Martinsville.

The speculation was that Gant had gone on his tear because his team had added a lot of camber to the rear tires. Andy Petree, who was Gant's crew chief, was one of the first to get really aggressive with rear camber, using a lot of specially made parts and pieces to make it work. Eventually, because of Andy's work, NASCAR added a rule that regulated rear camber.

We ran side by side with Harry at Richmond for lap after lap after lap, eventually finishing second. There was not a mark on either car after the race.

As Harry went on to win at Dover, we lost an engine and suffered a DNF. And at Martinsville, we were involved in several early incidents. Davey came on the radio and said, "Man, I tell you what, I've been in the middle of everything today, and I ain't been able to dodge nothin'." We had the car in the pits for almost 100 laps making repairs. We finished the race, but it might as well have been a DNF. We were 29th in a 32-car field.

Those two blows finished off our hopes for the 1991 Winston Cup championship. As we left Martinsville, we were fourth in the title hunt and 299 points behind Dale Earnhardt.

In October Davey and I and our wives took some time to do something that brought our families even closer together. Before the race at Charlotte, we had our son, Brandon, and the Allisons' son, Robby, baptized together at the Speedway Club above the track.

The ceremony was performed by Father Dale Grubba, a priest who closely follows racing and even wrote for *Stock Car Racing* magazine. Linda and I became Robby's godparents, and Liz and Davey became Brandon's godparents. The speedway president, Humpy Wheeler, helped us arrange the ceremony. In his office today, he has a large photograph of our families and Father Grubba as we were having our sons baptized.

When we got back to racing in the Mello Yello 500 at Charlotte, we had the race in the bag, or so we thought. Davey took the lead on lap 261 and was cruising until we had to make a final stop for fuel with only 17 laps to go. Geoff Bodine took the lead. And he didn't stop. He just kept going and going and going, right under the checkered flag. He had run the final 114 miles on a single tank of gas. The best we could do on one tank was about 98 miles.

As the laps were winding down, Davey got on the radio and said, "If he makes it, they need to check that fuel cell."

I headed straight to the gas pumps after the race. That's where the top five cars have to go to be refilled with gas before the car is weighed. It got pretty weird there pretty quick. Nosy reporters were ushered away from the pumps. Some of car owner Junior Johnson's crew guys tried to stand in front of the pump to obscure the meter. I wasn't having any of that. I even wrote down the figures.

Before they started pumping gas into Geoff's Ford, the meter showed that 18,176.6 gallons had been dispensed. When they shut the pump off, the meter showed 18,199.8 gallons. That meant that 23.2 gallons of gas went into Geoff's gas tank. Junior had been nailed with a big engine at Charlotte in May, and now he was nailed with a big gas tank.

Except nobody did anything this time. One NASCAR official told reporters they "forgot" exactly how much gas went into the tank, but insisted it was less than 22 gallons.

"If you get beat by a lap or two, that's one thing," I told the press. "But you don't get by with 17 laps with a legal car." It was frustrating to know that the only reason you got beat was because someone had blatantly cheated.

In hindsight, I wished I hadn't become caught up in it. What I did went totally against Robert's "live and let live" philosophy. His attitude was that instead of complaining, you needed to go back to your shop and figure out how you could make your own fuel cell hold that much.

But there wasn't much time to worry about it. We had three more races to run in 1991, starting with the AC Delco 500 at North Carolina Motor Speedway at Rockingham. And Rockingham was one of those tracks that hadn't been too good to me. It's a tough little one-mile high-banked track, and it was hard to get a handle on it. The track surface is rough, and it wears out tires. It's hard for the cars to get a good grip. And it's very unpredictable.

We were struggling before the race. We didn't qualify all that well (10th), and we didn't get much better during Saturday morning's practice. But Davey had his Busch series car down there, and he and Red Farmer, who worked on that car, had come up with a setup that had some really strange weight percentages in it. Now, when Davey got something in his head, you might as well just go ahead and do what he wanted, because he wasn't going to leave you alone until you did. But I always put a lot of faith in what he said. So when Davey said we should change our Winston Cup car's setup to match his Busch series car, we did it.

We changed the car for the last practice session on Saturday afternoon. We set it up with more weight distributed toward the front of the car (about 52 ½ percent instead of the normal 51) and added a lot of "wedge" (more weight on the right front and the left rear, which keeps the car from being loose). Suddenly, we were pretty fast. And then we won the race on Sunday. What made it really interesting is that when we went back to Rockingham in February 1992 that setup no longer worked. What we did for that race in 1991 worked one time and one time only. The only reason we could come up with for this was that Goodyear's tire compound changed slightly, so the setup wasn't effective the next year.

Two weeks later, we took Phoenix by storm, leading 161 of the last 166 laps to win by almost 12 seconds over Darrell Waltrip. The back-to-back victories vaulted us into second place for the Winston Cup championship, but it was too late to catch Dale Earnhardt. We were 156 points behind, which meant all Dale had to do to win his fifth Winston Cup championship was to start the final race at Atlanta.

We were all pretty amazed by the victory at Phoenix because the day before the race, we were lost. Davey couldn't get the car to turn. On Saturday night before the race, our sponsor Texaco had held a lavish steak fry under the stars at the Mummy Mountain cookout area at Camelback Inn Resort.

It was a beautiful night and a wonderful affair, but I couldn't get the setup problems off my mind. The car wouldn't turn a lick in the middle of the corner, and then it would be loose off the corner. I even took some notes to the steak fry and talked a bit there with Robert and Davey. We left soon after Texaco's little ceremony, and I couldn't wait to get back to the hotel to huddle with Davey and Robert and review our game plan. I knew if we could fix the problem of difficult turning in the middle of the corner we would probably also fix the looseness. Even after they retired, I continued working until midnight. Then I grabbed a few hours of sleep and was up at 3:30 a.m., working on our plan some more.

On race morning, as the usual mob of race-day visitors wandered through the garage, we went to work on that Ford Thunderbird, focused on the right rear as the source of the problem. We changed two springs, two shocks, the sway bar, the camber in the front wheels, and the wedge.

As Davey said after the race, "If somebody was in there watching us, they would have thought we were crazy—all the stuff we were doing. But it worked. As far off as we were yesterday afternoon, for it to be as good as it was today was so unbelievable."

That sort of thing was becoming routine for us. We raced—and worked—flat-out 100 percent all the time. It had *always* been that way for me. What was so incredible was that now I had a driver, a car owner, and an entire team who felt that way. If I'd told that team to take the front bumper and put it on the rear, I don't think there was a member who would have questioned it.

In the final race of the season at Atlanta, we lost a bunch of laps on pit road changing a dead battery. We finished 17th and slipped from second to third in the Winston Cup championship, only four points behind Ricky Rudd.

But we didn't care all that much. The battle for the title was over after Phoenix. "Let the points fall where they may," Davey told the media at Phoenix. "This is already the very best year I've had in my life. We're going to leave 1991 with our sights on 1992."

When the smoke had cleared at Atlanta and we had loaded up, I was standing next to the NASCAR transporter when I ran into Richard Childress. I shook his hand and congratulated him for winning the championship with Dale Earnhardt. It was Dale's fifth title.

"Well, we won this one," Richard said. "But we know you guys are going to make us work hard to win another one. You're the guys we have to beat next year."

CHAPTER NINE

Winning One Week,
Crashing the Next

With the power we were getting from Robert's restrictor plate engines, we all felt we had a good opportunity to win the Daytona 500 and get the 1992 Winston Cup season off to a flying start. We built a new superspeedway car for Daytona and Talladega and worked meticulously on the body design to make it as aerodynamically slick as possible. We spent an awful lot of time in the wind tunnel at Dobbins Air Force Base in Marietta, Georgia. We would test body modification, then go back to the shop and make changes, then go back and test again. We did this four or five times.

The 10 or so guys in Robert's engine shop began working ridiculously long hours on the engines. In the weeks leading up to Daytona, they were working seven days a week, 16 hours a day. They never quit trying to come up with one or two more horsepower. With a restrictor plate engine, five or six horsepower is equivalent to one mile per hour, which is two-tenths of a second at Daytona. So when you find a couple of horse-power you get pretty excited about it.

We tested our guts out during the two Ford tests at Daytona in January. But we struggled. So we went back to the shop, cut the bodies up and changed the body configuration, and did a few things differently. Back then NASCAR used fewer body templates so there was a bit more leeway to make changes. And on a track like Daytona or Talladega you want to "hide" the rear spoiler from the air as much as possible so there's less drag. We also worked on front fender shapes and the nose, because these parts see the air first and its important that they be as efficient as possible. The week before we were to go to Daytona to begin Speedweeks, we scheduled a final test at Talladega.

Davey was racing in Phoenix at the Copper Classic, so we had Red Farmer drive the car. Red was an exceptionally good test driver. He would repeat perfectly everything he did, which is critical when you're testing different setups and components. He did everything the same—leaving pit road, getting through the gears, staying in the same groove—one lap was a carbon copy of the next.

After two more days of testing at Talladega, we finally had a fast car. We looked at each other and breathed a sigh of relief. But there was still a lot of work to do. We had to be at Daytona in only five days, and we hadn't even painted the car. I knew as well that the engine guys would want to work on the engines right up to the point when we absolutely had to leave.

Davey had won three pole positions in 1991, including the Daytona 500, which he won a few weeks before I joined the team. So we were in the Busch Clash (now called the Budweiser Shootout) at Daytona, a non-points race for the previous year's pole winners that's run a week before the big race. Unlike most teams in that race, we elected to run our Daytona 500 car because we wanted to learn more about it. We ran competitively and finished fourth.

Then in the last practice on Wednesday afternoon before the Thursday 125-mile qualifying races—with maybe 10 minutes left—we got into a wreck on the backstretch and tore that car up.

We went into a frenzy of activity getting our backup car ready. Robert was warming the engine as we lowered it on the back platform of the transporter. We got about five laps in and we didn't learn a lot, but what we did learn wasn't good. Something was leaking in the motor. The next morning, we fixed the leak, got the car ready, and started dead last in our 125-miler. We finished third.

We continued to work on that backup car as we got ready for the Daytona 500. For the first half of the race, our toughest competition was Bill Elliott and Sterling Marlin in Junior Johnson's Fords, and Ernie Irvan in the Morgan-McClure Chevy. Davey took the lead for the first time on lap 56 and stayed there until Elliott repassed him on lap 84.

A heck of a battle broke out at the front on lap 92. As the pack roared off the second turn, Elliott, Marlin, and Irvan went three wide. Then all hell broke loose. As the "big one" started, Davey darted to the outside, hit the gas, and flew past all the carnage.

Fourteen cars wrecked, including nine of the 16 cars on the lead lap. When I saw Davey come back around, and not the other three, I knew our chances were really good. That's not how we wanted to beat 'em, but let's face it, we wanted to beat 'em any way we could. I told Robert, "If nothing falls off this car, we can win this race."

We led all but 10 laps of the rest of the race. At the end, Morgan Shepherd was chasing us in the Wood Brothers Ford. But he didn't have much for us.

Earlier in the week, one of our radios was stolen. We felt like it might have disappeared from the top of a toolbox or the workbench in the garage. With about 10 laps left in the race, we found that radio—in a manner of speaking. Somebody, somewhere, had that radio and was talking to Davey.

"You'd better get going, he's coming!" the mysterious voice warned Davey. "He's gonna pass you. Better get going!" We didn't know who was talking, we just knew it was *our* radio. But I think all of us immediately knew there wasn't a thing we could do. If we acknowledged the problem and acted like it was bothering us, the thief would talk even more. So all of us, including Davey, ignored it.

You can't see much of anything from pit road at Daytona. But when I looked out there and saw Davey's car come into the tri-oval on the last lap, I knew we were going to win the Daytona 500.

It was the most awesome feeling in the world. I had won the Daytona 500. It didn't seem that long ago that I was a wide-eyed kid from Alabama, sitting in line all night to get tickets just to *see* the race. I felt so fortunate. My wife and kids were down there, and they came to victory lane and were part of the celebration.

Davey had shown a lot of maturity and skill avoiding the big crash. He said as much himself: "Probably a year ago I might have gotten involved in a wreck like that. I followed Ernie at first. But then I said, 'Whoa, this is enough for me. I'm backing off.' I saw it coming. They all just ran out of room there."

Until that day, the only father and son to win the 500 were the Pettys—Lee and Richard—who were perhaps the Allisons' biggest rivals over the years. Now Bobby and Davey shared that distinction with the Pettys.

Bobby joined all of us in victory lane. "I'm very, very proud," he said. "It's really a special pleasure when you think about fathers around the country who would like to feel this way about their sons." Davey said, "Probably tomorrow morning, I'll be floating when I wake up."

I drove home after that race in our little Chevy Astro minivan. We had my winning crew chief trophy in the van with us, and I couldn't take my eyes off it. We spent the night at a motel somewhere in Georgia, and the next morning, we stopped on the way out to get gas.

A family was there with a little boy who was mentally challenged. They recognized me, so I went over to talk to the little boy. It dawned on me that one of the hats I had worn in victory lane was in the van. I got it and gave it to that little boy. I never will forget the gleam in his eyes. That's what makes things special, right there.

After Daytona, we were on a roll. We finished second at Rockingham, then strung together three straight fourth-place finishes. My watchword for Davey, which I repeated like a mantra, was "Look at the big picture." We all wanted our first Winston Cup championship, and we knew that the only thing we needed to improve on in 1992 was consistency. But after Darlington, we still only had a 48-point lead on Bill Elliott, who was on a tear. Elliott had won four in a row.

The special kind of dedication of our team was demonstrated again at Richmond, where we changed an engine on Friday after losing the pole to Elliott. We'd change an engine as quickly as most people take out the trash. A reporter came up to Robert as he was rolling the old engine back toward the transporter and asked him why he was making the switch. "We got beat," he said. "Gotta change something." Our own cylinder heads were coming back to haunt us.

It seemed like all the top Ford teams got a big boost after they started using our heads. Alan Kulwicki was faster. Mark Martin was faster. And now Elliott was taking us to the cleaners. Robert just shook his head when he recalled how much money he had spent and how many thousands of hours he and his son, Doug, and the engine room guys had worked since 1986 to get those heads as good as they were.

"We've been brave," he said in his usual soft-spoken way. "We took chances. We fell out of a lot of races, burned a lot of pistons, and blew up a lot of engines to prove this stuff works." Steve Hmiel, Mark's crew chief, said it best: "I think everybody had their own little tricks with the engines, but his worked the best."

Our string of five straight top-five finishes ended at Bristol in the sixth race of the season. But all our hearts were heavy even before all the trouble we had during the race. Davey's grandfather, Edmond J. "Pop" Allison, had passed away a couple of days earlier after battling cancer. Pop Allison, who was 87, was probably Davey's best friend. Before Davey reached Winston Cup, Pop Allison was with him every step of the way as he ran all of those races all over the Southeast. The loss weighed on Davey's mind that weekend, but the Allisons were probably the best in the business when it came to putting their emotions aside and doing their job. Davey was no different.

We qualified sixth at Bristol and ran with the leaders. On lap 181, we took the lead from Dale Earnhardt and stayed in front for 49 trips around that half-mile, high-banked bullring. Bill Elliott was finally having some trouble, and the yellow flag came out on lap 252 when he spun with two other cars on the backstretch.

We came into the pits for a routine yellow flag pit stop on lap 253. NASCAR had come up with some different rules on pit road. One of them was that your car couldn't be hanging over the pit box lines. But because it's so tough to pull into the small pit boxes at many of the tracks, NASCAR said the right rear tires could be partly over the line.

We were actually leading the race when we pitted. When Davey stopped, I saw that our front bumper was right on the front line of the pit box. I looked at it from the pit box. Walt Green, the NASCAR official who supervised our pit, looked at it. Then he looked up at me and shrugged his shoulders as if to say, "Looks like you're OK to me."

We finished our stop, and Davey drove off pit road. We ran another caution lap and the next thing I knew, Walt was standing below me, motioning for me to come down off the pit box and talk to him. So I jumped off the pit box.

"Larry," he said, "We need to bring him back in. We're giving him a one-lap penalty. He was over the pit box line."

I went ballistic. I was out on pit road, just screaming at Walt and waving my arms and hands up at the tower. The fans started going crazy. On the Motor Racing Network radio broadcast, anchorman Eli Gold said, "Now we have Larry McReynolds out on pit road, and for whatever reason, he's doing his Bobby Knight impression."

I felt like we had really been screwed by NASCAR. If Walt Green had said something on the spot, I would've understood. But he didn't say a thing. Obviously, NASCAR made the call from the tower. And at that point, Walt was just the messenger.

Actually, Walt loved it. Because of the scene I made, we were on the cover of just about every racing newspaper and magazine in the next couple of weeks. So it was kind of Walt's claim to fame.

Fortunately, the Raybestos Chevrolet owned by Bobby Allison was pitted next to us. Bobby was in the pits, and he saw what was going on. Bobby came over, put his hands on my shoulders, and said, "Larry, you will lose this battle. I've been losing these battles for years. Trust me. You won't win it. So you might as well take it, accept it, regain your composure, and go on."

If it hadn't been for Bobby, I'd probably still be standing there ripping the pits apart. But I didn't change my mind: it was a dead wrong call. Things got worse. I was still furious when Davey flew down the backstretch about 30 laps after the incident, trying to make up lost ground. A moment before he entered the third turn on lap 282, an oil fitting broke loose. Oil spewed onto the track and under Davey's tires, and he crashed hard into the outside wall in the third turn.

A tow truck dragged our wrecked car into the infield beside the third turn as Davey went to the infield care center. He was hurting pretty badly. His right shoulder and ribs were killing him. It wasn't too long before he was back by the car, quietly standing out of the way.

"Going into the corner, the back end just took off," he said. "I tried to correct it, but the next thing I knew, I was in the wall."

In the meantime, we swarmed over the car like bees on a spring flower. Several of the guys worked on the rear end damage. One crewman was inside the car. Others struggled to fix the oil line. We had to replace a broken windshield as well. And I sent more team members searching high and low through the infield for someone to relieve Davey. "We'll take about anybody," I told them. It was obvious that Davey wasn't going to drive any more that day.

We found Sterling Marlin, who had crashed on lap 17 and dropped out. Sterling had already changed into his street clothes, but since Bristol had no crossover or tunnel then, he was stuck inside the track with all the other drivers and teams who were out of the race. Sterling agreed to put his driver's uniform back on for the relief duty.

We spent more than 100 laps in the pits getting the car ready to go back out. Finally, around lap 440, we sent that wrecked Ford back out there with Sterling behind the wheel. We hoped to gain at least a few positions in the standings, which would give us a few additional Winston Cup points. We were looking at the big picture.

But even before we got that desperate effort started, we ran smack into another typical NASCAR deal. After we'd finally got the car patched up, Sterling drove out onto pit road and headed back onto the track. A moment later I got back to our pit. Walt Green came over and said, "You need to bring him back in, Larry! Speeding on pit road!"

I remember thinking, "You people just don't quit, do you?"

We made 48 more laps around the track, but in the end we gained nothing. We finished 28th—the same position we would have had if we had dropped out. But you just can't look at it that way. The minute you start doing that, you'll drop out of a race where you could have made up some positions.

Bristol had been an all-around bad weekend, and it ended just as badly as it had started. When they got back to Birmingham on Sunday, Davey went for an examination and X-rays at the Norwood Clinic. Fortunately, he hadn't broken any bones, but he did have muscle and cartilage damage. On Monday, the entire Allison clan gathered for Pop Allison's funeral.

Later that week, Davey brought his sore shoulder to North Wilkesboro Speedway for the First Union 400. When we got there, Competition Director Dick Beaty called me into the NASCAR trailer.

"You know Larry," he said, "Bill France was in the tower watching your little temper tantrum down on pit road. And you almost became the first crew chief to be ejected from the racetrack at a race. He wanted to stop the race, open the crossover and have you put outside. But I stood up for you. I told Bill it was just a 'heat of the moment' thing. But you'd better watch it. You don't know how close you came to being ejected."

"Yes, sir," I told Dick. He was very much from the old school. Dick Beaty could cuss you out and make you think you were pond scum. But after he got done with you, he'd put that arm around you, tell you how much he liked you, and say, "Now, get back to work." He never held a grudge.

Davey was still in a lot of pain, so Jimmy Hensley hopped in the car to qualify for us, and he did a good job, putting us seventh on the grid. Jimmy was ready to relieve Davey on Sunday, but Davey never used him. Before the race, in order to ease the soreness in his ribs, we fitted him with a chest protector and hooked him up to an electrical nerve block device.

Davey was one hurting race car driver during that event. It didn't help when Kyle Petty got into him and spun him out on lap 128. The only reason we didn't lose a lap is because Dick Trickle spun behind us and NASCAR had to throw a yellow flag.

Davey said afterward that he could never have made it if the car hadn't handled as well as it did. But our secret weapon on this day was not behind the wheel or under the hood. It was in the pits.

Our team had spent hundreds of hours during the off-season and during the week practicing pit stops. I let Joey Knuckles handle the pit crew, and he was a big inspiration as far as getting the team to perform fast stops. Our over-the-wall crew was a mix of regular employees and Sunday-only crewmen. They worked hard because they wanted to be able to beat any team out of the pits when it really mattered.

At North Wilkesboro, it really mattered. During a round of yellow flag pit stops about lap 266, a fast stop by our crew moved Davey from fifth to third. Then, on lap 312, another yellow flag came out when Kyle Petty smacked the wall in turn four. Everyone headed to the pits once again. We were second at this point, trailing Rusty Wallace. But when the jacks dropped, ours came down a split second ahead of Rusty's. And we were out of the pits in first place. It was the first time we had led all afternoon.

We led the rest of the way after taking the lead on lap 313. But there was one more big moment in the pits. Another yellow flag flew on lap 346, setting up a final showdown with Rusty's crew on pit road. Our team and his team were considered the two fastest crews in the pits.

It was the duel of the day. The frontstretch crowd was primed and ready for the drama to be played out in front of them, and we beat Rusty out of the pits again. The fans went nuts. As Davey later said, it was as simple as this: "If we hadn't beat Rusty out of the pits when we did, we would have finished second."

It was our second win of the year and Davey's 15th career victory. "I didn't have much left over," he said. "But we told everybody last week after Bristol that the sign of a good race team is bouncing back from bad things that happen to you."

But Davey was still feeling the effects of some of those bad things. Unfortunately for our team, there were a lot more bad things to come in 1992. Davey was in so much pain after the race that he finally had to sit down in victory lane. Davey may have been hurting, but a victory is huge medicine. He told the media after the race that he was sticking around North Carolina for an extra day to keep an appointment with his friend who owned a flying service in nearby Mt. Airy. "I'm going to take some helicopter flying lessons," he said.

And then he stuck around the track for hours after the race. After the victory lane ceremonies and the press box interview, after post-race teardown and inspection, and even after we'd loaded up and shut the doors of the transporter, Davey was still there, sitting on the back of his pickup truck, signing autographs. And he continued to sign until every blooming one of those fans had an autograph and was gone. I was always proud to work with Davey because of the way he drove a race car. But that made me proud to work with him for the person he was.

We had a weekend off between North Wilkesboro and Martinsville, which gave Davey's ribs and shoulder some extra days to heal. But at Martinsville, we had more trouble. We qualified way back in 23rd, which meant that we pitted on the backstretch.

Then, on lap 386, Davey's right front tire went down suddenly, and he slammed the wall hard in turn two. The same old Martinsville problem had slapped us down one more time: Davey had got the brakes too hot, and the right front brake had cooked the bead of the tire, causing it to blow.

"Oh, no," I thought, "Not this again." Davey slowly got out of the car and got in the ambulance. "I'm fine," he said. "I rebruised my ribs a little bit, but I'm OK." Davey was tough as nails.

The Winston 500 at Talladega was the ninth race of the 1992 season, and despite two DNFs (and a victory) in the past three races, we were still leading the points for the Winston Cup championship. We were only 16 points ahead of Harry Gant, but we still had that big picture first and foremost in our minds.

Before the Talladega weekend, some of the Ford racing people had called Robert on the phone and basically told him, "Don't run any faster than a 49.70 in qualifying." That's about 192.6 mph on the 2.660-mile oval at Talladega. It was a pretty questionable request, since everyone drives around Talladega flat out and it's not exactly easy to slow down just enough. But Ford was lobbying NASCAR for some aerodynamic changes at the superspeedways, and they didn't want the Fords to look as if they didn't need them.

I talked with Davey about it, and he said, "Let me tell you something. When I leave pit road, I'm not lifting. If you want to slow down this race car, you better figure out a way to do it. Because I'm not going to play a role in it."

I couldn't blame him. So I had the spoiler raised just a little bit and made a few other minor changes. Davey went out and qualified at 49.705 seconds, or 192.657 mph. And we lost the pole to Ernie Irvan, who made a lap at 49.66 seconds, or 192.831 mph.

I was so sick at myself for making those changes. In fact, on that very same day, Wayne Estes, Ford's public relations man for the Winston Cup series, had dropped by to tape interviews with Davey and me. I told Wayne: "Our game plan hasn't changed since I walked in the door over at the Texaco Havoline team, and that's to go out and try to lead every lap we can, win every race we can, and the points will come to us."

As far as we were concerned, qualifying was another race that we needed to win. We still hadn't won a pole position up to then in 1992. And to have "tanked" in qualifying because of a Ford political deal made me sick to my stomach and angry at myself. But this was a matter best kept within the family. When the media came back around to interview Davey after qualifying, he never said a thing about the phone call and the adjustments I'd made. "It just wasn't our turn to sit on the pole," he said. But the truth was that we could have won the pole and won it by a big margin.

What really counted, however, was that we won the race on Sunday. Davey grabbed the lead from Ernie on the first lap. And we went on to lead 110 of the 188 circuits. Davey was never more than a car length ahead, but he was never seriously challenged as he led the final 71 laps with "that 95-foot wide Ford Thunderbird," as he put it.

It had been a lot different than our last visit the previous July, when the Fords wouldn't cooperate, Davey was left hung out to dry, and he broke his hand in frustration after the race trying to punch out the hauler. This time the Fords worked well together. I even went up to Mike Beam, Sterling Marlin's crew chief, with about 20 laps to go and said, "Mike, whatever the outcome of this race, we worked good together today, and that's the main thing we've been trying to accomplish with the Ford teams."

Linda had come to Talladega for that race, and she celebrated with us in victory lane. After we left victory lane, she looked at me and said, "You know, Larry, Liz has been talking about getting together tonight over in Hueytown for a little party."

I looked at her and said, "Linda, we won today, and we're tickled to death. But we're done celebrating now. There's another race in two weeks, and it's in Charlotte. It's a big deal. We have to get back and work on those cars." We didn't go to Hueytown. We loaded the kids in the van and drove back to Charlotte that night.

Linda was disappointed, but I think she understood. I had to keep working on winning the next race and not relax until the championship was within our grasp. That was just my frame of mind in those days. And Charlotte *was* a big deal. Now we had a 67-point lead, and we'd been leading all year. We'd won the Daytona 500 and the Winston 500, and now we had two legs up on the Winston Million. All Davey had to do to win that $1 million bonus was win the Coca-Cola 600 at Charlotte in three weeks or the Southern 500 at Darlington on Labor Day weekend. The only driver who had ever won the Winston Million was Bill Elliott in 1985.

Working at Robert's shop on Dwelle Street was a joy. There was no time clock. There was hardly even a regular clock, at least not one that any of the guys watched. We'd work all hours. On warm nights, we'd throw the doors open to let the breezes in. AC/DC would be blasting on a boom box. Gil Kerley, our shop foreman, used to call me "Hoot Owl." He'd tell me, "Larry, I know you're here at the crack of dawn, but you really don't get going till the day end. You're just like an old hoot owl."

The problem was, as crew chief, I just couldn't get anything done during the day. It was, "Larry, call on line one," or "Larry, line two" or "Larry, please come to the office." But along about 5:30 p.m., those phones would go quiet, and everybody would stop asking me questions and the front office employees would go home. And finally I'd be able to get in there myself and get some work done on those cars.

Raymond Fox, the grandson of legendary NASCAR mechanic Ray Fox Sr., was my right-hand man. He'd hang in there with me and work the hours I worked. Most nights, the crew would dwindle down to myself and Little Raymond (that's what we called him). We'd usually work on setting up the chassis for the next weekend's race. It could take as much as six hours. I'd check everything on the car and then go through the whole chassis setup procedure. You never take anything for granted on a race car because if you go to the racetrack without checking something, that thing you didn't check will be the very thing that fights you the whole weekend.

Little Raymond used to get irritated with me because I was always so precise. If we wanted .025 of an inch of bump-out in the right front steering and it measured .020, we might spend another hour getting it just perfect. If we wanted the rear end housing ahead a 32nd of an inch on the right rear and it was a shy 32nd or a heavy 32nd when we measured it, we'd restring that thing and adjust it until we got it exactly right.

We were defending champions when The Winston cranked up two weeks later. This event was going to be different than the 1991 race because Bruton Smith, the owner of Charlotte Motor Speedway, and Humpy Wheeler, the president of the track, had spent $1.7 million having a huge lighting system installed so we could race around that one-and-a-half-mile track at night. No speedway anywhere near as big had ever been lit for night racing.

We had won The Winston and the Coca-Cola 600 in 1991 in our favorite car, James Bond 007. Now we wondered whether we should risk it again in the all-star race. Davey, Robert, and I had the same attitude. The next race, no matter where it was or what it was about, was the most important race, and we were going to race the best piece we had. So 007 was going back to The Winston.

In the twilight of a beautiful spring evening, Davey went out and won the pole position for the second straight year. There was a Sportsman race after qualifying, and during that event, a South Carolina driver named Gary Batson was horribly burned over 80 percent of his body in a fiery crash on the frontstretch. The next afternoon, we learned that he had died.

Despite that tragedy, Charlotte Motor Speedway was alive with excitement on Saturday night. It was another beautiful spring evening, a full moon was out, and Humpy Wheeler had promoted the event as "One Hot Night." An estimated 133,500 fans poured through the gates to see the spectacle.

Since no points were on the line, the drivers were more inclined to let it all hang out. And the fans knew it. They packed the frontstretch grandstands, ready for action. The place was buzzing with electricity. It was an unforgettable sight as the cars lined up on the frontstretch before the race. The grandstands glittered with camera flashbulbs. The crowd was roaring all through driver introductions. Michael Kranefuss, Ford's top racing official, who had seen racing all over the world, called it an "unbelievable atmosphere."

The race was supposed to get started after the explosion of a gigantic skyrocket blasted almost a half-mile into the moonlit sky, so high it would be visible from Mt. Mitchell 100 miles to the west. But the rocket barely got off the ground before blowing, as if it couldn't wait for the fun to begin. Even today, there is no other night like it in Winston Cup racing.

The race was run in three segments—two runs of 30 laps each and a final 10-lap sprint. Davey led all 30 laps of the first segment, but the field was inverted by a vote of the fans and Davey finished sixth in the second segment.

Then in the third segment Davey did some hard driving in the final laps, but the car just wasn't that good. With two laps to go, he was third. I was happy to settle for third place. I got on the radio to Davey and said, "We're going to finish third here, but that's OK. We've learned a lot about this car, and we can come back next week and win that million-dollar bonus."

As the field took the white flag, Kyle Petty and Dale Earnhardt were having a hell of a race for the lead. It was one of the wildest last laps in NASCAR history. Dale led Kyle by about two car lengths as they flew under the white flag. Kyle made up that gap in the first and second turns when Dale's car pushed up a bit into the banking. With Kyle right on his bumper, Dale took him down to the inside edge of the backstretch, nearly running him off the track in an effort to prevent Kyle from passing.

Dale carried too much speed and a bad line into turn three. He lost control and went for a long slide through the corner. Kyle had to let off the gas to get past that spinning black No. 3 Chevy. Davey got a great run on Kyle and came roaring up on him as Kyle reached turn four. Then Davey went low and dove under Kyle.

I was on ground level during that last lap. One of our crewmen, Roman Pemberton, was standing on top of the tool cart, watching the cars go down the backstretch. Suddenly, the fans started going crazy. I looked up at Roman and this look of sheer excitement had spread across his face.

I thought, "What the hell is going on over there?" I looked toward turn four and a second later here came Davey, leading the race, with Kyle right beside him. "God all mighty, looky there," I said. They were coming toward us, side by side and banging against each other, with Davey a nose ahead. He kept it ahead, too, and shot across the finish line half a car length ahead of Kyle as we exploded over pit wall to celebrate.

But after they crossed the line and got to the second part of the double dog-leg in the tri-oval of the frontstretch, the left front of Petty's car hit the right rear of 007, sending Davey spinning toward the outside wall at a bad angle. I saw our car slam hard into the outside wall, driver's side first. There was a shower of sparks. The car slid on down toward turn one, just missing Elmo Langley in the parked pace car before coming to a stop.

All of us on the crew began sprinting down pit road toward Davey's car. When we got there, all out of breath, what we saw was a scary sight. Davey was slumped over in his seat. His hands still gripped the steering wheel. He wasn't moving. But suddenly he started coming to, and we could see his arms moving.

When I finally got close enough to see his face, he looked at me through the broken front window and gave me a thumbs up. I kept telling the doctors and workers about his injured ribs. I was worried that they would reinjure them trying to get him out of the car. Davey heard me and called out, "My ribs are fine."

The rescuers cut a hole in the roof, got Davey out of the car, and put him on a stretcher. As they were getting Davey out of the car and onto the stretcher, I kept looking back at the scoreboard. It still had the 42 car (Petty) leading and the 28 second. I was thinking, "Man, I know we won this race. Am I going to have to do something about that, too?" But just as they got Davey out, the scoreboard numbers flipped.

Yes! It was a huge relief. Davey was OK, and we had won the race. When they loaded Davey into the ambulance, Bobby Allison and I got in there with him. On the way to the infield care center, Davey must have looked at me four or five times with the very same question.

"What happened?"

"Well, Davey, we wrecked. But you won the race."

Every time, Davey's response was, "You're kidding me."

Then he would ask me again.

In the meantime, a crazy scene was unfolding in victory lane. Robert was down there, but he was in no mood to celebrate. It was one of the few times in racing that a car had won a race, but there was no driver and no team in victory lane to celebrate. For some reason, the speedway decided to try to put the car there. The speedway tow truck that had picked up our car was now trying to drag it into victory lane.

Robert went ballistic. He was going to fight the tow truck driver. "You will *not* take this car to victory lane," he said. "We are not celebrating. Our driver is hurt. We are not celebrating nothing." They finally hauled our wrecked and ruined 007 back to the garage.

As this scene was being played out, a Medivac helicopter with Davey inside lifted off from the track and flew over turn four on its way to Carolinas Medical Center in Charlotte.

The next morning, The Winston's newest winner was lying in a hospital bed with an IV needle in one arm. He looked around, broke into that Cheshire cat grin of his, and said, "This is the darndest victory lane I've ever seen." At least we could laugh with him.

CHAPTER TEN

A Summer of Pain and Sorrow

The Winston in 1992 had been one of the most exciting races in recent NASCAR history, but we had paid a heavy price for giving the fans a memorable show. The season wasn't even a third of the way through, and our driver had been beaten up and battered. Davey had wrecked hard three times in only six weeks. On top of that, we had lost our favorite and best car. But Davey had also won three times.

Davey was released from the hospital around noon the day after the race, but he was hurting. He didn't have a concussion, even though his bell had been rung pretty good, but he did suffer a bruised left lung, left ankle, and left knee, and was generally beat up.

"We've got to quit knocking on this boy like we've been doing lately," Robert told the media. "He's our most valuable asset."

As for 007, it came to a sad end. After winning five of its previous nine races, the car was headed for the scrap yard. We took the wreckage back to the shop. On Monday, two days after the race, we removed the motor and transmission and what few good parts were left. Then we drove a forklift through 007, put it up onto the back of a flatbed, covered it and sent it to a salvage yard.

"I never want to see that car again," Robert said. "We won a lot of races with it, but Davey got hurt in it, too." Robert saved only the hood, so it could be auctioned off at a Coca-Cola 600 charity benefit. Some guy called to propose that we make a business arrangement with him to cut the car up, encase the pieces in solid plastic, and sell them. Robert told the guy he thought the idea was pretty sick.

By Wednesday, which was qualifying day for the Coca-Cola 600, Davey was back at the track, looking better than he felt. None of his injuries were visible, but hidden under his driver's suit, that slender 31-year-old body of his, as he put it, "looked like somebody beat me up with a baseball bat."

But he added, "I actually hurt less than I did after the crash at Bristol. I reinjured some of the ligaments under my right shoulder. Right now, that is the tenderest spot. And I've got a lot of bruises." What made him sadder was that 007 was gone.

Davey ran about 10 laps of practice that day and qualified 17th. This was a brand new backup car, and it was loose. The rear end wanted to spin out when Davey drove into the corners. We were suffering from what I call the "new car blues."

Davey already had a nickname for the car. He called it "Bo," after the actress Bo Derek. This name was inspired by the serial number, which ended in "10," the title of the movie she had starred in. Neil Bonnett agreed to run the car in practice on Wednesday, so after Davey made several practice runs Neil practiced the car for one run. Neil was quite a bit slower than Davey, so Davey would have it no other way but for him to qualify the car himself.

At the time, the car was basically all we had. "Bo," which I always referred to as "010," was destined to become one of the most memorable cars ever to come out of Robert Yates Racing. But her debut created another problem. Now we didn't have a backup car.

We were only 10 races into the season, and we'd already wrecked three cars. We simply didn't have any more. In fact, we had had only one car on the transporter when we sent it over to Charlotte Motor Speedway for The Winston. We finally got 010 finished in time to send it over to the track on Saturday morning. The next day, of course, it became our primary car.

On the night of The Winston, after I'd returned from the infield care center, I saw Tim Brewer, who was Bill Elliott's crew chief. Their transporter was parked next to ours. I had told him about our car shortage.

"I don't even have a backup car for the road race at Sears Point next month," I said.

"Well, we have plenty of cars up there at Junior's," Tim said. "You can borrow one if you want. It may not be what you want, but at least you'll have a car. All you gotta do is put a motor in it and paint it." So we sent a truck up there to borrow Junior Johnson's spare Ford Thunderbird.

The generosity of Tim and Junior made a pretty big statement about the quality of people in the NASCAR Winston Cup garage. They'd be trying to run circles around us on Sunday, but they were more than willing to lend a hand when we needed help. We never had to use Junior's car, thank goodness, but at least we had a backup car for a few weeks until we could get some more new cars built.

If you're really pushing, it takes two-and-a-half to three weeks to finish a new car from the time you get the rolling chassis into the shop. With a moderate pace, you'll finish it in three or four weeks. You take three or four days to get everything attached to the chassis—the suspension, the steering components, the seat. Since it's easier to mount just about anything on the car without the body on it, you try to attach everything you can. Then it takes another four or five days to hang the body, two or three days to get the paint and bodywork done, and another three or four days to put the car back together.

In the Coca-Cola 600, Davey ran all 600 miles and finished fourth. He even led some laps. We didn't win The Winston Million. We just weren't quite good enough. But we had one more big shot at the prize at Darlington in September.

Because of our good finish, we had to go through a thorough post-race inspection. As they measured the car, the inspectors found that the front air dam was too low. I about went into a panic. I didn't know what kind of story to come up with. I honestly didn't know what happened. I had no idea why it was too low.

Then I remembered that we had gone through the grass once on the frontstretch during the race. This was at the time Gary Nelson was slowly but surely taking over the job of Winston Cup director from Dick Beaty.

"The only thing I can figure," I told them, "was it happened when he went down through the grass that one time." I didn't really believe it myself, but I was just trying to come up with some fairly plausible explanation.

Thank goodness Dick picked up on that. "You know, I do remember that happening," he said. "That's probably what the deal is." At one point, they were talking about putting us dead last in the finishing order. That would have cost us the lead in the points race. But they let us keep our fourth-place finish and all the points that went with it. We left Charlotte 101 points ahead of Bill Elliott.

When we got back to the shop, we discovered that the left front jack bolt that adjusts the left front spring had unwound itself about four or five rounds, which lowered that left front corner a good quarter to three-eighths of an inch. That's what made the car tighter.

I've always had a saying: If you make a mistake once, it's not your fault. But if you make the same mistake twice, it's nobody's fault *but* yours. This was a little wake-up call. From then on, we put a jam nut or safety wire or something on the front jack bolts to keep them from lowering themselves. We could lock them down because you don't adjust wedge on the front jack bolts during a race.

After Charlotte, we had a mini slump. At Dover, we were penalized for supposedly speeding on pit road. We thought NASCAR made a questionable call, but it didn't matter what we thought. We finished 11th, three laps down. At Sears Point, where Davey had done so well the year before, he went off course on lap nine and hit a tire barrier. He spun out again late in the race. We finished 28th.

In June, Davey finished fifth at Pocono. Then we headed back to Michigan, where we had been having so much success. We didn't have 007 anymore, but we did have a brand new car—011. And it seemed to be just as good a car as 007. We won the pole for the Miller Genuine Draft 400 with a track record speed of 176.268 mph. The car was perfect. Davey said he couldn't have driven it any faster. "If anybody can beat that, they deserve the pole," he said.

It was our first pole of the year, excluding The Winston. And when Davey woke up on race day, he felt so good it made him nervous. At the track, we were busy with yet another engine problem. We had found an oil leak after the final practice on Saturday, so we decided to pull the race motor on Sunday morning and fix it.

We could have switched engines, but Robert and Doug said that was the best motor we had. Our backup was probably as powerful as any Ford motor out there, but Robert said this one had probably 30 to 40 more horsepower than the backup. So we needed to fix it.

After we pulled the engine from the car, we took it over to Jack Roush's transporter, which carried Mark Martin's cars. Jack's transporter had an engine stand. So we flipped the motor upside down, took it apart, and discovered that one of the engine guys had put the main seal in backwards. We replaced the seal, put the motor back together, put it back in the car, and pushed our Texaco Havoline Thunderbird out to the grid.

As the race got going, we were almost unstoppable. We led 158 of the 200 laps and beat Darrell Waltrip by 3.31 seconds. But the race was no walk in the park. As the laps wound down, fuel mileage became a huge concern. To win, we needed to finish without stopping. But it appeared that we might run out of gas before finishing 200 laps.

In the final 20 or 30 laps, I coached Davey around the two-mile oval. "Shorten the racetrack up," I told him. "Back off the throttle early, get back in the gas later. Let the thing coast through the corners. Keep those [carburetor] butterflies closed." I wore him out. We weren't going to make it unless he bought us a little fuel.

"Larry," he radioed back at one point, "if I back off anymore or get in the gas any later, I'm going to be coasting around the whole dang track!"

"You're doing good," I replied. "In fact, when you back off earlier and get back into it later, your lap times are quicker. That's actually helping you run faster." As it turned out, another yellow flag ended the threat and allowed us to top off.

After the race, when we were tearing down our engine during post-race inspection, NASCAR President Bill France came by. He looked at us and put his hand over his mouth, as if he was yawning. "Is the race over yet?" he asked. "I kinda took a long nap up there awhile ago."

That was Bill's way of saying, "You guys are stinking up my show, and I don't like it." I understood where he was coming from. It's not healthy for NASCAR for one car to run away from everyone else, even though it feels pretty good to a crew chief and driver.

In July, we finished 10th in the Pepsi 400 at Daytona. Davey's car had developed a severe push in the last laps. The car's front end wouldn't stick in the turns and wanted to push up the track. But we left Daytona then as we had left in February—still leading the Winston Cup points championship. We were 46 points ahead of Bill Elliott.

In the heat at Daytona, Davey was bothered by severe headaches. There was an off weekend between Daytona and the next race at Pocono, so Davey had agreed to run in the Busch series race at New Hampshire International Speedway. He went ahead and raced, but the headaches persisted in New Hampshire and continued after he flew from New England to the Bahamas for an outing with the France family. "Sitting out there on that boat rocking back and forth, I don't think that really helped out," Davey said.

On Wednesday, July 15, two days before pole qualifying at Pocono, Davey checked into Carolinas Medical Center in Charlotte for tests. His head hurt so bad he was worried that it might have been caused by the crash in The Winston, and that he might have other problems. The cause turned out to be a virus, though, and the doctors prescribed a course of antibiotics.

On Friday morning Davey checked out of the hospital and flew to Pocono for qualifying. He still didn't feel good, but we caught a break. Qualifying was postponed because of a thick fog that enveloped the track. The next day, he went out and won the pole at a speed of 162.022 mph. "That's not a bad lap for a sick puppy," he said. It just proved once more, in our up-and-down year, that you couldn't keep Davey down for long.

Davey showed his characteristic perseverance in an interview. "There's some things that you just can't do anything about and those things have happened to us: the crash at Bristol, the crash at Martinsville, the wreck at Charlotte in The Winston. Those are just things that happen. When they do, you have to bounce back and bounce back strong."

On race day, Davey told another reporter that if we could just keep things steady through the race in Charlotte in October we'd be in pretty good shape.

After the green flag fell, Davey led the first 30 laps. We gave up the lead during the first round of green flag pit stops, but took over at the front again after everyone else made their stops. We led lap after lap after lap after lap. By lap 139, we had led all but 19 laps. But on that circuit, Wally Dallenbach Jr. spun in turn two and brought out the second yellow flag of the day.

Like everyone else, we hit pit road for four tires. But one of the tire changer's air guns failed, and we had a long stop. When Davey got back out, he was seventh. When you give your driver a bad pit stop and cost him track position—he can be tough to deal with. I got on the radio and told Davey, "Be cool here. We've still got a good race car. And we've got over 50 laps to go."

Davey was with me. He wasn't going ballistic. He was upset, sure, but he understood. And after the restart on lap 148, he was ready to start picking 'em off one by one, starting with Darrell Waltrip in the No. 17 car in front of him.

On lap 149, Davey had a run on Darrell going into turn one, and Darrell chopped him off pretty severely. Robert said later he almost got on the radio to tell Davey, "You've got plenty of time. Be careful with each and every one you come to, including D. W."

The field came by us one more time and disappeared into turn one. We could hear them as they flew down the straightaway and through the tunnel turn. Suddenly, the flagman was waving the yellow flag. I didn't know what had happened, but our spotter, Terry Throneburg, came on the radio and said, "Oh, my God!" The tone of his voice was devastating.

And then he said, "Davey, are you OK? Talk to me, Davey. Are you OK?"

I chimed in as well, "Davey, are you OK? Davey, are you OK?" One of the biggest nightmares a crew chief can have is a driver not answering after a crash. Of course, the radio cord could just be unplugged, or the driver might be knocked out, so you can't immediately assume the worst if he doesn't answer.

"Terry, what's the deal?" I asked.

"Larry, it's bad," he said. You could hear the fear—almost panic—in his voice.

When your driver has crashed, standing in the pits is one of the most helpless feelings in the world. You can't see a thing, and you can't do anything. We knew our spotter must have seen something really horrible. Pocono could be a brutal track. Just four years earlier, Bobby Allison nearly lost his life and had his career end in a bad crash at Pocono.

I looked at Robert, and he was almost white as a sheet. He said later that he felt like his knees were going to buckle. Robert usually scanned the radio channels of a few other drivers during the race, and now he was hearing comments from other drivers. Robert said he heard Mark Martin tell his crew, "Davey looks like he's in bad trouble. They may need to get a body bag."

Terry was trying to keep us abreast of what was going on, and after a time he told me they'd gotten Davey out of the car and into an ambulance. I sprinted just as fast as I could run toward the infield care center. As I was running, a second-rate, out-of-work driver caught up to me and was running beside me. He shoved his phone number into my hand and said, "If you need me to substitute for Davey, here's my number. Call me."

At that point, I didn't know whether Davey was dead or if he'd walked away from the crash. But had I been dumb enough to actually stop and take the time to talk to him, I would have said, "Buddy, if I have anything to do with it, you'll never drive in a race car of mine."

I got to the infield care center well before the ambulance arrived with Davey. Robert followed me. After the ambulance backed up to the care center, the driver got out and told Robert, "He's going to be all right."

When they unloaded the stretcher, Davey was sitting kind of halfway up. He looked at me, and I could tell he was OK—at least as far as surviving. It was the greatest thing in the world to see. But he was holding his arm, and you could tell it was hurting him pretty severely.

They flew Davey by helicopter to Lehigh Valley Hospital in Allentown, Pennsylvania, which is only about 30 miles south of the track as the crow flies. After he left, the team loaded up our demolished car. Robert and I talked to the press. One of the first questions, of course, was about next weekend's race at Talladega.

"I don't care about Talladega," Robert said.

"Regardless of where we go and what's going on," I added, "as long as he's OK, that's what matters. I don't know how many more licks we can take. I hope that's all of them."

The crash had occurred after Davey had gotten past Darrell. When they came out of the tunnel turn, Darrell made a run on Davey. The right front of Darrell's car hit the left rear of Davey's car, sending him into a spin into the infield grass.

It was terrifying to watch the video. As Davey's car slid sideways in the grass, it lifted off the ground and did a reverse half barrel roll onto its roof. That pitched it violently forward into a series of barrel rolls. He flipped at least three times before rolling onto and over the guardrail between the track and the infield. The car continued to flip through a small ditch behind the guardrail and then did one or two end-over-end flips before crashing to a stop onto its roof. His car flipped as many as 11 times. It tumbled so violently, it was almost impossible to count the number of rolls, even while viewing a replay in slow motion. The sheet metal was flying off the car as it rolled. The roof came off, and Davey's right arm came out through the opening. As the car rolled down the guardrail, Davey's arm was crushed between the car and the rail.

We didn't leave the track until the race was over, so we were still there to see Darrell take the checkered flag for his first victory of the year. To us, it was adding insult to injury. I thought it was so unfitting for the race to end that way.

Some of us had been planning to fly back south with Davey after the race, so we had to drive down to Allentown. Robert, Raymond Fox, Ryan Pemberton, and I got in a rental car and drove straight to the hospital.

Davey's little brother, Clifford, had run in the ARCA race at Pocono that weekend, and he had already been in to see him.

"How do I look?" Davey asked.

"Like crap," Clifford replied.

Davey's response was to extend his middle finger.

Outside the room, Clifford told the others, "He'll be all right. He flipped me off."

When we got up on the floor, Davey's mom, Judy, met us outside. "I'm going to tell you, he looks pretty rough," she said. "His head is all swollen just from the beating he took. And his arm is torn up pretty bad."

She was right. Davey looked awful. In fact, he looked so hideous it was almost funny. His little old head was swollen like a pumpkin. His ears looked like they were way back around on the back side of his head. His hairline looked like mine—about at the top of his head. When we walked in, he didn't say hello. All he said was, "I'm going to kill that son of a bitch. I swear I'm going to kill him. I'm going to kill him next time I see him."

It was the same, familiar voice, but it looked like it was coming out of the wrong face. It was obvious Davey had inherited the bad blood that had existed between the Allisons and Waltrip going back more than 20 years.

"No, Davey," I said. "All we need to do here right now is just figure out what to do." Almost forgotten in the chaos was that Davey had finished 33rd at Pocono and had lost the Winston Cup points lead for the first time all season. Heading to Talladega, we were now nine points behind Bill Elliott.

"Let me tell you what you need to do," Davey said. "You all need to get on home and get that Talladega car ready. Get Sam [Manze, Davey's pilot] to fly you guys home. And get that car ready. Because I plan on being at Talladega, and I plan on racing that race car. I'm down, but I'm not out."

And that's exactly what we did. We went home and got our Talladega car ready.

Davey had the same spirit as his father, who stayed in Allentown with him. "All I can tell him is he's gotta pull himself together as best he can," Bobby said. "The sun comes up again tomorrow whether you're ready for it or not."

When the injuries were tallied up, Davey had broken and dislocated his right wrist, broken both bones in his right forearm, fractured and dislocated his right collarbone, and received a severe contusion above his left eye. He had gone into surgery Sunday night, and during a two-hour operation, doctors had inserted two pins in the top of his right hand and two plates with 13 screws in his right forearm. Most of the facial swelling had gone down by Monday, but he still had two black eyes.

Davey's facial injuries had come despite the fact that he used a full-face helmet. But the crash was truly a testament to the advisability of using a full-face helmet, because Davey's helmet was cracked and gouged in a number of places, particularly below the visor.

From the shop, as we prepared the Talladega car, we kept in touch with the hospital on a regular basis. Davey had some headaches on Tuesday, but awoke at 4 a.m. Wednesday feeling as good as he had since the crash. He turned on a TV and happened to tune in to a rebroadcast of the race. He gave nurses a play-by-play of the action. Moments before the crash was broadcast, monitors showed that his heartbeat increased. But as they showed it, Davey told the nurses exactly what happened and how it felt. Once the crash was shown, he said, "You might as well turn it off. If I can't win, I don't want to play."

On Thursday, four days after the crash, Davey went back into surgery to receive bone grafts, to allow doctors to close the incisions from his earlier operation, and to have a cast put on. By then, we had picked Bobby Hillin to drive in relief for Davey. But Davey was already expanding his driving plans. Instead of coming in after the first lap, which would certainly cost us at least a lap making the driver change, he told us he now thought he might be able to make it to the first caution period. That way we could get Hillin in without losing a lap.

On Friday morning, Davey was released from the hospital and immediately flew to the Talladega airport, which is right next to the speedway. We were over at the racetrack working on the car when he arrived. We had a show car over at a hangar at the Talladega airport so that he could make sure he could get in and out of the car before coming to the garage and trying it in front of everyone.

Dr. Harry Stephens, a Pennsylvania neurosurgeon who had also treated Bobby in 1988, was with Davey, along with Bob Grimes, who had fashioned his cast to facilitate driving. Davey could still move his fingers and thumb, which were not covered by the cast. When he came into the garage, he had sunglasses on. When he took the glasses off, his eyes looked like four Georgia road maps. We called him "Beetlejuice." The whites of his eyes were so bloodshot they were almost black. That was the scariest looking thing about him. He could see fine out of them, but looking in them was a pretty wicked sight.

I spoke with Les Richter, NASCAR's vice president of competition, and explained our strategy of letting Davey drive to the first yellow flag. Les, in his very quiet, polite way, stopped me in my tracks. "Larry, we will make the call as to whether he can run to the first caution or whether he runs one lap and gets out," Les told me. "You guys are not going to make this call."

By 4 p.m. Friday, Davey was in the air again and on his way to Hueytown, where he planned to rest before making the mandatory practice laps the next morning. When our time to qualify came, Bobby Hillin did a great job and put the Texaco Havoline Ford Thunderbird in the third starting spot.

At 10 minutes past eight that Saturday morning, Davey came out of our transporter, his eyes covered with those sunglasses, and eased into the car to run the practice laps he needed to run in order to meet NASCAR's requirements to compete in the race.

He took about 10 practice laps, reaching more than 189 mph, which was faster than the qualifying speeds of most of the cars in the field. The plaster cast kept his broken bones in place. Velcro kept his right hand on the steering wheel and allowed him to shift gears. And guts kept his desire burning as strong as ever.

Although Davey had vowed to kill Darrell, during the press conference he didn't even blame him for the crash. "I don't think there was anything intentional there," he stated. "There are times when you over-extend yourself or underprotect yourself. When that happens, you have to be willing to accept the circumstances. I don't have any animosity at all."

Bobby was not so forgiving. His comments reflected how most of us on the team felt. "It was really a pretty small contact and I really feel Darrell did not mean to hurt him bad, but he did mean to get him," Bobby said.

Davey told the press he felt fine in the car. "I ran with cars on every side of me and didn't feel any discomfort at all," he said. "Just a little pressure on my arm and collarbone. When I left pit road, I had a smile on my face. And the more I ran, the more I smiled. If Larry hadn't called me in, I would have stayed out there another five or six laps."

The race started with Davey in the car and barely a cloud in the sky. We had to start from the rear because Bobby Hillin had qualified the car. It was pretty obvious that day how God works in mysterious ways, because, on lap five, a tiny little rain shower showed up over the track and spit rain out for about two minutes. Out came the yellow flag. Davey hustled into the pits, and we made the driver change. Bobby Hillin drove a heck of a race that day. We finished third and took the lead back from Elliott, if only by a point.

We had a weekend off before the road race at Watkins Glen. There, Davey drove 18 laps before giving way to road-racing specialist Dorsey Schroeder. He ran well for us, but overshot the pit during a stop late in the race and fell back. We finished 20th, and lost the points lead once again.

On Thursday, August 13, I left the shop early that afternoon at about 11 a.m. and ran home to get cleaned up and changed. Robert and I, along with most of the team, were taking a commercial flight to Detroit for the Champion Spark Plug 400 weekend at Michigan International Speedway.

We didn't really know what to expect at Michigan. We had won two out of the last three races there, and had lost the other one by a few inches to Dale Jarrett. We knew we had a fast car, but it was less than a month since the Pocono wreck. Davey still had a cast on his right arm, and his eyes were still bloodshot.

When I got home, Linda had a terrible look on her face. "Call Libby," she said. "Clifford Allison has crashed at Michigan, and it doesn't look good." She was pretty torn up.

When I called Libby Gant, our office secretary, she was almost crying. "Larry, Clifford had an accident up at Michigan while practicing for the Busch race," she said. She said it sounded pretty serious. She said Robert wasn't there, but she had left a message for him. I finally reached Robert at his house just before I left for the airport. Robert told me Clifford had died. I was in shock. Davey's little brother was gone. It was almost impossible to believe. "My God," I thought. "What next?"

On the flight to Detroit, Robert and I tried to figure out what to do. We couldn't get in touch with Davey. When we finally got to our hotel, the Hampton Inn in Ann Arbor, Michigan, we spent all evening trying to get in touch with Davey. We found out later that Davey had heard the news soon after the crash. He was at the airport preparing to fly to Michigan. At first, he learned that Clifford had been in a very serious accident and that rescue workers were having a hard time getting him to breathe.

As Sam Manze started one of the engines on Davey's plane, Davey's cousin and agent, Tommy Allison, arrived with the worst news of all. Liz was there, too.

"Tommy, don't tell me that!" Davey said, weeping. Sam cut the engine off, and they all cried together for some time. Then they all got themselves back together, and Davey said, "Let's go."

Bobby Allison was at the track when Clifford died. He tried to get to the car, but NASCAR officials held him back. Clifford's wife, Elisa, also was there. They had three young children.

Although few people saw the crash, the story that emerged was that Clifford began to lose control as he entered turn three. He tried to correct the spin, lost control, and went backwards toward the wall. The left rear of the car struck the wall first, and the left side pancaked into the cement. The impact broke Clifford's seat, and he died instantly of a massive head injury. The upper bolts that held the driver's seat to the roll bar apparently broke, and he was found lying sideways in the car, still in the seat.

Davey was staying with some friends in Michigan, and he finally got in touch with us at the hotel that night. I approached the idea gently. "Look, Davey, if you want to go back to Alabama with your brother, we understand," I said. "We'll get someone to practice and qualify the car, and maybe you can come back Sunday and start the race."

Davey straightened us out real quick. "Let me tell you guys something," he said. "Yeah, my brother was killed today. But I came up here to do a job. And I'm going to do my job. I'm going to do my job when we qualify tomorrow. And I'm going to do my job Saturday. And I'm going to do my job when we race on Sunday. And then I'm going to go home, and I'm going to bury my brother on Monday."

Davey Allison was one of the most determined individuals who ever walked the face of this earth. He was such a role model. He had his priorities in order. And the next day this boy had to drive off in the *very corner* where his brother had just been killed.

The next day, he went out on that track and turned a lap at 178.112 mph, which won the third starting spot. Our team's public relations man, Brian VanDercook, had asked the media to not ask Davey questions about Clifford. But Davey did talk about his qualifying lap.

"It's not bad," he said. "But I don't have a whole lot of self-confidence right now. We'll have to build that up." But Davey was pleased that for the first time in five weeks, he had qualified his own car.

Since the media didn't have Davey to talk to, they came to Robert and me. "We're just trying to support him and make him understand that, whatever he needs, the whole team is here for him," I said. "With everything we've been through as a team this year, you just wonder when it's going to stop. And whether we're sitting at the head table at the NASCAR awards banquet in New York this December or at table 42 in the back of the room, it's been a year we'll never forget. For sure."

"You get over the wrecked cars, and even the broken bones," Robert said. "This is something you don't really ever heal from."

On race day, Davey went out and finished fifth. After the race, he drove his car to the gas pumps, crawled out, took a deep breath, and told the gathered media, "I hope everybody understands, but I'm going to the truck and I'm going home."

CHAPTER ELEVEN

A Championship That Wasn't Meant to Be

As the 1992 Winston Cup season entered its stretch run, we still had a chance to win the Winston Million. If we finished first in the Southern 500 at Darlington Raceway on Labor Day weekend, we would have our third victory in the four designated races, and we would win the million-dollar prize.

A couple of weeks before the Southern 500, we went down to Darlington for a test and ran it well. But before competing for the Winston Million, we had to run the Bud 500 at Bristol, the track that had bitten us so badly in April. This was the first race on the speedway's new concrete surface.

At the Bud 500, I think everything bad that had happened in 1992 finally caught up with Davey. He was running fourth on lap 201 when he spun in turn three and slammed backwards into the wall.

"It was my fault," he said. "I guess I was running a bit harder than I thought I was." He came into the pits with the car's gas tank dragging on the ground. We went to work, calling a wrecker over to try to jerk the back end into some semblance of shape. At one point, we tied it off to the infield care center, and I thought we were going to yank the building down.

We finally got him back out to crawl around the track in search of a few extra points, but this desperate effort ended on lap 329, when he lost it again and went head first into the frontstretch wall. We were done. We finished 30th, and the only saving grace was that Davey wasn't hurt in either crash. But that race was a good example of how playing hurt can bite you. At his peak, Davey would not have crashed like that.

Then we went to Darlington and lost the Winston Million. It was one of the most disappointing races I've ever been involved in. We qualified sixth, led some laps, and stayed with the leaders. It was a blustery, stormy day, and rain was a threat all afternoon.

Davey took the lead on lap 195 and stayed there for all but one of the next 69 laps. But as we reached lap 260, two forces were coming together: we needed a pit stop, and the sky was getting blacker and blacker.

I faced a tricky decision. Should we stay out and wait for rain? Or should we make a pit stop? Our tires were worn out. Our fuel was almost gone. But it looked like the rain was going to start to fall any minute, and it didn't look like it would be stopping any time soon. If it did come down, I knew the race was probably over.

I called over Gil Kerley. "Gil, run over to the NASCAR transporter and look at the weather radar they have there and tell me what you see," I said.

Gil came running back and said, "Larry, it looks good."

"OK," I said. "We're going to pit."

I called Davey in on lap 286. By this time, Davey's worn tires had allowed Mark Martin to grab first place. But we were still second. The points leader, Bill Elliott, was struggling along in 12th place.

Nine laps later, the bottom fell out of the sky. It was a monsoon. But Darrell Waltrip had stayed out there, milking his fuel for all it was worth. And Elliott had stayed out. He was now second. We had managed to get back to fifth. If we had stayed out, we would have finished no worse than second.

Three laps after the rain started, NASCAR red-flagged the race. And that's where it ended.

I looked at Gil and said, "Tell me about that radar again?"

He said, "Larry, I don't understand it. It showed green. It was good."

"Gil, don't tell me that radar was showing *green.*"

"Yeah, it showed good."

"Green?" I said. "Gil, do you know what green means on radar?"

"Yeah. It means clear."

"Green means *rain,* Gil."

You couldn't help but laugh about it. We laugh about it today a lot harder than we did back then. We could have gained as much as 43 points on Bill Elliott that day. Instead, we lost 10 points and now trailed him by 119 points. But what can you do? You pick up and move on.

This was D. W.'s first and only victory in the Southern 500, and he was delighted, even if he had backed into it. "I gotta give Davey credit, too, because he drove hard and gave it a good shot," Darrell said afterward. "Mother Nature just had another plan."

The Miller Genuine Draft 400 at Richmond International Raceway just brought more frustration. We qualified fifth and started out pretty strong, but as the race wore on, we were not contending for the lead. With 86 laps to go, we were 11th—two places ahead of Elliott—when

Ernie Irvan got into Davey and sent him on a long slide through the grass on the inside of the frontstretch.

"Ernie's got one coming," Davey told us on the radio as he got going again. NASCAR didn't throw a yellow flag, so we lost a lap and had to stay out there on flat-spotted tires. Davey gave Ernie a couple of mild shots about 40 laps later, but Ernie kept it going. We finished 19th, two laps down, and lost a few more points to Elliott, who was 14th.

A week later, we qualified 29th at Dover. Davey got out of the car and told the media what all of us had come to realize. "We're missing something," he said. "And we've been missing something. We've been missing something since the second race at Michigan. But I don't know what was wrong."

We made some changes before the race, and those got us going in the right direction. Of course, those pins and plates were still in Davey's right arm. But Davey ran hard at Dover and fought his way through the wrecks. At the end of 500 long miles and almost four and a half hours of racing, he was fourth, a lap down.

Elliott dominated the race, but he was snookered at the end by Ricky Rudd. He still finished second, and now his lead over us was 154 points as we headed to Martinsville.

When we all got to Martinsville, Davey couldn't wait to show us the pins that had been removed from his arm at the beginning of the week. He carried them around in his wallet.

On pole day, we were terrible. Davey was 32nd fastest among 34 cars—almost a full second slower than pole winner Kyle Petty. We had to run in the second round of qualifying, which means you have almost a full day less to prepare for the race than the other top teams. We managed to pull ourselves up to 22nd in the second round, but that still put us in a pit on the backstretch.

The race was rained out on Sunday, so we had to return and run the Goody's 500 on Monday. We caught a break when Elliott stumbled and suffered a DNF. He was already a lap down when his engine blew on lap 158. He finished 30th.

Davey was in a position to make up a bundle of points, but we got spun out. He worked his way back through the field. With 60 laps to go, we were fifth. Then Davey started having his usual Martinsville brake problems.

We finished 16th, four laps down, and managed to gain 42 points on Elliott. Now we were 112 points behind. Davey said, "We've obviously got some things to change on our short-track program."

But we weren't getting much time to make any changes. We were in the middle of seven straight weekends of racing. And at North Wilkesboro, the race was rained out for the second week in a row, and we had to return on Monday.

Even though we were usually strong at North Wilkesboro, this time we couldn't get the car right in practice, even though we had qualified 14th. We were fighting a lot of the same things we had fought at Martinsville. Even worse, we were beginning to look at each other and to question everything.

But we kept working. And all through the race at North Wilkesboro that Monday, we worked on that car and made it better and better. Unfortunately for us, there was not a single yellow flag. It was the first caution-free Winston Cup race in eight years. So we could never get caught up. Davey finished 11th, three laps down.

But Elliott was even worse. He finished eight laps down in 26th. We gained 45 points, and now we were within striking distance. If we had a good Mello Yello 500 at Charlotte and Bill had a bad one, we could take the lead. We felt pretty good about it, because it was one of our very best tracks.

We had almost no time to prepare, but neither did anyone else. Qualifying at Charlotte back then was on Wednesday, which was only two days after the race at North Wilkesboro. Still, I figured that, with our engine and our driver, there was no reason we shouldn't qualify in the top five.

We didn't even make the top 20. We started 22nd. After qualifying, I was about to pull out my hair. If the problem wasn't the engine and it wasn't the driver, it had to be the car, which was my responsibility.

All I knew for sure was that we weren't going to give up. We were going to keep on making changes and throwing stuff at our problem until something worked. Finally, on Saturday morning, the day before the race, our car started running better. The bewildered looks on our faces disappeared. Part of it was just getting back to communicating like we had been.

In Happy Hour we had one of the fastest cars. Based on what we saw in that final practice, we made a few more changes. But when the green flag fell to start the Mello Yello 500, the car was worse than it had been all week. We were junk. The car was so loose, Davey could barely drive it. We were a wreck waiting to happen every lap. We did everything we could do to tighten the car up. We put spring rubbers in the right front and left rear. We added six or seven rounds of wedge.

Finally, during a pit stop, we discovered that the right rear spring was out of its bucket. We later figured out that it had happened during the first pit stop. When we pulled a spring rubber out of the spring, it had yanked the spring from its bucket.

The minute we corrected that mistake, of course, the car was way too tight, and we had to start undoing all the changes we had made trying to correct the previous condition. When the checkered flag fell, we were 19th, five laps down.

But thankfully Bill Elliott refused to let us suffer alone. He was running along in eighth place and about to put a hurting on us in the points when his track bar pulled loose from the frame and his Junior Johnson Thunderbird became impossible to drive. He dropped out and finished 30th, which allowed us to gain another 28 points on him. Now we were only 39 points behind.

The new problem was, after three consecutive bad races for both Davey and Bill, both teams had lost so many points that there were now *four* other drivers in the thick of the championship battle. We trailed Bill by 39 points. Alan Kulwicki was right on our tail, only 44 behind Bill. Mark Martin was in fourth, 88 points back. Harry Gant was 95 points back. And Kyle Petty was within striking distance, 111 points behind Elliott.

It was pretty strange having Kulwicki breathing down our necks. Just a few weeks earlier, after Dover, he was 278 points out of the lead. Alan was a driver with an engineering degree, who'd come South out of Wisconsin to start his own team and try to make it on his own in the Winston Cup series. He was considered a huge underdog.

Rockingham was the 27th of 29 races, and a record crowd of more than 62,000 fans jammed the place to see the showdown. We ran well in practice, but Davey's car got loose during his qualifying lap, and we qualified 15th.

It was another tough race for us. Kyle Petty ran away with it, while we struggled to a 10th place finish, two laps down. We were down a lap by lap 120. We never made it up. During the race, tensions were high between me and my driver as I coached him from pit lane. At one point he snapped, "Talk to me, don't cuss at me!"

After the race, Robert, Davey, and I spent an hour and 20 minutes talking about our problems in the back of the team transporter. When Davey finally left, he was still mad. He walked right past the reporters who had been waiting for him there the entire time, and Davey didn't tell them a thing.

So I was left to speak for him. "We're all frustrated," I told them. "We're all tired. We're all under a lot of pressure. This race team—we're beat up. We've had no breaks—no relief—just about since the season started."

When the dust settled, we found ourselves 70 points behind Elliott, who had run a steady race and finished fourth. Kulwicki finished 12th and was now 85 points behind Bill. Petty's victory allowed him to move into fourth place in the points race, 94 points behind Elliott. Harry Gant was now 113 points behind. Mark Martin was 172 points behind and out of the title chase after crashing in the fourth turn late in the race.

Just a few days after the Rockingham race, we all headed for Phoenix. I had a new plan for PIR, and I was hoping it would pull us out of our slump. I took a new car with a different chassis.

Mike Laughlin, who builds chassis for a lot of Winston Cup teams, including Robert Yates Racing, had a new type of chassis called a "three-quarter low snout." A Winston Cup chassis has three primary components—the front snout, the rear snout, and the center section. The only difference in the low-snout chassis was the geometry in the front section. The suspension points in the front snout were lowered to make the roll center lower. Mike said it would allow the car to turn better on short and flat tracks. He had hammered on me to try one for probably close to a year. But our stuff had been so good we were hesitant to go out on a limb and try something that much different.

After we finished three laps down at North Wilkesboro, I was ready to give the low-snout chassis a try. I told Robert I wanted to try one. "That's fine," he said. "But we need to test it first."

We decided to have Mike Laughlin convert our 010 chassis into a low- snout car and sent it down to Mike's shop in Simpsonville, South

Carolina. Basically, all they did was cut the existing front section off with blowtorches and weld the new low snout back on.

We decided to test the car at Richmond in early October. We brought two cars—one with the conventional chassis and the other with the low snout. We ran more than 600 laps over two days. But it didn't take us more than two hours on that first morning before Davey knew.

He got out of the low-snout car, looked at it, and said, "That's my race car, right there. That's the car that is going to help us get out of the hole we're in."

In Phoenix, we ran a lap in practice that would have been fast enough to qualify second. But the car slipped again during the qualifying run and Davey started 12th.

Davey took it easy during the first part of the race. We were ninth after 50 laps. By lap 100, we were third. And that's pretty much where we stayed during much of the rest of the race.

On lap 239 of 312, Mark Martin took the lead from Alan Kulwicki and moved away from the rest of the field by several seconds. It looked like Mark was going to win the race, but a final round of pit stops started on lap 276. Mark came in on lap 283 and we took the lead.

Two laps later, just as we were about to pit, a regional driver named Jeff Davis spun as he tried to get onto pit road. We were right behind him, but Davey managed to stay out. The yellow flag flew. We came in the next time around. Because of the caution period, we remained in the lead.

The funny thing about the incident was that Davis was driving a Winston Cup car that was sold to him by Jack Roush, Mark's car owner. They sold the car because its former driver, Wally Dallenbach, considered it haunted. He said it was the worst car he'd ever been in. Davis's spin not only caught Martin, but Dallenbach as well.

The only laps we led in that race were the final 30 circuits. But it was a victory we desperately needed. We had already won four races and The Winston, but it had been so long since the last one, as Davey put it, "We just couldn't believe it could happen."

Davey was emotional about the victory and broke down a couple of times during post-race interviews when he mentioned his grandfather and brother. "It's been a real great season and a real bad season all in one," he said.

After stumbling through the races during the stretch run, we had finally regained that magic. And we had also regained the lead in the Winston Cup points championship. Bill Elliott had another bad race. He burned a piston, and as he put it, "killed about half the population of mosquitoes here in Phoenix" with the smoke pouring from his damaged engine.

With only the final race at Atlanta left, we had a 30-point lead over Alan Kulwicki, who had moved into second on the strength of his fourth-place finish at Phoenix. Elliott was now third, 40 points behind. Harry Gant and Kyle Petty were 97 and 98 points behind and pretty much out of it now.

To win the Winston Cup championship, all we needed to do was finish seventh or better in the final race. We had an off weekend before the race, which was on November 15, 1992, so we went to Atlanta to test after returning from Phoenix.

I made a point of not overworking the guys in the two weeks before the finale. I didn't think there was any sense in putting out a red alert. We probably worked closer to regular hours during that time than at any other time of the season. Some of the team flew to Las Vegas on the Monday after Phoenix. And everyone was off during that final off weekend of the season.

Even so, we put extra effort into getting ready for Atlanta. We tried to finish preparations early, and I taped a race-day checklist on that car while it was in the shop, just so we'd be sure to go over everything.

We had decided that we were going to race at Atlanta with the same car we'd just won with at Phoenix—the low-snout car. Just before the weekend off, we tested at Atlanta with three cars, looking for the one that was most consistent. We picked the low-snout car because of its success at Phoenix and because that's the car Davey wanted.

And the fact that Davey wanted that car meant a lot. By then I had worked with him for almost two seasons, and I knew his confidence level was worth a lot. Sometimes before a pit stop, if I wanted to take two tires and Davey came on the radio and said he wanted four tires, I'd give him four tires. Because he had so much confidence in four tires, he'd make those four tires work for him.

During the 1992 stretch run, Davey was starting to lose confidence in himself. But he was certain about wanting that low-snout car at Atlanta. And when Davey Allison made up his mind about something, trust me, you would be much better off at the end of the day if you went with him.

When Davey told me, "Larry Mac, that's the car right there that we need to take to Atlanta," that was good enough for me. I don't think Robert approved of this decision, but he let us do our jobs and didn't interfere. Truth be known, he *never* interfered.

In hindsight, using the low-snout car at Atlanta was probably a mistake. Robert knew it, but Davey and I didn't have quite enough experience to recognize it. On our team, the only two people who had been on a championship team were Robert Yates and our gasman, Norman Koshimizu, who were both with DiGard Racing in 1983 when Bobby Allison won the championship.

The low-snout chassis would turn better not only on the flat tracks, but on every type of track. But the problem on high-banked tracks with high-speed entrances to the turns was that the low roll center made the car feel too loose going into the turns. Even if the car wasn't actually loose, it would give the driver the sensation that it was loose because of the way the chassis rolled.

We paid pretty big money for Bob Latford, who was probably the premier statistician in Winston Cup racing, to formulate a chart that would enable us to track ourselves against all the other title contenders. We were looking for all the "what ifs," and to answer questions such as, "Where do we need to finish if we lead a lap?" and "Where do we need to finish if we lead the most laps?" It was a big numbers game, and we were doing all we could to win it. But I don't think Robert was too thrilled with our "numbers watching" strategy, either.

We ended up qualifying 17th. And we were pretty fast in practice. But on Saturday I think we got a little bit too cocky. There were three practices that day, one in the early morning, one at midday, and one final Happy Hour session late in the afternoon.

When we ran in the morning we were OK. We didn't have anything to stick out our chests over, but we were competitive. We didn't even run the second practice. We covered up the car and went to lunch. That was probably a mistake. That wasn't us. But we were trying to play mind games. We ran in Happy Hour, and I thought we were OK again, knowing all we had to do was finish seventh or better.

This race was to be Richard Petty's final event, and the night before the race, there was a big tribute to him at the Georgia Dome in downtown Atlanta. Linda asked me if I wanted to go. I told her I wanted to stay at the hotel and keep my mind fresh. I wanted to make sure we gave it all we could in the race the next day. We ordered pizza and stayed in the room. I slept pretty well that night.

The race got underway on a beautiful late-fall day in Georgia. We started moving up. By lap 30, we were 11th. But then we ran over a piece of debris that caved in the front air dam. We got it fixed during a yellow flag and managed to stay on the lead lap, but fell back.

Davey fought back through the field. Then we made a two-tire pit stop, which allowed him to take the lead on lap 86 and hold it for five laps. More importantly, by leading a lap, we got the five bonus points. That improved our chances. Now all we had to do to win the title was finish eighth or better.

After leading, we hung on in the top five for about 30 laps. But our low-snout car wasn't handling that well, and Davey slipped back. And for the next 150 laps, he hung there around sixth, seventh, or eighth—exactly where we had to be. By then, Bill Elliott and Alan Kulwicki had become the class of the field, trading the lead between themselves.

At lap 250 of 328, we were up to fifth, trailing Ernie Irvan, Rusty Wallace, Elliott, and Kulwicki. Three laps later, it all ended as fast as you could turn your head. As Irvan came off turn four, he cut a tire and his Kodak Chevrolet spun, hit the wall, and came back across the track right in front of Davey.

There was nowhere for Davey to go. I remember seeing Davey's black car with the red numbers spin and then hit the outside wall. My first thought was, "Did we tear up anything we can't repair?" Then Davey said to me over the radio, "It's bad, Larry. I can't steer it. We're done, guys."

I just walked out onto pit road and hung my head. It was out of our control. It was over. It was no one's fault. It was just racing fate. We took the car to the garage area anyway, determined to fix that thing and get it back out there.

While we were working on the car, Davey was having the routine checkup at the infield care center. When he came out, he calmly said,

"Well, that's just the way it goes sometimes. It just wasn't our year. It just wasn't meant to be."

Davey could have been mad at Ernie, considering their run-ins during the year. But he wasn't. He understood that the cut tire wasn't Ernie's fault. Ernie had his head rattled in the crash, and Davey checked on him at the care center and then twice more at his transporter. As Davey walked away from Ernie's hauler the final time, he said, "Don't worry about it. It's just racing."

Ernie said afterward, "The first thing I remember is Davey Allison coming in to find out if I was all right."

Elliott won the race, but Alan Kulwicki had won the championship by a slim 10 points after finishing second and leading the most laps in the race.

After our crash, we'd hauled the wrecked car back to the garage. I told the guys we had to fix it and get back out there. "I don't care if we don't get back out until three laps to go, we're going to go down swinging," I said.

So we sent Davey back out to ride around, and I went up to the top of the transporter to watch that poor, wounded, beat-up race car going around the track. The sight of that car almost made a statement about our whole damn year. I knew we had dumped a good season—a championship year. We had won four races by the end of June, and it seemed like there was no way we could lose the championship.

After Dover in September, Alan had been almost 300 points out of the lead for the championship. Now he was champion. For us, it had all slipped away. And to this day, I am certain of the exact moment when it all went bad. It was when Davey flipped 11 times at Pocono and crushed his right arm.

The other crashes hurt us as well—the crashes at Bristol, the crash at Martinsville, the crash after winning The Winston. But the Pocono crash was the crippling blow. Without that crash alone, there's no telling how many races Davey would have won in 1992. There's no telling how quickly he would have wrapped up the Winston Cup championship.

While other teams were testing and getting ahead, we were building new cars, nursing an injured driver, and just trying to hang on. In the middle of all that, we had to face the death of Davey's brother. We came back from it all, and came back from the crash at Pocono, too. We gamely clung to second in the points race and somehow went into that last race with a small lead. But it wasn't enough.

We had made arrangements to stay for the Ford Racing celebration after the race at the Hilton Hotel near the Atlanta airport. The whole team went to the party with our wives or girlfriends. And we probably had a better time there than any other group.

Yes, we'd lost. But it was a huge relief just to be done with it. And look how close we'd come despite everything that had happened to us. All of us were confident that we'd win the title in 1993. Surely to God, we'd never have another year like 1992. Of course, little did we know that 1993 would show us how insignificant it really was to tear up a few cars and lose a championship.

CHAPTER TWELVE

"Davey Has Crashed That Helicopter"

One of the most inspiring things to see in the wake of our loss of the 1992 Winston Cup championship was Davey's attitude. In the short few minutes from the crash with Ernie to the moment he stepped out of the infield care center to face the media, he came to terms with the disappointment.

"It just wasn't meant to be," Davey said. He repeated that time and again. He said it firmly and confidently because he really believed it. The loss simply didn't bother him that much. If not 1992, well, we'd win it in 1993, he thought. We all felt that way.

But we got off to a slow start in 1993. At Daytona, we were plagued by chassis problems. We just weren't very fast from the time we unloaded for the first test in January until the time we loaded up and left. During the race, we had to make several unscheduled pit stops. We finished 28th, three laps down.

At Rockingham Davey had ignition problems, and the car quit during our qualifying run. We had to start 39th in a 40-car field, which meant a pit on the backstretch. We finished 14th, two laps down.

The next weekend, as we arrived in Richmond to face the usual cold, early March weather, I told the media I felt like a truck driver who had missed a gear. "We need to pull this old rig over to the side of the road and start over in first gear," I said. But we felt good about one thing—we were using the same low-snout car at Richmond that had won at Phoenix. We had learned that the car was hard to get going in qualifying—that it could slip easier because it wasn't hooked up. But it would really shine on long green-flag runs.

We qualified 14th at Richmond, but once the race got started and that car got hooked up, we moved right through the field. Davey took the lead for the first time on lap 172 of the 400-lapper. There were only three yellow flags in the entire race. He led 152 of the final 157 laps, and we won by 4.36 seconds over Rusty Wallace.

"Considering what happened in the first two races of this year, I'm numb right now," I said afterward. "Our pit stops were the fastest on pit road. I think we had a couple of stops in the 18-second bracket, and the last stop was in the 17s." (Today's standard is 14 to 15 seconds for four tires and fuel, and some teams are even dipping into the 13s.)

At Richmond, I used to use a little trick to improve the downforce of the car that I used at most tracks. After we put the car out on the line on race morning, I took a pair of pliers from my pocket and pulled out the corners of the fenders just in front of all four tires, creating "Gurney lips" that increased front and rear downforce. I'd bend down and act like I was checking the tire pressure. Then I'd reach over and pull the fender out. It's a questionable move, for sure, which is why I waited until after pre-race inspection.

With about 30 to 40 laps to go at Richmond, and Davey holding a comfortable lead, I started worrying about those gurney lips. I knew if I didn't do something, NASCAR inspectors were going to see those lips during the tear down. And I knew they weren't going to like them, because I had gotten a little carried away on the starting grid and made them really big.

So there we were in victory lane, standing behind the car, smiling and posing for pictures. Except I've got those pliers out and every so often I'm trying to turn back the lips I could reach. I had to be careful; NASCAR officials were standing nearby. Our jack man, Jeff Clark, had gone to college for about eight years, and I always used to kid him about that. Once, after I had quickly ducked down to work on the lips, Jeff blurted out, "Oh, I was wondering what those pliers were for."

I said quietly, "Boy, Jeff, those eight years of college are really kicking in now, aren't they?"

But I somehow got all of them turned down. I didn't get them turned back perfect, but we made it through inspection. That win at Richmond was Davey Allison's 19th career victory. As we left Virginia, we felt like we were back on track. But five days later, at Atlanta, we struggled again. We took a new car down there, lost an engine in practice, and qualified 31st.

When we got up Saturday morning, it was snowing. We managed to get to the track before it really started coming down. A lot of people didn't make it. Back then, the garage was basically a shed, and we put up tarps and parked vans against them to protect our work area. By then, it was a full-blown blizzard. But we worked on that race car, trying to figure out what it was missing.

With snow falling sideways, the nor'easter brought Atlanta to a halt. It was called the Southeast's "Storm of the Century." Around mid-morning, NASCAR called off the weekend and rescheduled the race

for later in the month. Normally, we go the next raceable day, but everyone knew it would still be a mess on Monday. It took us forever to get
back to the hotel. We were staying at a Hampton Inn up in Morrow, off
of Interstate 75. Once we got back, all we could do was eat pizza and
drink beer. The power was off. We couldn't even watch TV.

Davey took off for Hueytown in a car. It's usually no more than two
and a half hours from Atlanta to Birmingham. It took Davey 12 hours.
He left at 10 in the morning and finally got home at 10 o'clock that night.
"We stopped whenever traffic stopped, and we'd throw snowballs for
a while," he said. I tried to tell that ol' hardhead before he left that he
was in for an ordeal, but he said, "Nah, I can do it."

My mom was stuck in the same blizzard in Birmingham. Her health
was not particularly good, and the electricity was off in her apartment.
I talked to her about every hour, but I was having a tough time getting
through because the phone lines were jammed. She kept telling me what
the temperature was in her apartment, and it kept dropping. It got down
to about 50 degrees. She lived at the bottom of Red Mountain and worked
at Baptist Medical Center, which was at the top of the mountain.
Fortunately, one of the hospital security guards got down to her and took
her back up to the hospital.

When we finally ran the race, we finished 13th, three laps down. We
didn't do much better at Darlington, finishing 11th, two laps down.
Davey's confidence was getting low, but they had an IROC race at
Darlington that weekend and Davey beat 'em like a drum. "I know I
can still drive a race car," he said afterward. It did all of us good to see
him win again.

Now it was back to Bristol, where we had gotten our first dose of mis-
fortune in 1992. The weather was cold and wet when we drove there
on Thursday, April 1. This was before the days of motorcoaches, and
Davey and I had adjoining rooms at the Bristol Days Inn. We were still

at dinner at a Mexican restaurant next to the hotel around 9:30 p.m. when we started hearing the sirens of fire trucks and emergency vehicles. And more sirens. And more sirens. We wondered what was going on.

At about 10:30 p.m., back at the hotel, Davey pounded on the door between our rooms. "Larry, something's happened. I think it's Alan Kulwicki and his plane," he said. We sat on my bed, him in his underwear and me in my sweatpants, watching the news on television. The plane carrying Alan had fallen out of the sky and crashed in a pasture while approaching the Bristol airport. Alan and the three others aboard were killed instantly. Alan had won the championship that we had lost in 1992. After everything we had gone through, I still didn't understand why. But that night, I think we got an answer. As we sat there, it seemed like Davey was now relieved that Alan had won.

It was cold and raining the next morning as we headed to the track. Even a little sleet was falling. It was crushing to see Alan's truck sitting there, and his guys, who looked so lost without their driver and leader. Alan was the most recent winner at Bristol, having won the Food City 500 the previous August. Before leaving the track, Alan's transporter made one final memorial lap. At 10:30 a.m., Alan's truck driver, Peter "Rabbit" Jellen, started the diesel engine of the Ford 9000 Aeromax hauler and eased down the frontstretch. All of us in the pits—the entire NASCAR family—lined pit wall and watched in silence. On the other side of the fence, in the grandstands, about 200 spectators also silently watched. It took Jellen several minutes to complete the lap. As he brought the big truck to the finish line, NASCAR flagman Mike Chaplin waved the checkered flag. Jellen wiped tears from his eyes. It was probably the saddest, slowest lap in NASCAR history.

Alan and I had gotten to know each other a little bit. I often saw him at Mass on Saturday evenings, and we'd talk at the racetrack. He had a dry wit, and he almost never changed his facial expression while talking. And he never quit interrogating you: "Are you using stickers or scuffs? What made you decide to use scuffs? How many laps do you have on those scuffs? Were those hard laps or easy laps?"

Once, after qualifying at North Wilkesboro, Alan and I were talking in the back of his truck. He went up to the lounge to change clothes, so I followed. We talked about race cars, racetracks, and race people. We just sat there talking, and all of a sudden I looked out the tinted window and noticed it was getting dark. I looked at my watch and realized we'd been there 90 minutes. The garage was closed. Everyone was gone. We were locked in the track. We had to find someone to let us out.

I thought about those things as I watched Alan's truck. But soon it was time to go back to work. It was one of those weekends when nobody wanted to race. But we did well, and finished fifth despite losing a cylinder.

Before race number seven at North Wilkesboro, we had the Easter weekend off. We headed right up to Martinsville for three days of testing before the holiday weekend. We were going to fix our qualifying and brake problems at Martinsville once and for all.

A fellow crew chief, Barry Dodson, clued me in on fixing the qualifying problem. "Larry, you just would not believe how much air pressure we put in the tires before we qualify at Martinsville," Barry said. We discovered that it did, indeed, take a lot of extra air pressure to qualify well at Martinsville. We had been adding four or five pounds. Barry said he was putting in 10 or 12 pounds. The extra air puts heat in the tires quicker at speed, which helps them hook up.

We took two cars to Martinsville and ran 675 laps. We not only solved the qualifying problem, we also learned how to keep the brakes on Davey's car. We had engineers and brake specialists with us and we tried different brake packages. We finally figured out that, to keep the brakes on the car for 500 laps, we needed a brake-fluid recirculator, which keeps the fluid constantly recirculating and helps keep air out of the line. But truthfully, the biggest secret to keeping your brakes at Martinsville is a good starting position near the front, so you don't have to use them so much.

The next weekend, we applied our knowledge at North Wilkesboro and finished fourth. Then it was back to Martinsville. We qualified sixth, and Davey ran really well, finishing second. In fact, when Morgan Shepherd wrecked with less than four laps to go, Davey just about caught race leader Rusty Wallace sleeping. Rusty only barely beat us to the line in the mad dash to the yellow flag. Most importantly, this time Davey finished the race. He didn't blow the bead of the tire, and he didn't lose his brakes. The first thing Davey did when he got out of his car was ask the guys to raise the hood, so he could look at the brake pads. He took a look and said, "There's as much pad now as we had when we *started* this race last year."

We didn't win any of the short-track races that spring, but unlike 1992, Davey didn't crash and hurt himself either. He had posted three top-five finishes, and moved to third in the Winston Cup points standings. Once again I began preaching, "Look at the big picture."

From NASCAR's smallest track we moved to the largest track at Talladega for the Winston 500, where Davey finished seventh, again one spot behind Rusty Wallace. During the mad four-wide dash to the finish line, Davey watched as Rusty's car was tapped by Dale Earnhardt and rose into the air, literally flying across the finish line on its way into a horrible, tumbling crash. Rusty suffered a broken wrist, a concussion, cuts, and bruises.

Davey went straight to the NASCAR trailer after the race, just raising hell about the racing conditions. "You guys are going to have to do something about this," he said. "You can't have people doing these things at the end of the race. We're going to kill someone." That was the Allison coming out in him. When he felt strongly about something, he wasn't afraid to voice his opinion very loudly.

At Sears Point, our fortunes began to slip again. We had a good run going until the final lap, when Dale Jarrett spun us out. We finished 15th. In the Coca-Cola 600 at Charlotte, we had a valve problem, something that doesn't happen very often on a Robert Yates engine. We finished 30th, 58 laps down. But we turned it around at Dover, where we finished third. And we had a good run at Pocono, leading a few laps and finishing sixth. After Pocono, we jumped from fourth to second in the Winston Cup championship. We trailed Dale Earnhardt by 225 points.

The next race was on June 20 at Michigan, and we were determined to get our speedway program on track. We qualified third. But early in the race, Rick Wilson, who was already a lap down, got into Davey in turn four and put him into the wall. We finished 35th—our worst finish ever at Michigan—and plunged to sixth in points.

The Pepsi 400 at Daytona marked the 15th of 30 races in the 1993 Winston Cup season. Since it was preceded by an off weekend, for two days we tested there with some front-end geometry changes that Davey wanted to try in hopes of regaining the edge we'd once had at Daytona and Talladega.

It certainly looked like the testing paid off, because in the practice session before qualifying, Davey ran a lap that would have won the pole. But we were all mystified when he slowed down in qualifying by three-tenths of a second—almost a full mile per hour. He still qualified third, but as Davey sarcastically noted, "All that test time certainly helped!"

We had nothing but trouble in the race. Early on, the engine shut off. We opened the hood and shut it. Somehow, that fixed the problem. I have no idea why. It was like a ghost at work. Then we lost the handle on the chassis. The car wouldn't drive a lick in traffic. We finished 31st, 11 laps down.

We just couldn't find that groove we had in 1991 and the first half of 1992. We'd run good one week but we'd be off the next, often at tracks where we had been good. Davey and I were beginning to get a little sideways with each other. But when you start struggling, you begin to question everything.

Davey was complaining that the cars weren't as good, and I was complaining that he wasn't helping much. We were struggling at Daytona, and when you struggle and you have something different on the car, it's obviously the first thing you question. "Damn it, I told you that goofy steering deal at Daytona wouldn't work," I told him. Davey had come up with the idea of leveling out the steering—normally the steering box and linkage assemblies are tipped at an angle. He thought making everything level might give us a bit of a performance advantage. Robert had questioned it the minute he heard about it. On the other hand, we could not sit still. We all felt like we had gotten behind on the body and aero technology and on the chassis technology. This is a common problem for a really good race team.

When your stuff is typically so good week in and week out, you don't want to change anything. Everybody else is changing everything to try to catch up. Eventually, they find something, and you fall behind. Another problem for us was that NASCAR's standardization of cylinder heads in 1991, which gave all the other Ford teams Robert's heads, was finally having a profound impact. In 1991 and even into 1992, we were beating some teams by 75 to 100 horsepower. That was no longer the case.

We were still searching for that special magic as we headed north to New Hampshire for the inaugural Winston Cup race at New Hampshire International Speedway. The track had opened in 1990 with Busch series races, but this was the first trip for the Winston Cup series. Although it was a one-mile oval, it was more like a short track because of the tight, almost flat turns.

The heat in New Hampshire during the Slick 50 300 weekend was almost unbearable. You expect cool breezes in New England, but we found ourselves in a stifling bake oven with temperatures over 100 degrees in some places. It was 10 degrees hotter than in North Carolina.

Davey qualified 7th in our low-snout car. But in Saturday morning practice, we struggled badly. Robert, Davey, and I huddled in that stifling garage, our faces streaked with sweat, and had a hard discussion about our problems. We talked about what we thought we were fighting and how we were at odds with each other. Bobby Allison joined in and made some suggestions. I said, "Look, we're junk. Let's make some big changes. What have we got to lose?" So we did. And in Happy Hour, the car hooked up pretty good.

Race day was July 11, 1993. It was another hot day, although the temperatures had dropped to the mid-90s. Before the race, they put the drivers in the backs of pickup trucks—two to a truck—for a parade lap around the track. I still have a picture on my wall of that parade lap, because in Davey's truck was Ernie Irvan, who had qualified eighth in the Kodak Chevrolet. The photo shows them standing in the back of the truck in their driver's uniforms, both waving to the crowd.

Ernie and Davey had had their run-ins, but I think Davey's sportsmanship after the crash at Atlanta went a long way toward burying the hatchet. Both appear relaxed and friendly in the picture. No one knew that in 48 hours Davey would be gone, and in less than two months, Ernie would be wearing that Texaco Havoline uniform.

We ran well in the race. Davey took the lead for the first time on lap 82. He led only 12 of the first 200 laps, but as the race wore on, Davey got stronger. Rusty Wallace had been leading quite a while, but we took the lead from him on lap 245 during a round of green flag pit stops. Soon, we were six or eight car lengths in front of Wallace, and he wasn't gaining any ground.

With about 30 laps to go, one of Michael Waltrip's hubcaps (which goes over the outer part of the hub to cover the bearing) came off and bounced to a stop on the backstretch. At almost the same moment that NASCAR starter Doyle Ford threw the yellow flag, a car hit the hub and sent it scooting out of harm's way.

"I didn't want to see no friggin' caution flag," Davey told us on the radio. We couldn't have agreed more. With that low-snout car, we were dead in the water for the first 20 laps of a run. Everyone pitted and so did we. We had enough gas to make it, but we'd been out there for 60 or 70 laps on those tires, and we'd be in even worse shape on used tires than new.

Rusty beat us off pit road. And he won the race by 1.31 seconds over Mark Martin. We finished third. But as we packed up the truck, we felt like the only thing that had stopped us was racing luck.

I flew home with Davey on his plane that evening. Robert was on the flight, along with Raymond Fox and Eli Gold, the MRN anchorman, and Bobby Allison. Davey was going to drop us off at Charlotte and fly on to Alabama. Davey always climbed up in that left seat in the cockpit and flew the airplane with his pilot, Sam Manze. But when we were boarding the plane, Davey told his father, "Dad, why don't you fly this plane. I think I'm going to sit back here with Robert and Larry and the guys. I'm going to drink me a beer and I'm going to enjoy myself."

That was very unusual. It was special to have him in the back with us. It was the old group again. We drank a little beer. We joked and cut up and talked. Davey was really looking forward to returning to Talladega in two weeks, and he was even upbeat about going back to Pocono the next weekend. We talked about being back on the same song page. Davey was more relaxed and confident than I'd seen him in awhile. I will always treasure those final precious minutes with Davey.

It was a two-and-a-half-hour flight back to Charlotte. If Davey was staying in Charlotte, sometimes I'd convince him to come over and spend the night with us. But this night, since Davey and Sam and Bobby were flying back to Alabama, they got out only to stretch their legs and refuel the plane. Robert and I grabbed our luggage and walked into the small private terminal at Signature Aviation at Charlotte-Douglas International Airport with everyone else. We said good-bye to Davey and walked out the door. It was the last time we ever saw him.

The next day was business as usual at Robert Yates Racing, as we prepared for Pocono. The transporters would be loaded that Wednesday night and would head out early Thursday morning.

Down in Alabama, Davey was taking the day off. Around midday, he and Red Farmer arrived at the Iceberg Restaurant in Hueytown, which had been an Alabama gang hangout for more than three decades. Allison pictures and newspaper headlines decorated the walls, and a sign above the entrance to the back dining room said "Allison Lane."

Davey and Red headed straight to "the Allison table" in the back room. Davey ordered a salad with vinegar and oil, fillet of catfish, and as always, the Iceberg's homemade french fries. No matter what else he got, Davey always ordered those homemade fries.

Davey and Red talked about how Neil Bonnett and his son, David, were testing that day at Talladega. Neil had announced that he was returning to competition in the DieHard 500. "After lunch, let's go over to Talladega and see how Neil and David are doing," Davey said.

They left the Iceberg and drove to the Birmingham airport, where Davey kept his new helicopter, a Hughes 369 HS turbine-powered craft. Just a few weeks earlier, he had traded one of his airplanes to get it. He loved the freedom it gave him to fly and land just about anywhere he wanted. He was building a helipad behind his house.

But quite honestly, Davey's helicopter flying made Robert and me very uncomfortable. He had received his helicopter pilot's license about a year earlier, but he didn't have a lot of experience in his new, five-seat Hughes. Months before, Davey had tried to get me to ride in another helicopter he was flying around Charlotte while in training. He'd flown to the shop several times and landed in the parking lot. "Davey, I'll fly around the world with you in an airplane, but I am not getting into a helicopter with you," I told him. I knew he had met all the criteria, but I thought he had done it way too fast. I didn't think he had enough seat-of-the-pants flying experience.

Robert had the same attitude, and wouldn't fly with him either. After several flights with an instructor, Davey had flown solo to the shop. Robert suggested that he keep an instructor with him for the time being. Davey assured us he'd be fine. But once, as Robert watched Davey take off, he had backed up as he lifted off and, as far as Robert was concerned, had come far too close to some trees.

At about 2:15 p.m., Davey and Red buckled into his new helicopter and took off for the short 50-mile hop to Talladega. They flew over the track from the east, circled above the first turn, and headed back toward the NASCAR garage in the heart of the huge infield. About 10 people saw what happened next.

Davey brought the helicopter in toward the media parking lot behind the track's infield media center. There are helipads at the track, but the speedway was nearly empty and had plenty of open places to land. Davey was maybe a foot or two from the asphalt when he decided to turn the helicopter around so it would be facing west toward home when he took off.

As Davey began to turn, he apparently backed up just a foot or two, and the tail rotor hit the fence behind him. The helicopter started rocking back and forth and shot up into the air some 25 feet. Then it started spinning, plunged to the left and crashed on its left side—Davey's side. The main rotors mangled the fence and gate to the garage area. The left skid broke off. The tail and rear rotor broke off and became entangled in the barbed wire from the fence. Tools, aircraft manuals, broken Plexiglas, and other debris littered the ground.

Red was hurt, but remained conscious. Davey was above him, hanging by his belt, unconscious. "Davey, let's get out of here. The motor's still running," Red yelled. There was still plenty of fuel onboard, and Red was worried about fire. Neil Bonnett was one of the first on the scene. As he arrived, the helicopter's turbine was still roaring. Neil pulled Red to safety and then helped ease Davey out. But nobody could figure out how to turn off the screaming engine. Someone finally had to get a mechanic from the adjacent Talladega airport to come over and turn it off. Davey and Red were airlifted back to Birmingham on another helicopter. Red suffered a broken right collarbone, two broken ribs, and other injuries. But Davey had a grave head injury.

In Charlotte, we were getting toward the end of the afternoon. Robert was in the engine shop. I was near the setup pad, which is just outside the front offices. Raymond Fox and Joey Knuckles were with me. Robert was paged to the office to take a telephone call. It was, as we soon learned, NASCAR President Bill France.

"Robert, are you aware of the situation with your driver?" Bill asked.

Robert momentarily wondered what Davey had done to upset NASCAR. But then Bill told him that Davey had crashed in his helicopter. "It doesn't look good," Bill said. Robert came back out in the shop looking like he had seen a ghost. He approached us at the setup pad and said, "We have a big problem."

"What is it, Robert?" I asked. He had trouble getting the words out. It was almost like he didn't want to tell us. Finally, he said, "That was Bill France. Davey has crashed that helicopter, and he's in bad shape." It was hard to comprehend what Robert was saying. My reaction was disbelief and shock. In racing, you get used to crashes. Even after hearing Davey had crashed, I guess the last thing I expected to hear Robert say is that he was next to dead.

We gathered all the guys together in the shop and told them what had happened. Then I called home and told Linda. She had been grocery shopping and had not heard the news. I told her Davey was still alive, but it didn't look good. Of course, she was pretty upset.

"We've got to get to Birmingham," I said. "Find somebody to watch the kids. Get some clothes together." Linda and I and Robert and Carolyn flew to Birmingham on a plane provided by Felix Sabates. The afternoon was such a blur, I have no idea how that came about. Knowing Felix, I'm sure he called right away and made the offer.

Linda was trying to stay positive, but she later said the moment she saw the look on Carolyn's face at the airport, she knew there was no hope. We arrived in Birmingham that evening. Somebody picked us up and took us to the Carraway Medical Center, the same hospital where I was born. They had Davey in intensive care, but the doctors said he had no chance of recovering. They were keeping him alive with machines.

I went in Red's room. He told me he didn't know what had happened. He said they were just a foot or so off the ground, and all of a sudden the helicopter started oscillating back and forth, went up in the air, and crashed down on its side. Red was still in a state of shock.

Liz asked Linda and me if we wanted to go in and see Davey. We quietly said no. We both knew he wasn't going to make it. And we remembered all too well what it had been like with Butch Lindley. I wanted to remember Davey how I had last seen him. Linda agreed. We stayed at the hospital all night. All of the Allisons were there. By then, everyone was pretty much accepting the fact that Davey wasn't going to make it. The mood was up and down. One minute, people would be chatting, even chuckling about something or other. The next minute, someone would be hysterical. It was an emotional roller coaster.

Like the rest of us, Liz seemed in a state of shock. Sometimes when she would go to look in on Davey she would come back just hysterical. But then she'd go back in there and come back elated because maybe she saw a little glimmer of hope, maybe he moved a hand, maybe he moved a finger or blinked an eye. But the doctors had told me, "Larry, so much of that movement is just reflexes. It's not a sign that Davey is getting better." And I was well aware of that from taking care of Butch.

Early the next morning, they took Davey off life support. He died around 7:30 a.m. We stayed until they announced that he had passed away. We flew back to Charlotte in the middle of the day. "I just want to go home and be with the kids," I told Linda. "I don't want to take any calls. I don't want to talk to anyone. I just want to be with the kids." By the time we left, many of the motorists driving around Birmingham had their lights on in memory of Davey.

When we got home and Linda saw our plastic playhouse in the den, she couldn't help but remember that it was Davey who had put it together. She could see him crawling around in there and sticking his head out the window just like a little kid. He had such a big heart, you couldn't help but love him. And then the next minute you'd be ready to pinch his head off because he was being stubborn or bullheaded or too preoccupied with whatever he was doing at the moment.

Davey was the most focused individual I have ever met. If he was eating lunch, he was totally focused on eating lunch. If he was thinking about hunting, you could forget about talking to him about the race car. He was extremely competitive, whether it was racing for the

Daytona 500 or flipping pennies during a rain delay to see who could get closest to the crack in the pavement. He did everything with the utmost intensity.

On Wednesday morning, Robert and I held a press conference to announce that we would not race at Pocono. Earlier, we had gathered the team together and told them. Some had wanted to race, but most didn't have the heart or the desire. "It was a tough decision to not race this weekend," I said. But I didn't get very far before I couldn't go on. We were standing beside the transporter, and I had to just walk away. I broke down in sobs when I got behind the transporter.

"This team has something missing right now, and I want us all to take the time to mourn that loss," Robert said. "We need time to grieve. When we go to a race, we go to win. We don't think we can win this race. I don't feel like we could get our car ready with tears in our eyes."

Robert told the assembled media that we would return, we just did not know when or where or with whom. We knew Davey was one very upset soul in heaven because we were not running Pocono. But Davey wasn't down here having to deal with this.

That evening, fans came by the thousands for Davey's wake at St. Aloysius Church in Bessemer. They filed by Davey's cherry-wood casket—rich and poor, black and white, people in their Sunday best and fans in T-shirts and blue jeans. The visitation was supposed to last 90 minutes, but they were still coming in when it was supposed to end.

We flew back to Alabama that afternoon for the next day's funeral. The team came down the next morning on a special US Airways flight—Flight 28. It was a hot day. The church was full more than an hour before the 11 a.m. service. Several hundred fans gathered in the churchyard under the hot sun to listen to the service on loudspeakers.

Father Louis Giardino delivered a wonderful eulogy. "If we were here celebrating the end of the season, Davey would look back and say that it had been a very successful life and season," he said. "Not that it didn't have its ups and downs, but he achieved a great deal of success." The priest talked about Davey's love for racing and said his school records were filled with comments like, 'Davey thinks too much about racing.' " That got a laugh.

I read a prayer during the service. But I had something else to say. The lump in my throat felt like a cantaloupe, but I told myself this time I was going to get through it. "As a close friend of Davey's, I know for a fact that he left this earth with all of his priorities in order," I said. "I just want to say one personal thing that's going to help me make it through this day. And as a personal witness, I know it's what made Davey make it through every day of his life. Just remember, there's nothing that can come our way that God and I can't handle together."

The funeral procession was more than a mile long. Bobby Allison himself drove a van behind the hearse. Judy was beside him. At the cemetery, we buried Davey in his driver's uniform, wearing a No. 28 baseball-style cap. The Allison family had not tried to close off the funeral to the public, so there were hundreds of fans among us. Every one of them respected our privacy.

After the priest finished his graveside prayers, country singer Joe Diffie sang "Ships That Don't Come In." Liz stood, placed a bouquet of red roses on top of the casket, and then bowed her head in a few moments of silence. Then, one by one, all of us walked past the casket and departed.

CHAPTER THIRTEEN

Ernie Irvan Takes Over

After Davey's funeral service, Robert and Carolyn and Linda and I flew home with the guys on the special US Airways flight. That night, all of the team members and our wives or girlfriends gathered at Robert's house. It was like a family get-together after a funeral. We all sat there in the basement talking about what to do from here. I don't think we reached any conclusions, but we knew we had to start talking about it. Actually, we did conclude one thing. We decided that Monday was our future.

We shut down the shop for the rest of the weekend and I told Linda, "I just want to turn the phones off and crawl into a shell for three days with you and the kids." And that's what I did. I couldn't help but watch the race on Sunday on television, but it was hard, especially when they showed the spot where our truck would have been parked. NASCAR left it vacant, and people had placed flowers and wreaths there.

The weekend seemed like it lasted a month. Robert and I talked several times by phone. "Robert, now we're really going to find out just how tough this race team is," I said. As with any family, Davey's death would bring us closer together or tear us apart.

The next week, we got back to work. We knew we had to move on, but the next race was at Talladega, of all places. We were not sure who we wanted to put in that race car. We felt like we needed someone who wouldn't feel the pressure of going to Talladega and driving Davey's car the first race after his death. At Ford's suggestion, we decided to put Robby Gordon in the car. Robby had some Texaco ties through Indy cars, but he wasn't so close to NASCAR that he would feel the weight on his shoulders.

The track had so many great tributes to Davey before the race. Probably the most touching tribute was a song by Alabama called "The Fan." It was so fitting, because Davey was such a fan-oriented driver. He treated the fans with so much respect, and he appreciated their support. As this song was played, Donnie Allison drove one of Davey's show cars around the track. Linda and I stood there and just held on to each other boo-hooing our eyes out. It was still almost impossible to believe that Davey wasn't with us.

Just before the song was played, Liz stood up and spoke to the crowd. "There have been times when we felt that we couldn't go on," she said. "I know that we can all hold on to the memories of Davey and try to go along with our lives."

When the green flag finally fell, we ran in the top five for a while. But Robby was inexperienced at Talladega, and on lap 57, he got his left wheels on the apron coming through the tri-oval. He spun, hit the outside wall and ended up sitting backwards at the start-finish line with the whole field coming past him.

"Robby, you OK?" I asked. "Robby, can you talk to me, bud?" For several long seconds, there was no answer. Finally, Robby said, "I can hear you, as long as nobody else hits me. I'm OK. What happened, though?"

We got it back to the garage and started to work on the car. Robert and I kind of looked at each other and thought the same thing: "We just need to load up and go home." So we elected to tell the world that we couldn't fix that car. "It's a tough way to end the day," I said. "We're loading up the car. The trailing arm mounts are bent pretty bad, and the car is banged up. We don't want to send Robby back out in a car that's not right."

It was a big relief to get out of there. On the way home, I listened to the rest of the race on the radio. It was a mess. Neil Bonnett's comeback race ended when he flipped in the frontstretch in a terrible crash, but managed to walk away unhurt. Later, there was a huge crash in turn one. Jimmy Horton's car flew out of the speedway entirely. Another driver, Stanley Smith, was nearly killed. I don't remember a lot about that. I was just glad to be heading home. Going back to Talladega less than two weeks after Davey's death was without a doubt one of the hardest things I've ever had to do.

Robert didn't seem too eager to put another inexperienced driver in his car again any time soon. "We're going to get an experienced driver behind the steering wheel, and we're going to go back to winning races," he said. By then, the wheels were already turning. While we were holed up at home, Ford's Lee Morse was already at work up there in Pocono. The night before the race, Lee telephoned Ernie Irvan.

"Ernie, what are the chances of you getting out of your contract so you can come drive the No. 28 car?" Lee asked. Ernie said he didn't know. He told Lee he was pretty happy where he was, driving the Kodak Chevrolet. But he didn't say no.

Lee and Ford weren't involved in paying Ernie's salary, although if Ernie joined the team, he would have a personal service contract with

Ford, as most drivers did with their manufacturers. They were helping Robert because they wanted the best driver possible for the 28 car, which was essentially Ford's number-one car. When Robert first mentioned to me that he was thinking about Ernie Irvan, I was horrified. "Surely to God, Robert, you ain't putting *him* in Davey's car," I said. "What in the world could you be thinking?"

Upon further consideration, I had to admit that Ernie was not a bad choice. He was aggressive and he knew how to win. In fact, the more I thought about it, the less opposed I was. Ernie was like Davey. Ernie was the type of driver who could actually challenge Dale Earnhardt. What better driver to put in your car than the one who had raced you the hardest? It didn't take long before I was all for the idea of hiring Ernie. Then I started worrying about getting my hopes up too much.

In those first weeks after Davey's death, it was all we could do to make it through each day. It felt so empty without him. We'd almost question why we were going ahead. It seemed so cold in a way. But there was really nothing else to do. We knew we couldn't just roll over and stop. Knowing how Davey handled it when Clifford died made it easier.

Davey's death also brought a ton of extra obligations. I was overwhelmed with phone calls. Robert and I would come back from lunch, and we'd each have a little stack of pink telephone message slips piled up like cordwood. Some of the calls were from drivers inquiring about our plans for the 28 car. Many were sympathy calls. I knew everybody meant well, but after a while, I really didn't want to talk about it.

There was so much to deal with. Robert agonized over whether to change the colors of the car. He had pretty much decided to change when Bobby Allison talked him out of it. I'm glad we didn't change. Many fans identified with that No. 28 Ford Thunderbird as well as with Davey. We'd lost him, and we didn't need to be losing the car, too.

Robert provided strong leadership, reminding everyone that this was a business and we had mouths to feed, so we'd better think about winning races again. Robert was my support, and I was his. Together we carried the team forward. I think it would have been a lot harder for either of us to handle without the other. Robert and I were best friends at that time. We had been close almost from the day I went to work for him. I could talk to Robert about anything. We often roomed together. We'd cut the lights at 10, but often laid there in the dark talking about anything and everything for several more hours.

We finally decided to hire Lake Speed for the time being. He was really our best choice among available drivers. At his first race, the road race at Watkins Glen, Lake gave us a lift when he qualified fourth. He moved up to second early in the race. Then he spun out. We really never recovered, because several laps later we tore up a transmission and had to replace it. We lost many laps and finished 27th.

Lake qualified second at Michigan and led a couple of laps, but finished seventh. At Bristol, Lake was running pretty good. But Bristol is hard on drivers, and Lake wasn't used to it. He had also been sick that weekend. Lake didn't really say a whole lot on the radio. About two-thirds of the way through at Bristol, he quit talking altogether. I kept noticing as he went past us down the backstretch that he was getting lower and lower in the car. Finally his wife, Rice (pronounced Reesa), came to me and said, "Larry, I think he is giving out. You need to start talking to him." So I started talking to Lake, but eventually he gave out and smacked the wall. We finished 16th, seven laps down.

By this time, the negotiations with Ernie Irvan were serious. In that first telephone conversation with him, Lee Morse had pointed out that Ernie would be driving for the number-one Ford team. Lee said the Kodak Chevrolet would never be the number-one Chevy team. It was not long before Ernie was eager to come. But his biggest problem was his contract. It extended through 1994. Ernie had built the Kodak Chevrolet team with owner Larry McClure and crew chief Tony Glover. They all won their first race together. Then they won the 1991 Daytona 500. Ernie and Tony were particularly close. When Ernie asked to back out of the deal, turmoil erupted.

Meanwhile, Robert made sure that everybody on our team, directly and indirectly, was content with Ernie as driver. He asked Bobby Allison. I think Bobby's reaction was a lot like mine. After he thought about it, Bobby gave it his blessing.

Robert wanted Ernie to finish out the year in the Kodak Chevy. But now feelings had been hurt, bitterness had set in, and Larry McClure decided to let Ernie go. About an hour and a half before practice was to begin on Friday at Darlington Raceway, McClure announced that he was releasing Irvan immediately. So Ernie came to us that very weekend as our driver. Back then a driver of Ernie's stature would have made about $500,000 a year (by comparison, he'd earn about $2 million now) and 40 to 50 percent of the winnings. Most teams that I was with paid the drivers 50 percent, but the driver gave 5 percent back to the crew.

We gave Lake Speed the news and put Ernie in a black driver's uniform. We pinned a Texaco patch on it. Ernie went out and made a few laps, and then he pulled into our garage stall. I knelt down next to the window just as I had done with Davey in our first session together in early 1991. We were at the same track.

I had the same instantly good feeling with Ernie that I had had with Davey. I knew this was going to be a special relationship. The communication was good right away. Ernie knew that he had crawled into one of the two or three best cars in the Winston Cup series, and he appreciated that. He loved the chance to work with me and Robert. That night, I remember calling Linda and telling her almost the same thing I had told her in March of 1991. "This is going to be good," I said.

We qualified 10th, but blew a motor at the start of Happy Hour. Ernie's jaw dropped after he watched our guys change the motor in about 30 minutes. We put him back out on the track with a good 10 minutes left in practice.

Ernie drove the dog meat out of that car in the race, and after 50 laps was racing Dale Earnhardt for the lead. We were pitted about two-thirds of the way down the frontstretch. On one lap, they came past with Dale leading and Ernie right behind him. One of Lee Morse's biggest selling points was that Ford wanted Ernie to be the driver to do battle with the great Dale Earnhardt. Now Ernie wanted to show us what he could do.

As they approached the first turn, Ernie drove up underneath that No. 3 car and picked its rear wheels off the ground. Dale looked like an octopus in the driver's seat trying to keep that handful under control. Ernie never said a word on the radio, and I never said a word. He just kept beating and banging with Earnhardt. After about 10 laps, Richard Childress finally had enough. "Cool it," he told Dale on the radio. "We need to finish this race."

We ran well in that race and finished fifth, one spot behind Earnhardt. Afterward, I mentioned to Ernie, "Man you jacked up the rear wheels on that three car one time."

"Did you guys see that?" he asked excitedly. "I tried my best to time it right where you guys could see it, but I wasn't sure if you did. Man, that's great!"

I was certain right then and there that Ernie Irvan was going to be one of the most awesome drivers I would ever work with. I knew he would be fun to work with, too.

The next race was at Richmond, and all of us were excited about going there. Ernie loved Richmond and always ran well there. We had always run well there, too. Before qualifying, we hit on a perfect setup. Ernie qualified second. But only 57 laps into it, the motor blew up as he came down the frontstretch. The only thing I could think to say to him was, "Ernie, don't get discouraged. This doesn't happen very often with Robert Yates engines."

Doug Yates apologized to Ernie, but Ernie wasn't upset. He told Doug he was sure he'd crash sooner or later and then they would be even. In fact, the next weekend at Dover, he did crash. But both Ernie and I felt it was only a matter of time before we started clicking.

On the Friday before the Goody's 500 at Martinsville Speedway in September, Ernie wheeled the No. 28 Texaco Havoline Ford onto the racetrack and ripped off a lap that won the pole. Then Geoff Bodine took the second spot driving Alan Kulwicki's old No. 7 Ford. It was almost like the front row was a memorial to Davey and Alan.

"I'm sure everybody in the garage area will probably look at that and think exactly the same thing," Ernie said. "They were both great race car drivers, and they had great cars."

Ernie told the press how he had chatted with Davey for the last time at New Hampshire. "He was talking about how long he was going to stay with this race team, about how much he enjoyed this race team," Ernie said. "I never knew I'd get a chance to find out from the side he was on. But this team is so strong and dedicated to what they're doing, I understand exactly what he's talking about now."

Ernie was handling the transition so well. He didn't bug us at the shop, but he did stop by. "Those guys don't need any help over there, that's for sure," he told reporters. "They know what their job is. And they don't need me there saying, 'Why don't we try this? Why don't we try that?' I don't want to interfere with what they're doing."

He explained how he worked with me: "I keep telling him to set it up the way he thinks it's right, and we'll go to the racetrack and go from there. The communication part has been awfully simple. Larry keeps a note on everything. And Larry seems to be able to ask me the right questions to get the right answers out of me. And that seems to be what it takes to be able to communicate."

Both Davey and Ernie were great race car drivers. And both were really good about being able to tell you what a car was doing. The difference was that Davey had a pretty good idea of what you should do to make it better. Ernie never really got into what he thought you ought to do. Ernie was probably the greatest driver I ever worked with in terms of adapting to a car. The saying "He could drive anything" applied to Ernie. That's the reason Goodyear wouldn't use him for tire testing. He'd adapt to whatever tire they put under him. He'd change his style to make the tire work.

Ernie knew he was never going to replace Davey in our hearts, or in the hearts of the fans. So he didn't try. All he tried to do was work hard with us, drive the guts out of the car, and get us back to winning again. He told me many times, "I didn't come here to replace Davey Allison. Nobody can replace Davey Allison. I just came here to pick up the pieces and help you all win again." The one thing he did demand was a different style for his Texaco driver's uniform. Out of respect to Davey, he did not want to appear in exactly the same design of uniform.

Race morning at Martinsville broke overcast and a bit cool, but as soon as the sun came up, temperatures soared. During the race the mercury rose to 91. But we went out and dominated that day, leading 402 of the 500 laps. We won by almost three seconds over Rusty Wallace. It was such a good feeling. This was only Ernie's fourth race with us, and we were running again like we had in our best days with Davey.

That day, I saw two of the most awesome sights I've ever seen at a racetrack. When Ernie took the checkered flag, he came down pit road to go to victory lane down in turn one. He was the only car on pit road when someone walked about halfway out and gave him a thumbs up. I looked harder and realized it was Bobby Allison.

Davey and Ernie had had their clashes. But this was the ultimate sign from Bobby that it was OK that we had put Ernie in the car. When Ernie got to victory lane, he was worn out. He sat down beside the car to do post-race interviews. He took off the top part of his uniform to get more air, and when I saw the T-shirt he was wearing underneath his uniform, it sent goose bumps up and down my spine. The T-shirt said, "In Memory of Davey Allison." Ernie said he was wearing it "right next to my heart."

"We're in victory lane here and Davey is in victory lane in heaven and I'm sure he's looking down on us and he probably shed a tear along with us," Ernie said. "The whole day today I kept telling myself, 'Man, don't screw this up for these guys. Be smart.'"

Ernie always had such a great attitude. I saw him mad at times, but I never really ever saw him down. I'd be pulling out my hair by the roots about something or other and he'd say, "Larry Mac, don't sweat it. We're going to be just fine." And I'd usually reply, "Please tell me how you've reached that conclusion, because I don't see it right now."

I don't think I ever became friends with a driver as quickly as with Ernie. After losing Davey, I had tried to put my guard up. I never wanted to get so close to a driver again. But Ernie broke down that wall like it was made of paper bricks. We were two totally different people but we meshed well together. Ernie is a lot like my wife. They live one day at a time, and whatever tomorrow brings, they'll deal with it then. I'm always worrying about the next five minutes *and* the next five weeks.

I wished Ernie would have treated the fans a little more consistently. He could be nice, but sometimes he'd embarrass me when he would blow off a fan. He could be awfully abrasive with people. Ernie was definitely much different in this respect than Davey, who knew that, in most situations, it was far easier and better to just go ahead and sign the autograph and be done with it. I really worked hard on Ernie about this.

"Ernie, he's your *fan*," I'd say.

Ernie would growl, "I'm trying to focus on something else right now."

"That guy didn't know that, Ernie," I'd say. "These are fans of our 28 car. And you just blew them off." I felt like we made some gains, but Ernie could be combative with people, even his friends, and ultimately this was one of the things that would cost him his ride in the 28 car after the 1997 season.

Ernie always called me Larry Mac. And he knew what buttons to push to irritate me. He knew I was a goosey person, and he'd sit there in the lounge and goose me in the side. Then he'd go out there in that car with this air of calm about him and just drive the hell out of that car.

We took our winning car from Martinsville to North Wilkesboro, and Ernie won the pole again. Afterward, Ernie was asked about Dale Earnhardt, who was leading the 1993 championship battle by a wide margin. "I plan on being his worst nightmare next year," Ernie said. We finished third in the race after losing a lap and regaining it.

The next race was at Charlotte, and we took car No. 015. We ran well in practice and qualified second, losing the pole to rookie Jeff Gordon.

The next day, Ford's Wayne Estes stopped by to chat. "It hurts so much knowing that Davey's not in that car," I said. But I told Wayne we were far, far ahead of where I expected to be. "I'm not talking about performance-wise," I said. "I'm talking about mental attitude on my part and everybody's part. I think we all know what our sport requires of us. We had to wipe our tears fast and press on. But there's not a single day that goes by that I don't think about him. It might be quick, or it might be for an hour.

"We're like the Allisons in a small way," I said. "Things keep coming at us, but we keep holding up our shield and letting the sparks bounce off. Hopefully . . . and hopefully it's this way for the Allisons . . . hopefully we've had our share and it's all behind us."

Three days later, Ernie went out and dominated the Mello Yello 500 probably like no one ever had, leading all but six laps. Other than winning the two Daytona 500s, it may have been the most phenomenal race I have ever been a part of. We beat everyone so badly that day. I don't know that I've ever had a more dominant car.

"We did have a miss in the car about halfway through the race," Ernie said afterward. "I thought the day was over. I started flipping switches, but I didn't know what they were for. There are three switches on the right-hand side (of the dashboard) and I flipped two of them down. Then it stopped missing.

"Robert said, 'Did you switch coils?' There's little, teeny labels on [the dashboard], and he acts like I'm supposed to read them going down the straight. And I said, 'I don't know, I can't read them while I'm racing.'

"With about five laps to go, it started missing again. I didn't ask this time. I just reached over and switched them all down. But it still kept missing. I don't know, maybe there's a little gremlin in the car or something. It's getting close to Halloween."

The night before our victory, Linda had asked me if I'd heard anything about the problem Mark Martin and his crew had at victory lane after they'd won the Busch race. "They wouldn't let the team into victory lane until almost the end of the victory lane ceremony," she said. Supposedly, the presence of the crew, all of them wearing their sponsor shirts, would overshadow the sponsor of the race.

"I'm not going to worry about that," I said. "You don't worry about those things. I've got 500 miles to worry about."

Well, lo and behold, it did become a problem. We got to victory lane, and the rent-a-cops let the car up there, but one of the track officials, Jim Duncan, came over and said, "Larry, you and Robert can come in, but you're going to have to keep the crew out." I was ready to blow. Victory lane is the only glory a crewman gets, other than a paycheck, for his 70-hour workweeks. And you only get to cherish it for about 20 minutes.

I looked at Jim and said, "Either we're all coming in victory lane, or that car is coming out and we're going out on the frontstretch and have a celebration in front of the fans. And you all can take pictures of yourselves in victory lane. It doesn't matter to me."

Finally, we just basically took over victory lane. My attitude was, "This is our race. We won this race. If you cops want to come in here with us, you're welcome to. But we're going in there." And sure enough, we did. But the conversation was pretty heated.

We finished off the 1993 season with three more good runs. In only nine races, Ernie had won twice, won two poles, and scored three other top-five finishes. He had jumped from ninth to sixth in Winston Cup points. Most importantly, he had revived our wounded race team. Because of what Ernie had done, 1993 was actually one of the few times in my career when I hated to see the season end. We would never forget Davey, but Ernie had lifted us out of our fog. Ernie had shown us the way.

In the mid-1970s, at about the age of 14, I proudly pose with King Richard Petty at the "Checkered Flag Dinner" in downtown Birmingham that I attended with my Aunt Noreen and Uncle Butch. Below is one of my childhood baseball teams. I'm standing at far right, next to my dad, Buck. My uncle, Alton Fowler, who wiped out all the stop lights with that load of scrap cars I'd stacked too high, is standing at left.

In my early racing days in 1978 (top left), I'm with Cale Yarborough when he came to Birmingham International Raceway to race Bobby Ray Jones's car. I'm wearing some pretty flashy racing slacks (top right) while posing in front of my Aunt Noreen's Chevy around 1976. I'm standing with Dave Mader III (lower left) after a Sunday feature victory at BIR, no doubt at the end of a long weekend of racing. And that's me third from the left (lower right) with the Bob Rogers Buick driven by Neil Bonnett at Bristol in March 1982.

National Racing Photo Services

David Chobat

I'm at the window of the No. 37 Bob Rogers Oldsmobile (left) at Martinsville Speedway in April 1981. Our driver, rookie Mike Alexander, set a track record in second-day qualifying and finished 10th. And on one of the greatest days of my life (above), I was married to Linda Giese on October 29, 1983, in Greenville, S.C.

I'm behind the wheel of our team's transporter (above), which I drove back to South Carolina with Linda after the 1984 Pepsi 400 at Daytona, where we finished 17th with David Pearson. And Davey Allison and I (right) give each other a genuine hug of happiness after he won the 1991 Coca-Cola 600, our first points race victory together. My son Brandon was born five days earlier, and I'm wearing my hospital bracelet and a button that says, "It's a boy."

Courtesy of Chobat Racing Images

Robert Yates, owner of the No. 28 Texaco Havoline Ford, and I (upper left) were like brothers during our years together from 1991 through 1996. Robert, Davey, and I (lower left) celebrate in victory lane at Phoenix International Raceway after our 1991 victory there. And we're in victory lane with our young families (above) after Davey won the 1992 Daytona 500. That's me with Brooke, Linda with Brandon, Davey with Robbie, and Liz with Krista.

This smiling portrait (left) is one of my favorites. Below is a shot of me during the great Blizzard of 1993 at Atlanta Motor Speedway. Two days before his fatal helicopter crash, Davey meets with Robert and me (upper left) as we struggle on Saturday at New Hampshire International Speedway. And on race day in New Hampshire, Davey and the hard-charging driver who would replace him, Ernie Irvan, share the back of a pickup truck during driver introductions.

*Linda and I celebrate with Ernie and his wife,
Kim (above), after Ernie's overwhelming victory
in the 1993 Mello Yello 500 at Charlotte Motor
Speedway. I'm with Brandon and Brooke (upper
right) during pre-race ceremonies at Pocono
Raceway in July 1996, about to receive the
Plastikote award (given to the winning crew chief)
after Ernie's tremendous comeback victory at New
Hampshire the week before. And I'm going over
practice notes with Dale Earnhardt in 1997
(lower right).*

Here's a couple of shots of me and Dale Earnhardt (right and far right) in victory lane at Daytona International Speedway after he won the 1998 Daytona 500. And I'm on top of the pit box tool cart (below) as driver Mike Skinner makes a pit stop in the No. 31 Lowe's Chevrolet.

Courtesy of Crider's Photography, Inc.

Our youngest, Kendall, is in front in the family portrait (above) for our 2000 Christmas card. Brooke is on the right and Brandon is standing behind us. And here's the FOX NASCAR broadcast team (right)—Darrell Waltrip, myself, and Mike Joy—near the end of our 2002 broadcast season. This is how we face the track when we're announcing.

Courtesy of Dick Berggren

CHAPTER FOURTEEN

A Crash on a Smoky Morning

t's always nice to have a fresh start at Daytona, especially after a year like 1993, but unfortunately that's not what happened after we arrived for 1994 Speedweeks. Less than 30 minutes after the start of the first practice session on Friday, Neil Bonnett was killed after he lost control of his car and hit the outside wall in turn four. Neil, who was 47, was pronounced dead about 30 minutes after the accident. At first I really didn't believe it. But it was just as bad as they said. It was another tremendous blow for the Alabama gang. Bobby Allison was at the track and went to the hospital soon afterward.

Neil was bound and determined to make a comeback in 1994 after suffering a debilitating head injury at Darlington in 1990. He was a great broadcaster and had a great career opportunity ahead of him, but Neil just had to race again. He was doing what he loved most, and I am a firm believer that when your time comes, your time comes.

They had a little memorial service at a funeral home in Daytona Beach and Robert and Carolyn and Linda and I went to it, along with a few members of our team. Then, on Monday morning, just three days later, Rodney Orr, a little-known driver trying to make his first Winston Cup race, lost his life in a single-car crash in turn two. In the Twin 125s driver's meeting, Rusty Wallace gave a stern lecture. "I've been upside down at Daytona and I've been upside down at Talladega and I'm telling you, it hurts," he said. "I think everybody in this room is running scared. I'll tell you, my wife is damn scared. So use your heads, please."

Ernie did just that in the first 125-mile qualifying race, leading 37 of the 50 laps to win over Rusty and Mark Martin. It was great to be back in victory lane at Daytona. "When you win a race here, it gets everybody pumped up," Ernie said afterward. "What we learned is we've got to make the car handle a little bit better. My car liked to stay to the bottom, but it was a little loose down there."

We ran very well in the Daytona 500. We led the most laps—84—and were in front seven different times. On lap 158, Ernie took the lead from Sterling Marlin, who had replaced him in the Kodak Chevrolet. Ernie was in front for the next 22 laps, but our Ford started getting loose. When Ernie got sideways coming out of turn four on lap 180, Sterling got past us.

"Got a little loose, Larry Mac," Ernie said on the radio. "He got by me." When I saw the replay, I said to myself, "That car wasn't loose, it was wrecked." But Ernie somehow saved it. Sterling led the rest of the way and scored his first career victory after 279 races. We finished second and were reasonably happy with that. We knew that, after losing Ernie, those guys at Morgan-McClure were on a mission.

We finished fifth at Rockingham, then took our reliable low-snout car back to Richmond. Ernie was qualifying in the top 10 nearly every race, which just tickled me to death. He qualified seventh at Richmond. But we had all sorts of problems working on the race setup. The setup I had used with Davey to win this race in 1993 didn't seem to work at all. We kept looking at the setup sheets and trying to figure out what was wrong. But we could never get the car around the track with that old setup.

We talked long and hard about it Saturday night before the race and decided to go with a totally different setup. We immediately started second guessing ourselves, but the setup turned out great. Ernie was fifth after 20 laps and third after 40 laps. He took the lead for the first time on lap 106. Ernie did a great job of driving the car just hard enough. The battle settled down to a duel with Rusty Wallace, and as Ernie said afterward, "It was won in the pits." Rusty could stay ahead of us if he was leading, but we got out first after the final stops during a caution period around lap 380.

As Ernie pulled away from Rusty in the final laps, our black No. 28 car had yellow wheels, and it was the ugliest Texaco Havoline car ever to run around that track. We were getting short on tires, and we'd bought a set from Michael Waltrip, whose Pennzoil team painted their wheels yellow. Ugly or not, we beat Rusty by 1.7 seconds for our first victory of the season.

That old low-snout car—number 010—had become quite a special car for us at Robert Yates Racing. I couldn't help but reflect back on the fact that Neil Bonnett drove it on its first day at the racetrack, and now he was gone, too. Then Davey had scored that huge victory in Phoenix with it. And he had driven it to his last victory here just one year ago. Now Ernie had it back in victory lane.

The next race was at Atlanta, and we qualified seventh there, too. But Ernie shot right to the front and took the lead from Terry Labonte on lap 14 and led the next 55 laps. We dominated the race that day, but did have our moments. We cut one pit stop too short trying to beat rookie Jeff Burton out of the pits. The left rear tire changer only got three lug nuts on tight. We didn't get bent out of shape about it. We came back in, tightened the other lug nuts, and went back to racing. We clawed our way back through the field and led 95 of the last 100 laps—207 laps in all—before crossing the finish line a few car lengths ahead of Morgan Shepherd. It was the only time I was the crew chief in back-to-back victories in points races. And it was my only victory at Atlanta.

We left Atlanta with a lead of 101 points over Mark Martin in the battle for the Winston Cup championship. I began to constantly remind Ernie about driving smart and finishing races. "Look at the big picture, Ernie," I said again and again. We finished sixth at Darlington, then we stumbled to 33rd at Bristol when a camshaft broke, but just to see Ernie Irvan drive that No. 28 car around Bristol was a sight. He drove that car so hard.

Ernie won the pole at North Wilkesboro and finished third there. He followed that up with a second at Martinsville behind Rusty Wallace. Then it was on to Talladega—our first trip there with Ernie. We were not really sure what to expect from the Alabama fans. Ernie and Davey had their run-ins, and Ernie certainly wasn't from Alabama. He was a native of California. When he took that car out to qualify, we weren't sure if the fans were going to cheer or start throwing chicken bones, beer cans, and seat cushions.

But Ernie was sensitive about the feelings of the Alabama fans. The day before qualifying, he took the time to appear on a number of local radio stations, and it was then that he realized that the fans in Alabama were still pulling for our car. When Ernie won the pole, the crowd went absolutely crazy. It was such a fulfilling moment. We had gotten so much negative mail when we first hired Ernie. "Now, there's not enough room in which to put all the positive letters," I told the press. "And I think 30 to 40 percent of the positive letters are from fans who wrote negative letters last year."

We finished second behind Dale Earnhardt at Talladega, then took a new car and a lot of confidence to the road race at Sears Point. I had won at Sears Point twice, with Ricky Rudd and with Davey, and Ernie had won in the Kodak Chevrolet. During practice before qualifying, we had a duel with Mark Martin. We laid down a fast lap, then Mark went out and went a little faster. Then we'd run a little faster than Mark. And he'd run a little faster than us. This went on for the entire two hours of the practice session. Finally, Ernie laid down one more fast lap in qualifying and won the pole. Mark qualified second.

After the race started, there was no question that if nothing bad happened, we were going to win. Geoff Bodine finished second that day, and at one point, we had such a lead on him we were actually trying to slow Ernie down. But Ernie knew exactly where he was. Just before entering turn one, if the driver looks to his right, he can catch a glimpse of cars coming through the esses, probably 20 seconds behind. Ernie said he'd watch Geoff coming through the esses on each lap to judge what kind of lead he had.

We led all but six of those 74 laps and won by 9.5 seconds, despite one scary moment for me. If you were leading, you always wanted to be the first to pit under the green flag. That way, you'd still be in the lead if a yellow flag came out. But it took drivers almost a minute and 40 seconds to lap that 2.52-mile course. On lap 57, Geoff Bodine and Rusty Wallace slipped into the pits before we did. The next 100 seconds were the longest seconds I've ever experienced at Sears Point, holding my breath and hoping that we got to the pits before a caution. On that very lap, in fact, Ted Musgrave smacked the tire wall in the Carousel turn, but he kept going and the yellow flag did not fly. We hustled in for our final stop on lap 58 and led the rest of the way.

The day we won the pole, May 13, 1994, was Linda's birthday. She didn't happen to come on this trip. In fact, she skipped every trip where I ended up winning the race. And just about every time she came, we had disastrous results. So when I got home, I joked with her about not

213

ever coming to Sonoma again. Then I gave her a bottle of California wine I'd bought for her. Ernie signed it to her. Here we are, more than eight years later, and that bottle of wine is still sitting in our wine rack at home in Mooresville.

When we returned to Charlotte, Ernie started second in The Winston and was determined to win all three segments of the all-star race. He won the first 30-lap segment, but then the field was inverted for the second segment, so Ernie had to start from the back. Ernie charged back to second and was trying to pass Geoff Bodine to win when he got all four tires into the grass along the frontstretch. Drivers sometimes recover after getting two tires in the grass there. We've seen Dale Earnhardt recover after getting all four tires in the grass. But our four tires in the grass didn't work. When I saw Ernie go down there, I said to myself, "We're in big trouble." Ernie crashed hard into the outside wall, sort of like Davey had crashed in 1992. But Ernie wasn't hurt. "I just made a mistake," he said. "I shouldn't have tried to pass him like that. I made a bad mistake."

Geoff won the second segment and went on to win the final 10-lap segment and the race. It was disappointing because I felt like we could have easily won that last segment. But a good part of me was proud to work with a driver like Ernie. He never was satisfied with anything short of winning. It's one reason he put so much effort into qualifying. Ernie wanted to sit on every pole of every race and *then* worry about getting ready for the race.

We brought a new-style chassis to the Coca-Cola 600 the next weekend. And we had trouble with it. We qualified 14th, but we were three mph off the pole—a half second a lap. I was still working with the Indy car engineer, Bob Riley, of Riley & Scott Engineering. At one point on race morning, I was up in the cab of our transporter, talking on the truck's mobile phone to Bob, who was at the Indianapolis Motor

Speedway working on a car he was getting ready for the Indianapolis 500. We were backtracking to make the car better, and Bob gave me some of the old measurements so we could redrill the pivot points in the chassis. We even moved a bunch of suspension points around in the garage at Charlotte, which is something not many teams would be willing or crazy enough to do.

We always tried to get everything we could out of every performance element of the race car. At night, NASCAR used to let us load our cars in the transporters for safety and security. Because the car had already passed tech inspection we would take the opportunity to put a slightly larger spoiler on the back to generate more downforce. It was only about an inch or so wider, but every bit helped on race day.

We were doing a lot of work in the wind tunnel to understand how to get more downforce. Our fabricator, Gary Beveridge, designed a dummy radio antenna that went alongside the regular antenna on the roof. We called it the Space Shuttle, because that's exactly what it looked like. It was like a vortex generator that put more air on the rear spoiler. It helped the rear downforce a bunch and provided such a gain that when we first tested it in the wind tunnel we took it off and put it back on again to double-check our results to make sure we weren't getting a false reading. We would put the car on the line with a regular antenna, and right before NASCAR would give the order to start the cars Gary would change the antenna to the Space Shuttle. Eventually NASCAR came up with a rule that said you could only run one antenna and that it had to be standard and placed in the center of the roof.

Another thing we would do just before the start was send a crewman into the car to help the driver cinch up his belts. But while he was in there he would take a small pair of pliers and turn an adjustable brace that pulled the back of the roof down some. This also helped get more air on the spoiler to generate more downforce. We were able to do this because roof height wasn't checked after the race.

Another questionable technique we used was to take an air hose and fill the fuel cell with air like an air mattress to expand the fuel cell just slightly. The minute we got our car loaded on the hauler at the end of the day, our gasman, Norman Koshimizu, would hook up the air hose to the gas tank and fill it with air for the night. We even installed an air line on top of the transporter just for this purpose.

One Saturday after Happy Hour, Norman crawled up there and was filling the tank with air. I heard a big bang. Norman came down and said, "Larry, I may have put too much air in the fuel cell."

"What do you mean, Norman?" I asked.

"Well, I may have bent the rack a little bit." The rack bolts on top of the cell to hold it in.

"Well, no big deal," I said. It was just one more thing to cover the next morning. Since we were struggling, I knew I'd be making changes anyway. When we unloaded the next morning, my jaw dropped when I saw the fuel cell. It looked like Norman had blown out almost the whole bottom of the cell. No kidding he put in too much air.

I wasn't sure what to do about it. I finally decided to track down Jackie Whitimore, the NASCAR official in charge of fuel cells. I was honest. I looked him in the eye and said, "I have a problem. We tried to blow the fuel cell up with air last night and it did a lot of damage. If you need to go to Gary Nelson about it, if you are going to fine me, if you're going to suspend me, whatever, I've gotta deal with this problem right now." I think Jackie appreciated that I had been honest with him. (It would have been hard to slip a new fuel cell through inspection because we had to reweld the mounting bars below it, and NASCAR puts two seals on each fuel cell to prevent teams from changing them.)

"Larry, get this fixed," he said. "Get that damaged cell out of there and get a new one in and get it fixed. Then come get me, and we'll make sure everything is right and all the bars are straight and all the welds are fixed. And we'll keep this between you and I."

Ernie managed to finish fifth that day, but we never really got the handle on the car. Still it was a good finish for the problems we had. It was one of those days I was telling him to look at the big picture. We left Charlotte with a 62-point lead over Dale Earnhardt in the battle for the 1994 Winston Cup championship. At the next race at Dover, we won the pole—our fourth of the year—and finished second to Rusty Wallace after leading 313 of the 500 laps. "It would be hard to have any more confidence than I have with this race team right now," Ernie said.

We finished seventh at Pocono for our seventh straight top-10 finish, but we finally stumbled again at Michigan and finished 18th. In the Pepsi 400 at Daytona, though, we were right back on track. We started fifth, but took the lead for the first time on lap 31 and began to dominate. With 40 laps to go, we were leading, when some of the cars in the back of the pack crashed in turn two. The yellow flag came out, and I couldn't make up my mind whether or not to pit. Ernie said, "Larry Mac, why don't we just get four tires now? You know everyone else will follow us."

So, Ernie hit pit road. I kept looking for more cars to come—and looking. Only Jimmy Spencer came in with us. Everyone else stayed out. I thought I had screwed up royally. I had given up all that track position. We'd never get it back with only 20 laps to go. Ernie drove off pit road. I went right over to the toolbox and started digging through the drawers. David Gray, a good friend of Robert's, asked me what I was looking for.

"A friggin' razor blade, so I can cut my wrists."

But if you gave Ernie what he wanted, and at that time it was four tires, well, he was the kind of driver who could work magic. Ernie and Jimmy came through that field like two men possessed. And I'll be a son of a gun, but seven laps after the restart, we retook the lead. Ernie had bailed me out again. We dominated that race, leading 86 of the 160 laps. We led 26 of the last 27 laps. But we didn't lead the last one. Jimmy Spencer beat us by a few feet. Without any drafting help, Jimmy passed us on the last lap with a classic slingshot pass you never see in restrictor plate racing.

There was no doubt in my mind that Junior Johnson and his guys were cheating. Somehow they'd figured out a way to suck more air into the engine. There must have been 12 or 18 ways to do it in those days. Teams would do everything from putting slide washers under the manifold spacers to drilling out the area around the mounting studs. Ernie said on the radio once, "I'm killing the son of a bitch through the corners because he's backing off the gas. But when he hits the straightaways and mashes the gas, it's like comparing a rocket to a go-cart." But Jimmy's car sailed through inspection, and it was time to prepare for the next race at New Hampshire.

The weather in New Hampshire was dreadfully hot and humid again. The racetrack was really slick on pole day, but we had it hooked up better than anyone and Ernie won the pole—his fifth of the season. It was still hot on race day, but we were really good and led more than half the race. By this point, of course, we knew that the black No. 3 car driven by Dale Earnhardt was the car we had to outrun week in and week out. Earnhardt struggled at New Hampshire. We put him a lap down after only 40 laps.

About halfway through the race, Ernie did something that made me realize how good he really was. I was watching the stopwatch, and Ernie's lap times suddenly began to increase. He was slowing down. Just about the time I was fixing to ask him about it, he came on the radio.

"Larry Mac, for some reason this groove I've been running—it's not there anymore." In the turns, the track surface was breaking up under the heat of the sun and the stress of the cars. Ernie's low groove was becoming too slick to run.

"OK, Ernie," I replied. "Just be smooth. You've got a good lead. Don't try to take more than you can get. Look at the big picture."

He ran another 10 or 12 laps, and I noticed that his lap times were getting better. Then he came on the radio and said, "Hey Larry Mac, I've found me another groove." Ernie had switched from a low groove to a higher groove, and he was making it work. But it was a brutal day at New Hampshire. As the track came apart, car after car crashed. There were 17 yellow flags for a total of 83 laps—more than a fourth of the 300-lap race. And NASCAR didn't seem to do a very good job of dealing with the problem. The least they could have done was sweep both grooves really well during those yellow flags. That didn't happen, even though we pleaded with them to do it.

Earnhardt, as it turned out, was down but not out. He made up his lost lap during a caution period and took the lead from us on lap 257. Another caution soon followed, and on the restart, Ernie charged into turn one, took the high groove he'd been using, hit the marbles, which hadn't been swept away, and slid right into the wall. He made it back to the pits. The left rear fender was caved in on the tire. We got the tire off and I began beating and banging on the fender to clear it out of the way so it wouldn't rub the tire. I didn't realize, however, that during all that beating and banging, I had knocked one of the posts off the battery, which sits in front of the left rear tire.

When the car wouldn't start, we tried to push start it. We pushed and pushed and pushed, but it was not going to crank. It was *never* going to crank. We sprayed ether into the cowl to try to help it crank, pushing it down pit road and then rolling it back to our pit. We tried so many times, and it was so hot I thought I couldn't push anymore. But adrenaline kept me pushing. Finally, I gave out. I'd had one too many breaths of ether. I collapsed on pit road. One of our crewmen grabbed the can of ether from my hand, left me lying there, and kept trying to start the car. Rusty Wallace's crew hauled me back over the wall. People talked of a heart attack. One guy wanted to give me a nitroglycerine pill. I said, "No, man, I'm not having a heart attack! I'll be fine. I just blacked out."

They got me behind the pits and gave me oxygen and wet towels. I began to feel much better. Then they put me on a golf cart ambulance to take me to the care center. Off we flew. The driver about threw me off twice. Finally I had to say, "Look, buddy, how about I get off this thing and *walk* to the care center. I believe I'll be a lot safer."

The team finally got that car started again, and we went out and managed to run a few more laps and actually gained three positions. But instead of another top-five finish, we were 30th. Earnhardt finished second and took the lead for the Winston Cup championship. Dale was now ahead by four points. Ernie and I were furious after the race. "I might as well go race on dirt, so we know what we've got to do," Ernie said. "Nobody raced today. You just rode around and saw who could stay out of the marbles."

I told reporters we had begged NASCAR to sweep that upper groove. "I normally keep my mouth shut about our sanctioning body, but son of a gun if they didn't do everything in their power to tighten this points battle up today," I said. "They got what they wanted, so we'll just have to work harder. It sure does get old, though."

We qualified fifth at Pocono, but broke a timing chain and finished 37th. It was only our third DNF of the year, but it was our second in a row. We fell farther behind Earnhardt in the points as the series headed back to Talladega for that hot race in July. There, we got beat by Jimmy Spencer again after leading 90 of 188 laps. I believed, and still believe, that we were beaten again by a car that was cheating the restrictor plate. But our third-place finish put us back in the Winston Cup points lead by 16 points over Earnhardt, who had blown his engine at Talladega.

The next race was the inaugural Brickyard 400 at Indianapolis Motor Speedway, and it was amazing to see all those people fill up those grandstands on race day. Ernie slipped during qualifying, and we started 17th. It didn't shake his confidence. "I'm coming to the front," Ernie said. "I'm going to pass at least 16 people." And that's exactly what he did, although it took him most of the race to do it. By the 80th of 160 laps, we were running fifth. And by lap 139, we were challenging leader Jeff Gordon. Ernie was right on his bumper. Jeff told his crew chief, Ray Evernham, "I'm getting loose! I'm going to have to let him go by. He's going to spin me out."

I was scanning Jeff's radio channel that day and heard him. I quickly got on our radio: "Ernie, Jeff is screaming that you get him loose when you get behind him."

"Oh, yeah," he said. "I see it." And I knew Ernie was going to use it to his fullest advantage, too. On lap 140, Ernie muscled past Jeff and took the lead. The only problem was, Jeff could make Ernie loose, too. Back and forth it went. Jeff led four laps. Ernie led five laps. Jeff led five laps. Ernie led six laps. Ernie was ahead as they went into the first turn with five laps to go. Jeff drove hard into the corner to try to make Ernie loose, but all of a sudden Ernie moved radically up out of the groove and slowed. We had cut a tire.

By the time we got to the pits, changed the tire and got going again, we were a lap down. We finished 17th. Gordon went on to win. It was a bitter loss. Ernie had Jeff's number and knew exactly what he was going to do with that kid. He knew where to pass him and how to make it work. Our car didn't drive the greatest with Jeff behind us, but I knew Ernie could handle that, too. It also really hurt to lose all those points.

We finished second at Watkins Glen, but never led a lap, which was rare that year. And we saw the next race at Michigan, event number 21 of the 1994 season, as another opportunity for a strong run. By then, we'd led at least one lap in 17 of the 20 races. We had led 79 times for a total of almost 2,500 miles. Nobody was even close to us. We'd won three races and five poles. We knew we could win more. Most importantly, we were in a tight championship battle, trailing Earnhardt by just 27 points.

Ernie struggled during qualifying and was 19th. It didn't bother him at all. "The car is driving so good, I'm really looking forward to the race," he said. "This car's going to be great on race day."

But after our just-average qualifying run at Michigan, we had some work to do. Robert and I were staying at a hotel in Ann Arbor. Ernie was staying in his motorcoach at the track with his wife, Kim. After the garage closed, we went out to Ernie's motorcoach to kick back for a while with Ernie and Kim as we worked on a game plan for Saturday morning. We had not qualified well, because our car was way too tight. It was pushing up the track something terrible. Normally, when you get a car ready to race at Michigan, that push will magnify. So you really have to go after it. When I showed my concern, Ernie said, "Don't worry about it, Larry Mac. We're gonna be just fine on Sunday."

It's an hour-long drive from the track back to Ann Arbor. Robert and I probably stayed in the room that night and ordered pizza. It was very common for us to do that. When we stayed together, I'd get up an hour before we were going to leave and shower, then I'd wake Robert up. I was up by 5 a.m. the next day, Robert by 5:30. We were at the track when the garage opened at 7 a.m.

At 8 a.m., we started a two-hour practice. I climbed to the roof of the hauler, but there were so many motorhomes and so much smoke and haze from the morning campfires, you could hardly see the track. At about 8:30 a.m., we finished making some more chassis changes, and Ernie went back out.

"Ernie, I betcha that car is still going to be too tight," I said on the radio. "But let's go out and run 10 more laps and see what we got, and we'll adjust from there."

When Ernie came around to complete lap 10, I got back on the radio and told him, "Ernie, I can tell that thing is still way too tight. That's 10 laps right there, so let's get on in here and go to work on it."

Ernie really didn't respond to me. He may have said something like, "10-4." Normally, at the end of a 10-lap run, Ernie would run it hard into one more corner before backing off. I saw him drive hard into turn one and disappear behind the campers and smoke. I turned to come down off the truck and saw the flagman at the start-finish line waving the yellow flag. Raymond Fox, our car chief, waved his hands frantically at me. He had been up on the truck with me, standing a little higher. He had seen Ernie crash.

I thought Raymond was just trying to tell me that the caution was out. I came on the radio and said, "Ernie, caution's out! Caution is out!" Raymond motioned at me like, "Hey, it's us." So I started the dialogue that is a crew chief's worst nightmare: "Ernie, you OK? Talk to me, Ernie? Ernie, are you OK?"

There was no response.

I knew the radio could have become unplugged. Ernie might be OK, just unable to communicate. I asked again, "Ernie, are you OK?" Again, no response. As I came down off the transporter, I saw NASCAR's pace car driver, Buster Auton, fly out of the NASCAR trailer and dive into his pace car. He was in a big hurry. Robert and I ran over to Buster and asked him if we could ride out there with him.

"C'mon, hurry," Buster said.

We jumped in. I got in the back, and Robert took the front. Buster drove around turn one at probably 100 mph. I could tell he'd been told something bad. When we drove up, the car didn't look torn up all that bad. I've seen a lot worse. Buster threw the pace car in park, jumped out, and ran toward the car. Robert and I hopped out and began to follow him. Steve Peterson, one of the NASCAR officials, walked over and stopped us. He was white as a sheet. "Guys, you don't want to go over there," he said. "It's not good." I'm glad he did, because I saw nothing gruesome.

Ernie was still in the car. We were about 15 yards from the wreck. Actually, I never even saw Ernie, for all of the people swarming over him. But I found out that he was bleeding from every orifice and that the interior of the car was covered in blood. After what I'd heard, I thought Ernie was dead. I walked over to the outside wall, leaned over it, and threw up. "This can't be," I said to myself. "This just *can't* be. It can't be for Ernie. It can't be for Kim. It can't be for Robert. It can't be for our race team. It can't be for me. This just can't be happening."

Robert and I got back in Buster's car and left before they removed Ernie from the race car. "It's bad," Buster told us. "But he's alive." Apparently, a tire had failed. Back at the truck, Robert and I told the guys what we knew. "Just sit tight," we said. "Don't unload the backup car. Don't do anything. We're going to the hospital, and we'll get back with you."

Even though we were in a tight battle with Dale Earnhardt for the championship, two of his crewmen, Danny "Chocolate" Myers and Danny Lawrence, came over and told us, "Look, if you guys want to get on to the hospital, we'll unload your backup car for you and get it through inspection for you." We thanked them and declined, but it showed the true spirit of the NASCAR Winston Cup garage. Our competitors were family first.

They flew Ernie in a helicopter to St. Joseph's Mercy Hospital in Ypsilanti, next to Ann Arbor. I found Kim crying in their motorcoach. She knew Ernie was in deep trouble. Don Hawk, Earnhardt's business manager, drove us to the hospital. Six of us piled into a four-door sedan: Don, Robert, me, Kim, Ernie's dad Vic, and Max Helton, the minister from Motor Racing Outreach. That one-hour drive seemed like it took four or five hours. Nobody said a whole lot. I sat in the back, next to the left rear door, and looked out the window, reflecting on all the tough times. I thought about Butch Lindley and how he'd been gravely injured and put in a coma just before he was supposed to drive our car. I never got to talk to Butch again. I thought about Davey and my two and a half years with him, and those accidents, and his brother getting killed at Michigan, and losing the championship and then losing Davey. And now, to know that me and Robert and our entire race team were going to have to deal with *another* tragedy, possibly another death, was devastating. I just wanted to see Ernie make it. I didn't care if he ever raced again. I just wanted him to still be able to be a husband to Kim and a dad to Jordan and a friend to me. I just wanted to be able to sit and talk with him again.

CHAPTER FIFTEEN

Dale Jarrett Fills In

When we got to St. Joseph's Mercy Hospital in Ypsilanti, they took Robert and me to an administrative office, where we could use the phone while we waited for word from the doctors. When we were the only ones in there, we had the same type of conversation we had after Davey died. What are we going to do about Michigan? What are we going to do about Happy Hour? Who are we going to put in the car? What about Ernie? We kept bouncing back and forth from worrying about Ernie to worrying about what we would do.

That afternoon, the surgeon, Dr. Errol Erlandson, came out and told us that Ernie was gravely injured. He had a skull fracture, swelling of the brain, and severe bruising of the lungs. His lungs had collapsed, and he had been given an emergency tracheotomy that allowed him to breath, right there in the car. It saved his life.

"He is not alert at this time, but he is stable," Dr. Erlandson said. "He has received some severe injuries to two major organ systems, either one of which in their severity as assessed at this time could be fatal. We'll just have to wait and see how things unfold."

Don Hawk took Robert and me back to the track, where we finally decided that we just couldn't race the next day. We drove back to Ann Arbor, picked up Linda and Carolyn at the airport, and went back to the hospital. That evening, Dr. Erlandson met with us again. Kim was there, along with Ernie's sister, his dad and mom, and Robert and me. The doctor looked at them and kind of hung his head. "We're looking right now at about a 10 to 15 percent chance of survival," he said.

That was devastating to hear. Those odds weren't good at all. And that wasn't a 10 to 15 percent chance of being able to come back and drive a race car. That was a 10 to 15 percent chance of *living*. Linda and I kept a vigil at the hospital the next day and watched the race on television. When Earnhardt crashed early, I couldn't help but think how good that race would have been for gaining points.

We flew home later that afternoon. We had to figure out what to do and move forward. We took the same attitude we took after Davey's death. We *had* to. Robert Yates Racing was a business. There were mouths to feed and sponsors to please and races to run. It was a business we wished we weren't in at that particular moment, but we had no choice but to continue. It was midseason, so we had few options as far as hiring a driver to fill in for Ernie. We hired Kenny Wallace, Rusty's youngest brother. Kenny had run his first full season in 1993, but lost his ride.

I flew back up to Ypsilanti on Thursday, five days after the crash, and saw Ernie for the first time. He looked terrible. His face wasn't distorted or anything, but I've never seen so many wires and tubes in a human being. He was semiconscious, but still pretty much in a coma. I squeezed his hand and said, "Ernie, we will be here for you when you come back. And you *will* come back. And we will win races again together."

About a week later, I returned for a second visit, this time with Robert. Ernie looked a little better this time. He seemed to be responding more, but I wondered whether he was really responding to me or whether it was the kind of spontaneous response we sometimes saw in Butch. By this time, I felt that Ernie would survive, but I still wasn't sure whether he would have any kind of a life.

Back in Charlotte, I'd call the hospital and talk to Kim every single night—sometimes twice a day—just to check up on him, and her. Kim was such a trouper. She never left that hospital. She was right there with him every single day. And about two and a half weeks after the crash, she called one night around 10. I was already in bed. "Hi, Larry," she said. "I got somebody here who wants to talk to you."

I heard a raspy but familiar voice say, "Hi, Larry Mac." It was Ernie. His voice sounded scratchy from all the tubes that had been down his throat. But there was no question who it was. I was so elated to hear his voice, I don't really have any idea what he said. He only talked for a moment, since it was such a struggle. But that was one of the most gratifying moments of my life. It looked like I would get my wish. Ernie was going to come back to us as a friend—a whole person—and that's what meant the most to me.

It had been hard to get back into racing until I got that call. But hearing Ernie's voice again brought back some of my enthusiasm. On the track, however, we struggled with Kenny Wallace. He just didn't have enough experience to do what Ernie or Davey had done. Kenny was doing better than he ever had, and he was qualifying pretty well at most tracks, but he just wasn't finishing races that well. His best run was at Martinsville, where he finished fourth. It was the first top-five finish of his career. He kept the car out of trouble and took care of his brakes. That made the difference at the end of the day.

At our Christmas party that winter, Joey Knuckles, who took care of the brakes and suspension, had one of the front rotors and brake pads mounted on a trophy stand with a little plaque that read, "Kenny Wallace – First Top-Five Finish – Martinsville Speedway – September 25, 1994." If we'd given Kenny a ton of money, I don't know that it would have meant more to him than that trophy.

As the season drew to a close, I began to get offers from other teams. One was to go to work for Roger Penske as Rusty Wallace's crew chief. It was an offer I couldn't ignore. Rusty was a proven winner. We still had no idea whether Ernie would ever race again. But I had made my promise to Ernie. I turned down everything.

Robert, meanwhile, had started working a couple of weeks after the accident to find Ernie's replacement for 1995. We had no idea whether Ernie would race again, but we knew we couldn't promise the ride on a permanent basis. Dale Jarrett's name and number was on one of those pink slips we picked up after lunch at the office. Dale had won three races, including the 1993 Daytona 500. He was driving for NFL Super Bowl champion coach Joe Gibbs, who had become a NASCAR car owner in 1992. Robert talked with Dale by phone. They briefly met in the parking lot of the Raceway Grill outside Darlington Raceway during the Southern 500 weekend, where Robert told Dale he wanted him to drive the No. 28 car and Dale confirmed that he wanted to drive it.

I wasn't opposed to hiring Dale Jarrett, but I certainly wasn't a big supporter. Dale just hadn't impressed me that much, especially on qualifying day. I didn't see the aggressiveness that Davey and Ernie had. As a person, they don't come much better than Dale, but sometimes I thought he was almost too nice, and that held him back.

Robert pointed out the obvious: "Who else are we going to get with that kind of experience? And he doesn't tear up cars. He's consistent. He's smart. He's levelheaded. He knows how to win."

But I wasn't convinced. I was afraid our team wouldn't survive if we couldn't find another driver like Ernie or Davey. I was fearful that we wouldn't be that lucky a third time. I saw how much of a beating team morale was taking with an inexperienced driver like Kenny Wallace. I wanted someone like Davey or Ernie, and Dale Jarrett just didn't fit the bill. This was frustrating to Robert, because I was basically saying, "Don't hire Dale, but I don't know who else to tell you to get."

One thing I did like was Dale's attitude. When Robert told him our plan was to have Ernie back in the car if he could race again, Dale said, "That's fine with me. If you'll just give me one year in that 28 car, I'll prove to everyone that I can drive a race car. I'm willing to take my chances about the future." At the time Robert had no plans to expand to two cars and was actually against the idea. The announcement that Dale would take over the 28 car in 1995 came at Charlotte in October. The deal got pretty complex before it was done. At one point, the only way Joe Gibbs was going to let Dale go was if car owner Bill Davis let Bobby Labonte go. So Robert was romancing Bill almost as much as Joe.

As we worked through September to put the deal together with DJ, Ernie made remarkable progress. Two weeks after the crash, Dr. Erlandson upgraded Ernie's condition from serious to fair and took him off the ventilator. The doctor called Ernie's progress "amazing." He said there was no sign of irreversible brain injury.

Ernie was able to get up out of bed and sit in a chair, even though he was still in intensive care. This was great news, and it lifted the spirits of everyone on the team. "I tell you, if his recovery continues as well in the next two weeks as it has in the last two weeks, by the time we get to Dover [for the September 18 race], Kenny Wallace will run the first 250 miles and Ernie will run the last 250 miles," I kiddingly told the press.

We were in Dover in mid-September when Ernie was released from the Michigan hospital and flown to Charlotte, where he checked into a rehabilitation facility of Carolinas Medical Center. After the race in Dover, I couldn't get back to Charlotte quick enough. I hadn't seen Ernie since he had been unconscious in the Michigan hospital about a month before. I drove straight from the airport to the hospital and saw him around 10 o'clock that Sunday night. I went in his room and hugged him and he kind of hugged me back. One of the first things he wanted to know was why we'd put Kenny Wallace in the car. He wasn't too thrilled about that.

"Hey, who else were we going to get?" I said.

Ernie asked me, "Who won the Southern 500 at Darlington?"

"Bill Elliott," I said.

"Damn, I have been asleep a long time, haven't I?" he said.

During the next couple of weeks, I visited him several times a week. Sometimes I'd grab lunch and have lunch with him in his room. On October 5, before qualifying at Charlotte, the doctors allowed Ernie to come to the track. He even held a press conference. "I sure would like to be racing," he said. "It's hard to sit there and watch everybody go out and practice. I told Norman [Koshimizu], 'I think I'd be good for one lap anyway. Go ahead and get my helmet.'" Ernie had a patch over his left eye, which was badly injured when his skull was fractured. Earnhardt told him he wanted a patch—that it was the new thing.

Ernie was soon released to an outpatient program. He returned to his home and began planning and working to race again. By the end of the year, we had come up with something of a plan to help ease Ernie back into racing. But he was skeptical. The afternoon before the 1994 Winston Cup awards banquet in New York, Ernie and Kim came up to Robert's suite in the Waldorf-Astoria. I was there, too. "Robert, I want to be back in that car next year at Daytona," Ernie insisted. "Either I'm going to run Daytona in that 28 car, or I'll drive for someone else."

"Ernie, it ain't gonna happen," I said. "You're just not ready yet. We've got a plan."

"I've got a contract," he said. "You *have* to put me in that car."

We calmed him down. We promised we'd work with him. And after that, we came up with a much more concrete plan for his return. We got a lot of help from Ford's top racing executive at the time, Dan Revard, who took Ernie under his wing and lent a fatherly hand to our task.

In January, we did a test at the Ford Proving Grounds track in Naples, Florida. Robert and I were there with Ernie, along with DJ, Revard, and others. Those cars are hooked up to provide a ton of real-time data acquisition. And as I watched the telemetry and watched Ernie drive the course, it didn't take long for me to realize Ernie hadn't lost a thing. Revard was grinning from ear to ear.

That same month, during Daytona testing, Ernie went to watch. He was about to claw his eyes out to get in one of the cars Dale was testing. We asked Robert if it would be OK. "Man, if y'all do something, I don't want to know about it," he said, and drove off on his scooter.

Late on the last day, we pulled a van into the garage with Ernie in it. He was wearing Norman Koshimizu's firesuit, and it looked like two Ernies could fit inside it. We drove up to the garage. Ernie got out of the van, and Dale Jarrett got in. Then Ernie got into the race car and off he went.

I stood on top of the transporter. I was really nervous. It was Ernie's first time in a race car since he was injured. He drove off pit road changing gears like nothing had ever happened. But I could hardly stand it. I could only imagine what NASCAR would do if they found out. Even worse, what if Ernie couldn't handle it and crashed?

Ernie ran five or six laps wide open. Finally, I made some excuse to call him in, like we had a lot of tape on the front end that would make the engine run hot. He came in. But it meant the world to him. It was a long time before we told anybody about it. Kim found out about it and wasn't very happy. But Ernie was overjoyed, and we were, too.

Back then, NASCAR used to have two tests at Daytona in January. During the second test, we started blowing motors left and right. This started on the first day of the test and continued all three days of the test. Finally, about midmorning of the third day, Doug Yates and I had had enough.

"Let's get the hell out of here, go home, regroup, and take everything down to Talladega and test there so we can figure this out," I said.

"No," Robert said. "We're going to figure this out right here."

We had been using a new approach to the short block—which is the bottom part of the engine, including the pistons, piston rods, crankshaft, and the block itself. We figured it had to be the source of the problem. Robert was leasing engines to car owner Bud Moore, who agreed to give back the old-style engine that was in his backup car. They gave us that motor about lunch time. Since testing was still going on, there was plenty of room to spread out, and we set up shop in the empty garage normally used for NASCAR inspections. We put blue tarps up to wall off our work area. Robert didn't want people looking at the guts of his engine, and he wanted to keep the dirt to a minimum.

Doug and I still weren't game for what Robert was fixing to do, but he went ahead. Needless to say, engines were his department. And in that closed-off space, we removed the blown engine from the car, took off the cylinder heads (which were undamaged), pulled the heads off Bud Moore's engine, installed the other heads, and put everything back together.

I can still see Dale Jarrett sitting there on a tire, wearing his driver's uniform, with his mouth just sort of hanging open, almost not believing what he was seeing. Of course, this particular effort even surprised me. But it was funny, and gratifying, to see the reaction new drivers had to the kind of effort we routinely threw at our work.

About an hour and a half later that afternoon, at 3:30, Dale steered that car back out on the track and ran a helaciously fast lap. We had beaten the problem. And when we came back to Daytona for Speedweeks, Dale went out and won the pole position with that same engine in his car. Dale was pumped up out of sight.

This was the first Speedweeks where teams used really aggressive shock absorbers. Instead of extending normally—what's called rebounding—after being compressed by a bump—these shocks had very slow rebound, so the car stayed sucked down on the track. This reduced drag and helped the car go faster, but it created a little problem for the driver. The car rode like a covered wagon. The driver got a teeth-rattling, bone-jarring ride. After we got through post-qualifying inspection, I saw Dale looking through the toolbox and asked him what he was looking for. He said, "Two three-quarter-inch wrenches so I can take those damn shocks off the car, so we don't have to run them again until we get to Talladega to qualify."

After winning the pole, we struggled all that week. The car had been handling terribly, but we kept working on it and never gave up. I don't think I've worked so hard during Speedweeks to make a car run well. On Friday night I went back to the hotel room and listed every setup piece on that race car, from trailing arm location to steering box ratio and valving. If it was something that could be changed I listed it and thought about it. "Could this be the problem? Could *this* be the problem?"

We went in Saturday morning and completely rebuilt the car, and by final practice we weren't bad. We ran fifth in the 500. One of the most rewarding things was to have Terry Laise, a GM engineer and technical advisor to its NASCAR teams, come over and say, "I just have to shake your hand. I watched you guys this week, and I have never seen a race team struggle so much during Speedweeks, and never give up, and have such great results on race day." That meant a lot coming from Terry, because we were a Ford team.

We finished fifth at Rockingham and Atlanta, too, and sixth at Bristol. But we struggled at Richmond and finished 25th, seven laps down. And we had our first DNF at Darlington, where we lost a transmission. After finishing 11th at North Wilkesboro, we headed to one of my strongest tracks—Martinsville Speedway. But we just weren't running that well. Dale had good finishes on race day, but he wasn't a contender and we weren't qualifying well. We had not even started in the top 10 since our pole at Daytona.

Dale had begun to complain a little bit. But he was pretty reluctant to come right out and tell us what he felt or what he thought he needed. And my problem was I was still living in the Ernie Irvan era. Dale said the motors just didn't seem to have the zip they had at the beginning of the year. At least we were able to deal with this problem. After we finished seventh at Martinsville, Robert and Doug realized they went down the wrong path on using a particular combination of intake manifolds and cylinder heads. Their engine dynamometers at the shop were showing great power, but the engines weren't running on the track. At Martinsville, you're so close to the track and you can see so much; I think Robert noticed some things. The engine shop went back to other tried and true combinations. Soon the engines started running better.

Ernie had been going to all the races with us. He would also come to the shop and take the guys to lunch once or twice a week. Just before

LARRY McREYNOLDS THE BIG PICTURE

Talladega, Ernie called and asked, "Is Linda Mac going with you to Alabama?"

"No," I said.

"Can I go down there and stay with you?" he asked.

I said sure. Ernie was a people person—even more so after the injury—and didn't really like to be by himself. We stayed at the Hampton Inn in Oxford. We got there Thursday evening, and I said, "Ernie, I really don't feel like going out to dinner. There's a Braves game on television. Let's order pizza in and watch the game."

"Sure, Larry Mac, that sounds fun."

The next day was qualifying day, which is always hectic. You work your guts out. By the end of the day, all I wanted to do was go back to the room. There was another Braves game on television. So that's what we did. And we ordered pizza again.

Saturday was a long day, too. Ernie said, "Don't tell me." For the third night in a row, we ordered pizza delivered to the room and watched the Braves on television. That night, Ernie finally rolled over on the bed and said, "You know what, Larry Mac, you live a pretty [expletive] boring life."

At Talladega, Dale qualified fifth. We were running really well in the race when, all of a sudden, Dale started complaining about the power steering. He said something was wrong, but I wasn't really buying it. Dale finished 19th. Dale and I still hadn't developed much communication. It was my fault. I was bitter over losing Davey and almost losing Ernie, and I'm not sure anyone could have satisfied me then. I missed Ernie. I wanted him back. Even if Dale had told me exactly how he wanted his race car set up, I probably wouldn't have paid much attention. I thought he ought to be able to drive the same stuff Ernie had driven. It was probably one of the few times in my career when I was close-minded.

But to be on the lead lap and finish 19th at Talladega was pathetic for a Robert Yates race car. I didn't think Dale was putting forth the effort he needed to. When Dale pulled in after the race, I would hardly speak to him. I checked this, checked that, and I didn't find anything. I said to myself, "He just didn't want to run today."

Later that week, we pulled off the power steering box and had it examined. Something internally was wrong with it. Up to that point, I was doubting just about everything Dale was telling me. But that opened my eyes a little bit. I began to think, "Maybe I need to listen to this guy closer."

Still, Dale was not being very forceful about his opinions. I translated that into a lack of confidence, so it was almost a stalemate. And Ernie wasn't a big fan of Dale either. He probably fed off of my attitude. I didn't bad-mouth Dale among any of the crew members, but looks and actions are worth a thousand words. There probably aren't a handful of people on this earth besides Dale Jarrett who could have put up with the hell that we laid on him—me in particular. We were very unfair to him in a lot of ways. Most drivers would have probably quit before the 10th race. But DJ kept smiling and kept his cool and kept taking it. He tried his best to be a team player.

In The Winston in 1995, Dale wrecked early. Even worse, he wrecked after getting hit from behind. I was the type of crew chief who would get irritated if my driver wrecked. But I got real irritated when my driver wrecked from behind. That means you weren't going fast enough. After that race, I would not even speak to DJ in casual conversation for a few days.

The next day I called a meeting, and Dale, Robert, and I tried to figure out what to do to get on track. I told them, "Look, gang, we're 12 races into this deal and we're junk. We're wrecking, we're not running well, and we're qualifying terribly. Something needs to happen here. I don't think time's going to heal this one."

I don't think we made a lot of headway. It got a little heated. We both got some stuff off our chests. Dale's big message was we were not giving him the feel he was looking for. Different driving styles dictate the package a driver looks for in a race car. With Ernie we had sat on poles, won races, and led laps, and we were a threat to win the pole or race every weekend. Our team had been very successful, and we were very reluctant to change the package. I was bullheaded and thought Dale ought to be able to adapt to our car and drive what Ernie and Davey had driven.

We continued to struggle before the Coca-Cola 600 and qualified 22nd. Nothing we did made the car go faster. And Dale couldn't really tell us what was wrong. During one of our practice sessions I finally said, "Dale, do you have a problem if we put someone else in this car just to see what's going on? Maybe they'll feel something you're not feeling."

"Go right ahead," he said. "Maybe they'll find something." Dale was as open-minded as they came. So we put Hut Stricklin in the car. Hut didn't run any faster than DJ. And in all honesty I didn't expect him to. But Hut came back in and gave us some specific information. He said he didn't feel like the left front tire was working. He said it gave him an insecure feeling getting into the corners.

We went to work and made some changes. Dale got back in the car. Not only was he faster, Dale liked the way the car drove. I think that was a major turning point for both Dale and me. It wasn't the last of our problems, but it opened our eyes. Dale saw that if a driver gave specific direction, we'd go to work on it. And I saw that I needed to get Dale to do what Hut had done. And then I needed to listen to him. Unfortunately, our luck continued to be miserable. We were swept up in a big wreck at Dover on lap two and had to drop out. The following week, at Pocono, we wrecked again and finished 38th.

At Dover, tires were a huge problem. This was the first race on the new concrete racing surface, and tires were wearing out after 15 laps. In an emergency move, Goodyear substituted another tire with a harder compound. They brought in a new batch of tires, but couldn't meet the demand, and all the teams called their shops to see if they had any of the same tires back there. Several guys on our team came in on Sunday morning, flying up on the special US Airways "race day express" that brings crews to the racetrack and flies them back after the race. All of our guys walked into the track carrying one or two tires on their shoulders. We were going to have all we needed, that was certain. Then we wrecked on lap two and didn't need any of them. The car was torn up so bad it took us 200 laps getting it repaired well enough just to load in the truck.

I had flown up to Dover with Ernie on his plane, along with several team members. Ernie was working as an analyst on the TNN telecast of the race. When we finally got the car loaded, there were still 253 laps in the race, but we were stuck because we were flying with Ernie. You could pretty much talk Ernie into anything. So I went out on pit road and found Glenn Jarrett, who was working pit road for TNN. I told him, "The next time you go to a commercial break, see if they will let me talk to Ernie."

When they went to a commercial, Glenn gave me his headset and microphone. I told Ernie, "I've got a deal for you. How about we take your plane back and we take one of the guys off the race day express and you fly home on the race day express?"

He said, "OK, no problem." So that's what happened.

The race had just ended when I got off Ernie's plane and into my car in North Carolina. Ernie didn't get home until midnight. He called the next day and said, "The traffic after the race was so bad, and I was stuck on that bus headed toward the airport, right in the middle of that traffic." Here we were, flying off in Ernie's airplane while he was sitting in traffic.

Throughout the month of June, my thoughts had been preoccupied with my mother, who had been diagnosed with cancer in May. She was getting worse and worse. I went to Daytona on Wednesday, June 28, but she took a turn for the worse and Dale Jarrett was kind enough to fly me back to North Carolina, where my mom had moved. That was the kind of guy Dale was. Even though we weren't getting along, he reached out to me.

My mother passed away on June 29, shortly after I got back to be with her. Two days later, while I was making funeral arrangements, we blew an engine 38 laps into the race. I guess that was the race to miss if I was going to miss one. We buried my mother on Monday, July 3, and Dale and his wife, Kelly, came to the service. I was very touched by that, especially in light of the rocky times we'd had.

I was still pretty down as we prepared for New Hampshire, which came a week after Daytona. But I was pretty confident we could do well at New Hampshire. We had the same car Davey had run so well with here in his final race and the car that Ernie had led so many laps with in 1994. With DJ behind the wheel, we struggled. We qualified 14th, but I think that the team and I, even Dale, thought that he just couldn't get around this track, even though he had a proven car. In the race, we wrecked on lap two—hit from behind by Geoff Bodine.

"Dale, for what it's worth, he said he was sorry, he just messed up," our spotter said on the radio.

"That does a lot of good," Dale replied.

The front end was all knocked out of shape. We got back out, but finished 30th, four laps down. It wasn't Dale's fault, but I thought to myself, "He just wasn't getting the job done. He just wasn't getting around that corner fast enough."

When DJ and I passed each other in the garage, I didn't even acknowledge him. It was later in the week before we talked again. It was a tough time. My mom had just died. My car wasn't running well. I was fuming as we loaded up. Charging into the truck with a double handful of radios, I slipped and hit my shin and ankle. It felt like somebody had hit me with a sledgehammer. I fought through that injury all week, but by the time we got to Pocono, I had a knot on my leg about the size of a golf ball.

In pole qualifying, Dale did no better at Pocono than he had in June. He was 14th in June, 15th in July. But the car ran pretty well in the race. A caution flag flew, and we pitted with 41 laps to go. We could go 38 to 39 laps on a tank. But it appeared the race might go green the rest of the way and become a fuel mileage contest. Almost from the drop of the green flag during that final run, I worked on DJ to save gas. "DJ, we can make it to the end if somewhere out there we buy us a lap and a half or two laps of fuel," I said. I repeated the usual instructions: off of the throttle early, roll through the corner longer, back on the throttle later, shift from third to high gear on the frontstretch earlier.

But you just can't seem to get good fuel mileage at that big two-and-a-half-mile track. I felt in my heart that we were not going to make it. But we had to go for it. We needed a victory. We weren't very high in the points, so we had nothing to lose. As other cars came in to top off their tanks, Dale took the lead on lap 188. The race went green the rest of the way. Somehow DJ bought us the fuel we needed. When he came off the final turn, his car sputtered. But it caught again and he finished just ahead of Jeff Gordon. The car ran out of gas on the backstretch, and Michael Waltrip pushed us back around.

After that victory, it felt like the weight of the world had been lifted from my shoulders once again. And I think Dale felt the same way. I think it took that victory to prove to ourselves and each other that we could do it. Another predominant feeling was that my shin was killing me. After victory lane, doctors in the infield care center cut that clot of blood, bandaged me up, and sent me on my way. I could hardly walk, but it was a sweet ride home. That was the only race I ever won at Pocono. It was also the first race I'd won in 14 months, since Sears Point in May 1994 with Ernie. So much had happened in those 14 months. But I was certain of one thing: It felt good to be a winner again.

We finished second at Talladega and third at Indy. Those performances, along with the victory at Pocono, helped Dale turn the corner at Robert Yates Racing. Perhaps more importantly, it allowed me to change from a doubter to a supporter. Maybe DJ wasn't another Ernie Irvan. But he knew how to take care of a car. He was brilliant at saving gas. He knew how to finish even if he wasn't running well. And those wrecks, well, they really *weren't* his fault. In short, I began to see that Dale was championship material, even if he didn't win as much or go as fast as a driver like Ernie Irvan.

In August, as we headed back to Michigan and the first anniversary of Ernie's crash, it was still very much in doubt that Dale was going to continue with Robert Yates Racing. The convenient and often-told story is that Robert started his second team to keep Dale. But by August 1995, we knew for sure that Ernie was returning, and we also knew that we were going to create a second team. And DJ was not on the short list to drive the new car. Johnny Benson's name had come up; John Andretti was on that list; but not Dale. We qualified 17th at Michigan, but Dale moved through the field and took the lead for the first time on lap 52. He led a bunch of laps. We were in front at lap 100, the halfway point. Two laps later our engine blew up, and we were finished. But as Robert and I headed to the airport, I said, "You know, Robert, we're being stupid right now."

He looked at me kind of funny.

"We've got two of something that many race teams don't even have one of," I said. "We've got Ernie Irvan coming back. And we've got Dale Jarrett, who can win races. Look at what he did today, leading lap after lap. Yeah, we had him in a good race car. But he still had to drive the thing and mash the throttle. We've got two good race car drivers, and we're fixing to let one of them get away from us."

Before long, we signed DJ as our second driver. And I began working some of the longest, hardest hours of my life creating a second team at Robert Yates Racing.

At Martinsville in September an amazing event had occurred off the track, and it was something that set me thinking about the incredible journey I had made as crew chief since I'd left Birmingham. It involved Felix Sabates, one of NASCAR's most colorful figures. Felix emigrated from Cuba as a teenager and became a self-made millionaire, in part through marketing Atari's Pong computer game and the Teddy Ruxpin doll. He's warmhearted, hotheaded, and known for throwing his money around.

On Friday Felix had corralled Robert and me in our transporter. "I want to offer Larry one million dollars to come be my crew chief, starting next year, for my 42 car," Felix said. I looked at Robert. Robert looked at me. Both of us were at a loss for words. Robert finally said, "Well, uh, if Larry won't take it, I will."

We all laughed, but then Felix went on to say that he'd give me private time on his yacht and his jet and plenty of other perks. "I want Larry to be the first million-dollar crew chief," Felix said. "Don't give me an answer now, Larry. Think about it."

My immediate reaction was "No way." But I had to think about it. I could pay off my home and every other debt I had. I'd be able to put money in the bank. But I knew how publicity-conscious Felix was. If I accepted this offer, I'd be in every newspaper and magazine as the million-dollar crew chief. In those days good *sponsorships* weren't much more than $4 million to $5 million. How could I gain the respect and support of all the guys on the team, who were working just as hard to make $30,000 or $40,000 a year? So in the end, it wasn't hard to say no. And I still felt a loyalty to Robert, Ernie, and the team. I'd given Ernie my word that his car and team would be there waiting for him when he came back.

CHAPTER SIXTEEN

Ernie's Comeback

When Robert decided to create two teams in the fall of 1995, the bulk of actually assembling the new team fell on my shoulders. One of the big reasons we started the second team was that we didn't know what things were going to be like when Ernie came back. We hoped for the best, but we needed to cover ourselves in case it turned out to be a disaster.

It was when I took on the responsibility of starting the second team that Robert also just about doubled my salary. That made me feel that I had finally come into my own as a crew chief. But I earned that extra money. I had worked insane hours in my career—starting Kenny Bernstein's team, building new cars in 1992 to replace wrecked ones— but from the end of September in 1995 until I left Robert Yates Racing in December 1996, I never worked so many hours, so many days, so many evenings, and so many weekends. Hiring people, ordering cars and parts, ordering tools—you name it, I did it. Everything we already had in place for the No. 28 car had to be duplicated for the No. 88 team.

On top of that, we were totally overcrowded at Robert's shop, which wasn't even big enough for one team. We had stuff stacked and packed all over that shop. Sometimes it wasn't worth climbing around and through all the stuff to get from wherever you were to the bathroom.

I'd wake up thinking about what I had to do that day and say, "There's no way I can get all of this done." Some nights I couldn't go to sleep for worrying about the next day's load. I was preparing a new team for a driver who I was finally getting comfortable with. At the same time, I was helping lay the groundwork for my old driver to somehow make a comeback after surviving a near-fatal crash. That was work enough in itself.

If you'd left it up to Ernie, of course, he would have come back at Daytona in 1995. He did that one secret test there in January 1995, and in March he did his first publicly acknowledged test at Darlington Raceway during a test with DJ. Dan Revard wanted Ernie to test his Busch car before trying the Winston Cup car.

Mark Martin came to the test, and Ernie had him jump in the Busch car and run a few laps to shake it down. Our crew was put off that Ernie didn't ask DJ to do it. I asked Ernie why, and he blew off the question. "I've already asked Mark," he said. I'd changed my attitude toward Dale, but Ernie never warmed up to him. Dale worked a lot harder toward being a good friend to Ernie than vice versa.

I was pretty nervous with Ernie in the car at Darlington, just as I had been at Daytona. But I knew we would never know if he could actually do it unless we let him get some laps under his belt. I stood up on top of our truck with a pit in my stomach. About the third lap, he came through turn four and let those left-side wheels drop below the apron, which made the car wiggle. But he stayed on the gas, as you have to, and drove straight and fast up off the corner. "Man, he hasn't lost a *thing*," I thought. In a few more laps, Ernie was running lap times as fast as DJ.

But at the end of the day, while driving his Busch car, Ernie scared all of us when he lost control in turn one and hit the wall. Thankfully, he wasn't hurt at all.

In April, Ernie took a couple of his Craftsman Truck series race trucks to North Wilkesboro. Ernie drove one, and he put Joe Ruttman in the other. They raced hard for a bunch of laps. Robert watched and was impressed with how well Ernie had done. Unfortunately, Ernie's medical recovery wasn't quite complete. In April 1995, doctors discovered an aneurysm in his brain. It was not life threatening, but it took three operations to correct it, and Ernie was sidelined for several months. Ernie began wearing an eye patch during 1995 because his badly damaged left eye was pointing at the wrong angle after everything healed. Without the eye patch, he had double vision. He later had more surgeries that allowed him to discard the patch.

Ernie finally received his release to drive on September 16, 1995, and promptly went to North Wilkesboro to test again. Ernie had planned to make his return at Martinsville in the Craftsman Truck Series, but qualifying was rained out and he was out of the show.

The next week, Ernie qualified seventh at North Wilkesboro. I was very nervous until he made that show. There were no provisionals for his car, and I felt greatly relieved when he qualified as well as he did. I had an ear-to-ear smile and puffed on a big cigar as I walked through the garage area afterward. We had successfully passed through the first level of battle in his comeback.

It was a tough weekend, because we were really trying to run two cars with what was little more than a one-car team. But Ernie did a hell of a job in the race. He started seventh, took the lead on lap 125 and led 31 laps. Later, he held off the leaders for dozens of laps to keep from going a lap down. He finished sixth, still on the lead lap. On the radio, he sounded like the same old Ernie—calm, collected, nonchalant. He said later that he became a little emotional with about five laps to go, when he knew he had done what he had set out to do—finish the race and post a top 10.

As he hoisted himself out of that Ford Thunderbird at the end of those 400 laps, Ernie looked fresh enough to drive another 400 laps, especially for a guy who'd driven with one eye all afternoon. More importantly, he looked really happy. The fans in the backstretch grandstands let out a huge cheer when Ernie lifted himself out of his car. Reporters were all over him immediately. Of course the first question was, "How do you feel?"

"Good,'" Ernie chirped.

Asked about the traffic, he said, "I'm glad I didn't have two eyes because it would have been tough to see with both of 'em." It was the same old Ernie.

"I wouldn't have done this if I didn't think I could do it," he said. "Normally we wouldn't be happy with a sixth-place finish, but this is like winning. Everything seems the same. I still made the stupid moves I used to. I bounced off the fence with about 20 to go, but that's about normal. It was just like I was racing last week."

Earlier, at Darlington, things weren't so happy, when we broke the news to Ernie that we were hiring Dale full-time and creating a two-car operation. Ernie was totally opposed. He got in his car, left the track, and went home. Eventually, he settled down and capped off his mini-comeback in 1995 with two more races, including a seventh-place finish at Atlanta.

Meanwhile, I had already hired most of the team members for DJ's new No. 88 Quality Care Ford. After the word had gotten out about the second team, I couldn't walk 100 feet in the garage area without five or six people ambushing me about coming to work for us. I built the team from scratch and handpicked a group that I thought would be young, aggressive, and would learn my way of doing things. Then I launched a campaign to get the man I thought most qualified to be crew chief. He was Todd Parrott, one of the leading crewmen on Rusty Wallace's team. Todd is a take-charge guy, and he had the same commanding presence as his father, Buddy Parrott, one of the most talented crew chiefs in Winston Cup history. I started talking to Todd on a regular basis and one day convinced him to come over to our house. We sat in the living room, and I fired every pitch at him I could think of. Finally I talked him into it.

When we got to Daytona to begin the 1996 season, Ernie qualified second and DJ was third. Dale Earnhardt did something he'd never done before—he won the pole position for the Daytona 500. "I really have to be honest with you," Ernie told the media. "Everything with my comeback surprised me. Sitting out as long as I sat out and going through all the trauma my body went through, it's amazing how I've been able to come back. All the prayers are answered because I never thought I'd ever be able to race again when I was laying in that hospital in Michigan."

Neither did a lot of people. Some of them apparently still didn't believe it. NASCAR Vice President of Competition Mike Helton took a lot of heat for letting him come back. But if Ernie didn't fully vindicate himself in pole qualifying, he certainly did in his Twin 125 qualifying race on Thursday before the Daytona 500. He won the race by about four feet over Ken Schrader after leading flag to flag. At the end, he somehow managed to hold off the double-team drafting move of Schrader and Jeff Gordon.

Seconds after Ernie took the checkered flag, the radio was a riot of noise as everyone tried to congratulate Ernie. DJ came on, as did Todd Parrott. Then I came on and said, "Ernie, like I told you Saturday. Now '96 has *really* begun."

Ernie had made such a statement. And he had beat three Chevys. Among those who came to victory lane was Helton, who busted through the people to get to Ernie to congratulate him. He looked so proud. Mike's butt had been on the line.

In the press box, Ernie was asked if his comeback was complete. "I don't think that'll be settled until about August," he said. "The day I got hurt, we were racing Earnhardt for the championship. There would be nothing better than to be racing Earnhardt for the championship again. That's when it'll be complete."

There were some tough questions, too. Why risk another head injury, like Neil Bonnett, who died in a comeback attempt? The scary thing about returning from a bad head injury is that you are extremely vulnerable to head injuries in the future. A hard hit that another driver would be able to sustain could easily kill Ernie.

"Everybody said, 'Well, Neil never should have got back in a race car,'" Ernie said. "Yeah, if he hadn't got back in a race car, he wouldn't have been killed that day. But he wouldn't have been happy. And I wouldn't have been happy if I never got in a race car again, either."

In the 500 itself, early in the race, Ernie was following Dale Earnhardt when the No. 3 car's engine quit because of ignition problems. Ernie got into Dale and he wrecked. DJ came through and won his second 500. Todd Parrott's first victory as crew chief was the Daytona 500. I was disappointed for Ernie and the 28 team, but overjoyed for Todd and Dale and the 88 crew, most of whom I had picked. I was like the dad who had two sons in the Little League game. One of them struck out four times and the other hit a grand-slam home run to win the game, but I was equally proud of both of them.

After Daytona, Ernie began to struggle. He had always excelled at qualifying, but now we were terrible. In fact, from the time we won the outside pole at Daytona to Talladega until late April, where we won the pole, we didn't start in the top 15. And we failed to qualify for two races and used provisional starting spots to make those fields.

Even worse, Ernie continued wrecking. At Richmond, in the third event of the season, Ernie qualified 26th, but crashed with just a few minutes to go in the final practice before qualifying. We got the backup car unloaded and had about 10 minutes to make a few laps. After I pushed it onto the truck's loading platform, Robert was actually warming the engine up as we lowered it on the gate. In the race, Ernie wrecked on lap 20. He had another incident late in the race.

I really began to have questions. Were we doing the right thing with Ernie? Were we doing the right thing with our race team? Ernie was questioning himself, too, and that added pressure. Ernie maybe wasn't as good as he was before the accident, but we knew in our minds that he still was probably better than 80 or 90 percent of those guys out there.

We qualified 32nd at Darlington. Dale Jarrett qualified third. In the race, Ernie was coming down the backstretch when I heard his dad, Vic, who was spotting, warn him about a wreck in turn four. We were pitting on the backstretch, and as I watched him get into turn three, it didn't look like he was slowing down that much. A few seconds later, I heard him curse in the radio. Somehow, he'd gotten involved in that wreck.

Ernie was tearing up cars faster than we could fix them. This was our fourth wrecked car of the season. We stripped it right there at the track and sent the chassis back to Mike Laughlin for repairs. I found Ernie in the transporter. "Ernie, what the hell is going on?" I asked. "You're hitting everything but the pace car." Was he trying too hard? Was his vision OK? We started yelling at each other. "Well, what the hell do you want me to do about it?" Ernie asked. "I'm not doing it on purpose."

By Monday, we had made up. But I felt pretty bad for making the crack about the pace car. Ernie was coming back almost from the dead.

Deep inside I knew that we were in a major rebuilding year. We had to get him acclimated to these tracks again. Maybe in the second half of the season we could shine like we had during the first half of 1994.

In the meantime, DJ and Todd were having a hell of a season. They had finished second at Rockingham and Richmond and were leading the Winston Cup points. From a racing standpoint, my pairing of Todd with DJ was one of the smartest moves I ever made. They ended up winning four races in 1996, including the Daytona 500, Coca-Cola 600, and Brickyard 400. In 1999, they would win the Winston Cup championship.

But not too long after I hired Todd—even before the 1996 season began—I began to get concerned about his way of doing things. As a crew chief, one rule I always lived by is never ask a guy to do something you wouldn't do yourself. Todd would demand that crew members be at work at 7 a.m. and then he'd come in at eight or 8:30. Todd also had a bad way of talking down to people. He tended to belittle them or make them look bad. And he had this beat-on-the-chest attitude of "I'm the crew chief and if you don't like it, you can leave."

During 1996, we began construction on a new building. Todd tried to convince Robert to put a wall down the center of the building to separate the 88 and 28 teams. Robert didn't share this with me, but when I found out, I fought tooth and nail against it.

"We're not going to be skins and shirts," I said. "We're one team building two cars." The new building was Robert's baby, and, as it turned out, he was against the idea. But eventually Todd got even more than a wall. At the end of the 1998 season, Robert agreed to split the two teams and move the 28 team entirely out of the original Robert Yates Racing facility. Today, the 28 team is in Ricky Rudd's old shop in Mooresville.

Todd was the type of guy who would always try to use you to his advantage. If we were running good and the 88 was struggling, I could not even turn around without running into Todd. But if the roles were reversed, he made me feel like I had the plague when I went to talk to him.

Todd was like the best gun I ever built, but then as I was putting the final polish on it, the gun went off and shot me. I pleaded with Robert to crack down on Todd and to help me get him under control. But Robert didn't step in. He hates adversity and confrontation and avoids it at all costs. I didn't mind confrontation. I told Todd once, "As long as you're running good, you'll get by with your tactics. But if you ever slip and fall, they'll be lining up to walk all over you and make you look bad." I was not surprised in 2002 when Jimmy Elledge was let go as DJ's new crew chief less than three months into the season. Jimmy had been hired to replace Todd, so Todd could be Robert's overall manager. But Todd refused to give up his power. He gave Jimmy no real authority and little to do.

Todd did not like the decision Robert and I made that both teams would use suspensions built by Mike Laughlin. I had used the Laughlin chassis most of my career. Todd wanted to use a chassis built by another car builder, Ronnie Hopkins. Of course, I wanted both teams to use the same chassis, so we could work off each other's notes.

We finally let Todd go ahead and build some Hopkins cars. What's the use of having two teams if you don't let one experiment? Dale and Todd had a lot of success with the Hopkins car. We were struggling. Eventually, I switched to the Hopkins chassis, too, but I probably let my ego get in the way for a while.

At Martinsville, where we usually ran well, Ernie could hardly get around the track. He was 35th fastest after the first round of qualifying, so we tried again Saturday and he was slower. We failed to qualify, but started 34th in a 36-car field with a provisional and had to pit on the backstretch. We had brought our usual successful setup, but it didn't work well, so we changed everything for Saturday and were still slow.

So Ernie, Robert, and I sat down on Saturday night and decided to change everything back to the setup that had worked so well in the past. I don't know that I have ever changed so much on one race car as we did on that Sunday morning at Martinsville. We changed springs; we changed shocks; we changed sway bars; we moved the trailing arms; and we moved the lead weights in the frame rails. So basically, we changed everything but the paint scheme. We almost didn't make it to inspection in time.

When they dropped that green flag, we had a pretty good race car. As it turned out, we were especially good on long runs. Ernie worked his way up through the field and finished second, two and a half seconds behind winner Rusty Wallace. To know that we could start almost dead last and work out of a backstretch pit and still be competitive and finish second was a great confidence booster for all of us.

DJ had qualified 12th at Martinsville, but struggled to a 29th place finish. It was his first really bad run of the year. That Sunday night, after I got home, DJ called. He said, "Larry, I just had to call you and tell you how proud I am of you and the 28 bunch. I know everybody struggled their guts out this weekend, and you changed everything you could have possibly changed on race morning. You guys never give up, and it paid off today." That phone call meant a lot to me. It shows why you won't find a classier person on this earth than Dale Jarrett.

But Dale was competitive, too, and five days after that call, I saw the side he could display in the heat of competition. We posted a time that ended up winning the pole position for the Winston Select 500 at Talladega. Dale qualified second. When he came in, he threw his helmet at the car and stalked off to his motorcoach. I told Robert he needed to get DJ's head screwed back on his shoulders. Robert talked to DJ, and he apologized. But it showed how deeply he really cared about winning.

In the weeks leading up to Talladega, Robert and Doug and the guys in the engine shop had worked all-out to produce two really good restrictor plate engines—one for Ernie and one for DJ. We had other good motors, but these two were the daddy rabbits. On pole day, NASCAR rolled in a trailer rigged with a chassis dynamometer. You'd roll a car onto the trailer so the rear wheels sat on rolling barrels. The machine measured actual horsepower at the rear wheels. But running a restrictor plate engine on a chassis dyno is pretty tricky. You can easily damage the motor. And this was the first time they'd ever done this.

I was dead set against the test. Why test now in the middle of a race weekend? I said we'd put both cars on the chassis dyno after Sunday's race if they'd just leave us be now. We warned NASCAR Technical Director Gary Nelson that he might damage our race motor. But he was going to do the test whether we liked it or not. Gary started running our car, and the next thing I knew, carbon was flying out the exhaust pipes. Gary had slipped the clutch during his first run through the gears. That had lugged the motor and burned a piston. He had blown it up right there on that chassis dyno.

As Robert explained, "We know you can hurt engines lugging them. All truck drivers in America know about lugging. When you go up a hill and miss a gear and go to the next one up and you don't have enough RPM, you have to start over. That kills these engines, especially these restricted engines. I'm not happy with what happened here. We just wiped the clutch out. It about half-snapped the crankshaft in two. It threw a lot of sparks out of the exhaust. We wanted to race this motor, but now it's questionable."

"It was a donkey show," I said.

To add insult to injury, the NASCAR computer failed during the test and lost all the information. This was one instance when Gary was totally out of line. He made things worse by telling the press we had had the option to not have our car undergo the test.

"That's a lie," I snapped.

"They didn't give us any option," Robert said. "They told us."

When Robert opened up the engine the next morning under a makeshift tent of tarps next to our trailer, the bad news was visible in the tiny craters and pockmarks on the tops of the pistons—the telltale evidence of damage. We had to have another block sent down there, and we worked late into Saturday night, long after the garage normally closed, to change cylinder heads and build a new motor. But of course it just wasn't as good as the motor we had.

"We built 23 restrictor plate engines this winter, and two of them turned out good," Robert said. "That was our best bullet. I hope they're happy."

But NASCAR was far from done with us. In the race, we were involved in the big 14-car crash in which Ricky Craven's car tumbled through the first turn. Ernie finished 31st. DJ finished second. We were loading up when Doug Yates came over and said, "Just thought you'd like to know. They're putting that 88 car up there on the chassis dyno right now. I guess they weren't happy with blowing up just one of our engines."

I went ballistic. I ran over there. They had the car about halfway up on the ramp, and I went over and began unhooking the straps they had attached.

"You guys are not putting this car up on that chassis dyno," I said.

The NASCAR inspectors looked at me like I had two heads. But Robert was standing beside me and he said, "No, you're not going to blow another motor up."

They took us up into the NASCAR trailer. Mike Helton and Gary Nelson were there. "You're not blowing up another one of our motors," I said.

Mike looked straight at me and said, "We are going to put that car up on the chassis dyno."

I said, "No you're not, either. Not our car. We have the right to say no. It's our car."

"We have the right to tell you guys you can't run in Sonoma next week, too," Mike said.

"If that's what you guys want to do, go right ahead," I said. "But you're not blowing up another one of our motors."

I was calling their bluff. Would they really ban us from running Sonoma, especially after screwing up so bad in front of everyone? I turned to Robert and said, "Robert, am I right?"

But Robert didn't stand behind me. He just said, "If NASCAR wants to put that car back up there, I guess that's what they're going to do."

The expression "so mad you can't see straight" does not do justice to how mad I was. I didn't know who I was more upset with, NASCAR for doing this or Robert for not supporting me. That moment was the beginning of the end for me at Robert Yates Racing. On the way to the airport, after they tested DJ's car on the chassis dyno, my chest started to hurt. Some of the guys on the team noticed something was not right with me. I said, "I'm OK. I just drank a cold soda too fast."

But one of them told our secretary, Libby Gant, the next morning, and all of a sudden, about halfway through the day, Linda showed up and she hauled me off to the doctor's office, where I had an EKG. Everything was fine, but with all that had gone on that weekend, no wonder I was hurting.

A week later, out at Sears Point Raceway in Sonoma for the road race, I was standing near our transporter when I had a sense that somebody was coming toward me. I looked up, and about 50 feet away, NASCAR President Bill France was headed my way. He walked up, took a drag off a cigarette, and said, "You know, Larry, you've got to quit taking this so serious. This is just a [expletive] *game*." Then he turned and walked away, leaving me standing there speechless, without a chance to reply.

Before the June race at Dover, we went up there in April to tire test for Goodyear. It was so cold the first day, it actually snowed. We never got on the track. The next day, water was seeping across the frontstretch. We kept putting sand and oil dry on the water, but we couldn't stop the seepage. Robert, a very persistent sort, sent our truck driver to get some Sakrete. We worked through lunch getting that seepage stopped. Finally, at about 1 p.m., we got on the track. But there was no rubber on the track, and it was hard for the cars to get a grip. Ernie was riding around, getting up to speed, when on the third or fourth lap, the car broke loose in turn one. Ernie hit the wall. I was scared to death. Ernie was pretty groggy when we got to him. He was OK, but was sore for a few days. The car was destroyed. It didn't look worth hauling home. I went back to the garage, and Todd Parrott was loading up the No. 88 car. "I'm getting this car back into this hauler while it's still in one piece," he said.

We went back to Dover for the race and had a good, solid run. We didn't have the best car by any means, but we were good enough to hang in the top five all day and wound up fourth. In the next five races, through the Pepsi 400 at Daytona, we continued to struggle in qualifying, but had good races. We posted four top-10 finishes, including three top fives. The exception was the June race in Pocono, where we crashed.

The Jiffy Lube 300 at New Hampshire on July 14 marked the beginning of the second half of the 1996 season. We qualified sixth. It was the first time all year, with the exception of the Daytona and Talladega races, that we had qualified better than 16th.

The New Hampshire weather was awful on Saturday. The storms were so bad they finally shut down the garage and made us leave early. We never got on the track for practice. After qualifying, we did a few old things to the car that we had done in the past at New Hampshire: We put a little stiffer right rear spring in it, changed the rear shocks, and made a few other minor adjustments and got the car ready to race.

Ernie ran really well that day and took the lead for the first time on lap 57. The last pit stop was critical. It came under green. I made the call: two tires and gas. Todd Parrott did the same for DJ. We actually gained on them in the pits. Both teams had good stops, but the 28 group really shined that day when they needed to.

Ernie took the lead for good on lap 278. I kept my fingers crossed. "Please don't let there be a caution," I said. A late yellow flag had cost Davey a victory here in 1993 in his final race. Fortunately, the race finished clean and green. And as the laps wound down, DJ was second. They finished one-two, with DJ about five seconds behind. It was incredible. Ernie had made it all the way back to victory lane in the Winston Cup series. It's certainly one of the most special wins of my career and ranks right up there with the two Daytona 500 victories and my first win back in 1988 at Watkins Glen.

After the victory lane ceremonies, when I walked in the press room for the winner's interview, I looked at all the reporters and photographers and TV people and I announced, "Ladies and gentlemen, comeback complete!"

CHAPTER SEVENTEEN

Leaving Robert Yates Racing

T wo weeks after Ernie's comeback victory at New Hampshire, we were blamed for a huge crash at Talladega that injured Dale Earnhardt.

The pack was coming through the tri-oval on lap 117 when the cars driven by Ernie and Sterling Marlin ran into each other. That turned Sterling into Dale Earnhardt, who was leading. Sterling and Dale crashed into the outside wall head on. Ten other cars were involved. Dale's car flipped up on its side and was clobbered by other cars. Dale limped to the stretcher, but he was hurt pretty bad. He was airlifted to Carraway Methodist Medical Center in Birmingham. He suffered a fractured left collarbone and a fractured sternum. It was one of the worst wrecks of his career.

Ernie took a lot of heat for the Earnhardt crash. He did not crash himself and went on to finish fourth. But I was watching the monitor for a couple of laps before the crash, and it was obvious that both Sterling and Dale were doing some pretty serious blocking. When they came off turn four and through the tri-oval—and I've told this to both Dale and Richard Childress—their tactics backfired, because Ernie didn't back off this time.

The next week, at Indy, Sterling walked in our garage and tossed a pair of glasses at Ernie. "You need these," Sterling said. They almost came to blows. I wished Ernie had coldcocked Sterling right there. Thankfully he didn't, but Sterling deserved it. Members of his team were passing out photocopies of an eye chart with a message that read: "Ernie Don't Hit Me You One-Eyed SOB."

Ernie certainly had no problems seeing at Indy. Both he and DJ were really strong, though neither had qualified that great. But as the laps wound down, it became a duel between the two of them. On lap 139, Ernie got past Dale on the backstretch. But DJ stayed right on his bumper. Ernie said after the race that his car handled better in turns one and two and DJ was better in turns three and four. It came down to the tiniest slipup, and that happened with seven laps to go. As Ernie explained it, "I got a little high in turn two. I got up in the marbles. It washed up, and I just about hit the fence, and Dale got by me. It was my race to win and my race to lose. I ended up losing it."

"My car slid, too," said DJ. "I almost hit Ernie because it slid, and I really had to cut it left to keep from getting into him."

I was really disappointed for Ernie, because if ever a track owed him one, it was Indy. He should have won that inaugural race in 1994. In a perfect world, I would prefer to have seen the order of finish flip-flopped. At the same time, I was thrilled to see those Robert Yates cars finish one-two at Indy. I remember looking at Robert with about five laps to go and saying, "Is this not the greatest problem in the world you could imagine ever having? Your car is trying to beat your car to win at Indy."

Robert just shook his head in amazement. Afterward, as he accepted congratulations from every direction, a little girl told him, "The only thing that could have been better is if they had tied."

That run at Indy capped off quite a stretch for Ernie. It was his sixth straight top-five finish. He had moved from 16th to seventh in points. But we lost our momentum when the transmission broke at Watkins Glen and we got in another big wreck at Bristol. That was followed by the usual Bristol madness, as we took our car to the infield to try to straighten the frame. We got a wrecker over there and tied a chain to the frame and another chain between the car and the infield care center. Robert got in the car and held the brake while the wrecker tried to yank the frame into some semblance of shape. The Bristol infield is so small that the wrecker looked as if it was going to pull itself onto the track. NASCAR was raising hell with us. If that chain had broken, there's no telling how many miles that wrecker would have gone.

Then chaos erupted in DJ's pit. Todd Parrott had gone over the wall during a stop to get a loose tire and had slipped and blown out his knee. I rushed over to help preserve their top-five run. While I was there, my radio was going crazy because Robert wanted to tie off the car to a concession stand for better leverage when the tow truck was pulling. NASCAR was screaming at him. It was just another night at Bristol. But we finally got back out and actually picked up a couple of spots.

Ernie won his second race of his comeback season at Richmond on September 7, after a great battle with Jeff Gordon. But there was little joy in victory lane that night. The gulf was widening between Robert and me. It was even larger with Ernie and Robert. Ernie was having a serious dispute over souvenir sales with Robert's wife, Carolyn, who was at the track that weekend. She and Ernie had been at each other pretty hard.

Ernie also had displeased some Texaco executives. As part of his Texaco contract, Ernie had to make a certain number of personal appearances on Texaco's behalf. After he had done the contracted number of appearances, he still had to do more, but he would be paid for them. When the Texaco bigwigs would come in for a race and take all of us out to dinner, Ernie wanted to count that as one of his appearances. I said, "Ernie, these are the people who paid your salary a full year, basically without you racing. They never let you down about money, and now you want to charge them to go have dinner with them?"

Robert was also getting pressure from Texaco about Ernie shunning fans. Ernie was often rude and would refuse to sign autographs, prompting the fans to complain to Texaco and threaten to never use their product again. That was just the way Ernie was. It doesn't make it right, but Ernie wasn't going to change and nobody was going to change him. When he was abrasive with people, he didn't care who they were. Fans, executives, the press—he could snap at anyone when in a foul mood. I began to see the handwriting on the wall. Ernie wasn't going to be with Robert or Texaco much longer.

It's so tough to win in this sport; you have to make the most of what little bit of excitement you get celebrating—that 15 minutes in victory lane. And at Richmond, I didn't get to enjoy that 15 minutes, because I had sponsor representatives asking me where Robert was. I found him in the lounge of the transporter. And I knew why he wasn't there. He just didn't want to be there. He was afraid Carolyn would be mad at him, and he didn't want any confrontation with Ernie. So he decided to stay away.

Right then and there, I realized, "Why do this if it isn't even fun to win a race anymore?"

Besides, I had something else in my racing life that was providing lots of satisfaction and fulfillment. That night, Ernie and I flew to New

Hampshire on Ernie's plane for a triple-header Sunday of racing that included a NASCAR Craftsman Truck series race. Ernie was going there to run in the truck race; I was going to broadcast the races as a color commentator in the booth for The Nashville Network.

During the off-season, I had been approached by Pam Miller, a television producer who specialized in NASCAR races, about becoming a broadcaster. I'd first met Pam in 1990, when she and Ned Jarrett did a story on me for ESPN. Since then, she had become good friends with Linda and me.

"What makes you think I can be a *broadcaster*?" I asked Pam. I'd never even given it a thought.

"Larry, I've watched you being interviewed," she said. "You tell the whole story, you're animated when you talk, you're not bashful. I think you'd be really good."

My first broadcast had been the Busch race at Rockingham in late February. I was a pit road reporter. I loved it. It was exciting and challenging. Pretty soon I was doing races every off weekend and nearly every Saturday. In July, I even did a race for CBS—the big network.

Unless something unusual was going on at the shop, an off weekend was really a mini-vacation for teams, and we wouldn't go into the shop at all. So while the broadcasting meant time away from my family, it didn't affect the race team. I can honestly say that, during all the years of my part-time broadcasting career, I don't ever feel that I shorted the race team. And the networks knew that my team came first. If I was scheduled to do a Busch race on Saturday, they would come up fifteen minutes after practice to confirm that I could still do it. And if we were struggling or the car had problems, I had told them I couldn't do it. For every two or three races I broadcast, I had to miss one because we weren't running well.

Broadcasting for me was like golfing for a lot of people—it was challenging and fun, and I enjoyed the heck out of it. In those first few years, being a full-time broadcaster was the farthest thing from my mind, and I wasn't sure where it was leading. But I told Linda, "I don't know how, but I think this is going to pay off some time."

The New Hampshire triple-header featured the truck race, a race for the NASCAR Modified Division, and a Busch North stock-car race. As Ernie and I flew up there, we said nothing about the hollow victory lane ceremony we'd just had. I don't think Ernie realized that Robert hadn't been in victory lane, and I wasn't about to tell him. I focused on my upcoming marathon broadcast. And a marathon it was. Mike Joy, Buddy Baker, and I were in the booth for about seven hours. The only breaks we got were during commercials. We did three races in a row. After it was over, Buddy and I raced each other for the bathroom.

The next Winston Cup race was at Dover. In Saturday's final practice, we discovered we had a good car. Ernie took the lead for the first time on lap 98. On lap 199, Ernie had been leading for 35 laps when he went to lap Derrike Cope in turns three and four. Derrike got into Ernie and put him in the wall. We destroyed another race car. That was the second car we had crashed at Dover in 1996.

After we loaded the car, the guys wanted to beat the traffic to the airport. "C'mon," they said.

"I'll wait and leave with the 88 crew," I replied.

Why wouldn't I leave early while the getting was good? I was so upset with Derrike I decided to stick around and get in his face after the race. I didn't care how long I had to wait. I hung out next to the infield care center, figuring he'd eventually show up there. Lo and behold, with about 100 laps to go, Derrike tore up his car in another wreck. He arrived at the care center to be checked out. When he came out, I was all over him.

"What's your problem with the 28 car?!" I screamed, grabbing his arm. We both unleashed a stream of expletives at each other. At first, only one person separated us. I began to realize I might have bitten off more than I could chew. Other NASCAR officials arrived, and I was thankful they did, because I might still be recovering from injuries. My ambush made Derrike irate. MRN Radio was getting ready to interview him, and the pit reporter described the confrontation. My guys were on the team airplane, listening to the radio, when they heard, "Here comes Larry McReynolds!" They couldn't believe what I was doing.

NASCAR hauled us into their trailer and pretty much read me the riot act. I got yet another version of the old "you need the sport more than the sport needs you" routine. But the NASCAR trailer had a revolving door that day, and about 48 hours later NASCAR announced fines for Jimmy Spencer, Kyle Petty, and Michael Waltrip for their temper tantrums. Theirs had been aired on television. I was not fined; my blowup had only made the radio. Later in the week, I realized what a fool I had been by getting into Derrike's face. I wrote him and the entire Allison team a letter of apology and requested that it be posted in their shop. Several of Derrike's guys later thanked me for it.

At Charlotte in early October, we had a brand new car for Ernie. Late in Happy Hour we decided to try a different set of shocks. Ernie went back out, blew a tire, and hit the wall hard. Ernie was OK, but we had to go to a backup car and he didn't run well in the race. On lap 209, Ernie spun in turn two. Robby Gordon, trying to make it past on the high side, tore off the right front of Ernie's car. That impact spun him back around into the lower groove. John Andretti, trying to get by on the low side, T-boned Ernie.

I went into that all-too-familiar routine.

"Ernie, you OK buddy?"

Our spotter interjected, "Larry, he took a pretty hard shot on the left door."

"Ernie, can you hear me?" I asked.

Ernie didn't reply.

Once again, I ran to the infield care center. As I ran, I saw the impact from Andretti's car on a replay on the big television screen in the infield. It scared me to death. But when I got to the infield care center, Ernie was alert. He was talking, but groggy. Ernie was taken to Carolinas Medical Center as a precaution. When I got there and saw him, it was obvious he'd had a concussion, because he had a bad headache and was vomiting. I was pretty scared for Ernie because he had taken two hard shots in two days. But X-rays and a CAT scan showed no more injuries.

By then, I'd already decided to leave Robert Yates Racing. It was not only the problem at Talladega and the joyless victory lane at Richmond. I'd painted myself into a corner. I am the world's worst when it comes to saying, "I can do that." I never say no. But in 1996, I took on too much. And I wasn't smart enough to say, "Guys, I can't keep taking these responsibilities on. I need some help." Robert probably would have given me that help if I had asked for it.

While trying to be the No. 28 crew chief, I also was trying to be team manager for both teams. I had to make sure all the tests were booked and that everybody had an airplane seat and a bed to sleep in and that all the wives had wives' passes at the track.

Robert had secretaries, of course, but you had to tell them what you wanted. I didn't actually book flights, but I had to go over the plans or make sure they knew that this guy's per diem was due or that guy was no longer on the payroll. I painted myself in the corner by accepting that job, and it burned me out very fast.

Of course, it didn't help that the crew chief I had hired didn't want to cooperate with me. From when I hired Todd to the time I left, trying to keep the 28 and 88 teams working together felt to me like I had two cords, and I had to stretch them to their max to keep them plugged into each other. Then I had to stand there and hold them together. I just couldn't hold them any longer. During the last third of the season, I had to make myself put both feet on the floor in the morning when the alarm went off. I knew then that, no matter how much I was making, I needed to be doing something different.

I talked to Robert at Martinsville in September 1996, two weeks after our victory at Richmond. Our motorcoaches were parked side by side in the lot behind turn one. After the race, I stopped in and told him, "Robert, I just don't think I'm going to be with you next year." Robert looked kind of surprised, but I think he was expecting it, too.

I never went out and pursued other opportunities. I didn't even nose around before I talked with Robert. Money certainly wasn't the issue. Remember, in 1995, I had turned down a million dollars from Felix Sabates to become his crew chief. That was a million dollars *just to go there*. We didn't even discuss salary.

Anyway, a couple of months after I told Robert at Martinsville that I didn't think I would be returning, Winston Cup Director Gary Nelson came up to me at Rockingham. Happy Hour was over and the garage was getting ready to close. Gary kind of just stood there, and I wondered what the heck he wanted.

"Ah, I don't need to get in the middle of this deal," Gary said.

"What the hell are you talking about, Gary?"

"I came over here to share something with you, but I don't know why I've gotten myself in the middle of this deal."

"Gary, what's on your mind?"

"Well, there's a race team that is very interested in you being their crew chief. They want to talk with you. And I'm talking about one of the best teams in this garage area across the board."

Then he added, "Childress and Earnhardt want to talk to you."

"Well, OK," I said. "All they gotta do then is track me down and call me up."

In the meantime, Linda had managed to come up with two tickets to one of the World Series games in Atlanta, which she presented to me as an anniversary present. She had worked through Danny Lawrence, the engine tuner on Dale Earnhardt's team, who was friends with Ned Yost, the Atlanta pitching coach. So we flew down to Atlanta to see game three on Tuesday evening. The next morning we were to fly to Las Vegas to meet Robert and Carolyn before flying over to Phoenix. When we got to our seats for the game between the Braves and New York Yankees, we found Dale Earnhardt's daughter, Kelley, and one of her friends sitting beside us.

About halfway through the game, Kelley got on her cell phone. I thought, "Why in the world would you bring your cell phone to a ball game? And who in the world could you need to talk to?"

No sooner did I think that than she handed me the phone. "Here," she said, "Somebody wants to talk to you."

"Hello?" I asked.

"This is Dale. What are you doing?"

"I'm at the World Series. What are you doing?"

"Listen, are you going to do this damn deal with me? You need to do it, Larry. I'm telling you, you need to come do it. You just need to tell Richard you're going to do it, and you need to tell him how much money you want and let's get this deal done and let's get going."

"Well, I understand, Dale, but I'm just trying to figure out . . . "

"What do you need to figure out!" he interrupted. "All you need to figure out is that you need to come over and do this deal."

"I need to figure out if I really need to leave the 28 car."

"Well, Irvan ain't gonna be there forever, you know. You've been there long enough. C'mon over and do this deal with me."

When we got to Phoenix, I was standing near the back of our truck by myself when Earnhardt walked up.

"Richard talk to you?"

"Well, yeah," I said. "We talked a little bit."

"Man, please come do that deal," Dale said. "Help me get that deal turned around. Man, Larry, I know we can win some races and we can win some championships."

I told him I was still trying to decide whether I really wanted to leave Robert Yates Racing. But as far as what I could bring to his team, I felt the same as Dale. I thought to myself, "If I can just take half of what I've got over to Earnhardt, it'll snowball with his talent."

I met formally with Dale's car owner, Richard Childress, for the first time at the season finale at Atlanta. We discussed a lot of things. We talked about what Richard felt was missing from the race team. He thought the team needed stronger leadership and somebody who could work closely with Dale and understand what he was trying to say.

"Dale is not going to be the easiest driver to read," Richard said. "He's not going to be one who comes in there and tells you to put a 1,800-pound spring in the right front. He's going to tell you what the car is doing, and you're going to have to read in it. And you're going to have to fix it."

"Well, that's basically what I did with Ernie," I said. "I love that kind of challenge."

Richard and I never discussed money at that meeting. Don't get me wrong, money was important to me. But it wasn't the most important thing. I wanted to go somewhere where I felt like we could win races and have a chance at a championship. Most importantly, I wanted to go somewhere where I could be happy. When that alarm went off in the morning, I wanted to jump out of bed and hit the floor running like I used to.

"Richard," I said, "I still need to do a little soul-searching. You know, the 28 car is my home and it's been a special place."

"OK," he said. "But we're leaving for Japan here right away, so let's try to get the deal done."

The opportunity to work with Earnhardt was all I could think about during the trip across the Pacific for the exhibition race in Japan in late November. While over there, Richard and I tried to sneak away into a little smoking room they had in the hotel in Suzuka, but while we were in there talking, I think just about every person related to NASCAR who was in Japan walked by that room. But I needed to ask Richard a few more questions. Did he think most of the guys were going to stay? What was the plan with David Smith, who had been the crew chief?

Richard told me Dale had a lot of faith in David, but not necessarily as the leader of the team. On the other hand, they'd won a couple of races together and finished fourth in points. I wondered what the real weakness was with the team. The next day, I was walking out of the garage when Dale walked by. He grabbed me by the arm, spun me around, and said, "How long is it going to take you to make up your mind on this deal. I want you to come do this deal! I'm telling you, you *need* to come do it."

"I talked to Richard last night," I said. "I told him I would call him when we got back from Japan, and I'd have an answer for y'all then."

"OK," Dale said. "But I'm telling you, you need to come do this deal."

Dale was always nice about it, but overwhelming. It was pretty flattering that a driver of his stature—in my eyes probably the greatest race car driver ever to grip a steering wheel—was on that much of a mission to get me. We were on the same flight home as Dale's team was. They didn't work on me, but they were all over my poor wife. Every time I'd get up to go to the bathroom, I'd come back to find one of them sitting in my seat telling her that she needed to convince me to come work for them.

That flight was miserable. All the way back, I agonized over what decision to make. One thing that didn't bother me at all was the prospect of the long commute from Mooresville to Welcome—one hour one way. That didn't bother me a bit. In fact, I never even saw Welcome until after I took the job. The agony for me was the thought of actually splitting with Robert. It all boiled down to leaving that 28 car.

The main reason it was so hard for me to leave Robert Yates Racing is that Robert Yates Racing is what put Larry McReynolds on the map in NASCAR. I had gone from "who's Larry McReynolds?" to being the person that many people considered to be the top crew chief in the sport. I was unknown in 1989, but by 1996, no matter where I went—the grocery store, movies, some place with the kids—people would come up and want to talk about racing and the 28 car. That team had gone through so much as a group, and the nucleus had stayed the same— Raymond Fox, Gary Beveridge, Norman Koshimizu, and Joey Knuckles. We had gone through so much, and by clinging together we had always made it through. Walking away from those kinds of relationships is very difficult.

After we got back from Japan, Linda's parents came in for the long Thanksgiving weekend. They told Linda that when they first arrived, they thought we were having trouble in our marriage. You could cut the tension with a knife. But we weren't having trouble. It was me, agonizing over what to do, and Linda was agonizing with me. Linda discussed the pros and cons, but she never suggested that I do this or that. Her attitude was "Whatever makes you happy, the kids and I will adapt."

It was hard to contemplate leaving Robert after the many wonderful times we'd had together. On Christmas Day, after the kids had opened their presents, we wouldn't go see the relatives, we'd go to Robert's house.

When Doug Yates was married in 1993, our entire family was in the wedding. I was a groomsman; Linda was a bridesmaid; Brandon was ring bearer; and Brooke was flower girl. Even though my relationship with Robert had deteriorated, I wasn't sure that I was willing to give up on it.

Back in Mooresville, I finally decided, "I'm not going to take the job. I'm going to sort out my problem with Robert. I'll just go in there and tell Robert, 'Let's make our minds up—am I going to be team manager for both teams or am I going to be crew chief for the 28 car? I can't do both anymore.'"

After all, my predicament wasn't Robert's fault. I just kept taking stuff on and wasn't smart enough to say, "No more!" After all we'd overcome—losing Davey and almost losing Ernie—surely we could figure out how to fix *this* problem.

Then I received a telephone call from Bobby Hutchins, the team engineer and general manager at Richard Childress Racing. It was the evening before Thanksgiving. Bobby worked me over pretty hard to take the deal. About halfway through that two-hour chat, it struck me: there was no way I *couldn't* do the deal with Dale. I'm not sure it was anything Bobby said. I came to the realization that the opportunity with Dale Earnhardt—the driver who had won more Winston Cup championships than anyone except Richard Petty—was one I couldn't turn down. Plus, the Earnhardt crew—the entire team—wanted *me* as their crew chief.

It was a no-brainer. I was unhappy as hell where I was. The team that wanted me was solid as a rock. All I had to do was walk in that shop and take the bull by the horns. With Dale's talent, it would just be a matter of time before I won a Winston Cup championship. Even better, I'd be helping the sport's greatest driver win his eighth championship, which would be a record.

I met with Richard Friday at his condo at Charlotte Motor Speedway and accepted the job. He matched my salary, but it seemed to be a difficult pill to swallow. There's no question I was making as much or more than every Winston Cup crew chief in 1996. I don't think it's proper to go into my own figures, but I can tell you that top crew chiefs in the Winston Cup series today make upwards of $600,000, or even a bit more.

I left Robert Yates Racing in November, just after the season ended. I left on fairly decent terms, although Robert and I really didn't speak for more than a year. On the evening I packed up my stuff, Ernie was there, as well as Doug Yates. They gave me a hard time. A calendar on the wall happened to show a picture of Dale Earnhardt. "Look at him smiling," Ernie said. "He knows what he's done over here."

I started work with Richard on December 15, but I spent the last week of November just hanging out at his shop in Welcome. I learned a lot about the place. I learned about the people and could see their good morale. I learned about the structure of the place, and I realized it was going to be very different than what I was used to. On that first day there, I looked up around 4:15 p.m., and the place was almost empty.

"Where did everybody go?" I asked Bobby Hutchins.

"They get off at four," he said.

And they were gone at four.

Bobby assured me, "They do everything they need to do." But the schedule was one of the hardest things to get used to. Everybody started at seven, but the guys on the road got off at four, while everyone else got off at five. It was far more regimented than at Robert Yates Racing. One of the first things I saw was a time clock. A time clock? It blew my mind. I'd never seen a time clock at a race shop. I think Richard had been advised that he'd better get one or the government might come down hard on him. Everyone was on a 45-hour workweek, and Richard paid overtime to the regular team members. And he kept pressure on Bobby Hutchins and David Smith to *keep* from paying overtime.

At Yates's, we had a set time we went to work—7 a.m.—but we really didn't have a set time to leave. We just kind of worked, and when it felt good to leave, we left. Usually that wasn't before 7 or 8 p.m. At RCR, the road crew usually took Tuesdays off. At Yates, the only days off would be on the off weekends.

Like Robert, Richard had two Winston Cup teams. Besides Dale Earnhardt's No. 3 team, Richard had Mike Skinner in the No. 31 Lowe's Chevrolet. Richard had more employees than Robert—probably 100 or more compared to 70 or 80 at the Yates shop. Richard's two teams were somewhat separate, and he often had different people doing the same job—one for one team and the other for the second team. Richard, for instance, had two body shops, and Robert had one shop doing the same work for both teams.

I didn't understand the regimented schedule at Richard Childress Racing when I first went to work there. But by the time I left four years later, I had learned just how important it was to have some discipline with the schedule. Richard was one of the biggest promoters of having a life besides racing. He pounded this into me for four years. He got on me because I never took a vacation longer than a few days. I never took a week off—maybe a three- or four-day weekend during Christmas. But Richard would try to give everyone a week off during Christmas and a week during the summer as well.

One Christmas after I'd been there a couple of years, Richard was adamant about everybody taking a week. He told me, "You *will* take a week. You will not come to this place. Larry, you've *got* to do that. If you don't, you'll be burned out before you're 40."

You know what? He was 100 percent right. I learned from Richard that you could have a good race team and a good operation but also have some solid structure to it, with good scheduling and good planning.

Many a night at Robert Yates Racing, nine guys would be there at midnight while we were setting a car up. Two would be doing the work, and seven of them would be watching. I wasn't smart enough to say, "Why are you here? Go home and be with your families. Get some rest." For some reason, I thought everybody needed to be there. It took me a while to get acclimated to the RCR way of doing things, but two things helped. One, I saw that it could work, and, two, I saw how I needed it.

I realized I had a little boy who was growing up really fast, and all he wanted from his daddy was to play pitch for a little bit, or watch TV with him—just a little time. And I realized I had a little girl who was growing up really fast, and all she wanted was for her dad to go to her dance recitals every once in awhile. Our youngest, Kendall, was born in September 1997. She really didn't know she had a daddy when she was a baby. When she would get up in the morning, Dad had already gone to Welcome. And many, many nights when Dad got home, Kendall was already in bed.

I guess it just dawned on me one day that I was missing out on a lot of really important things, and I probably needed to become a partner in Richard's way of doing things. So I did. And it meant a lot to our kids.

CHAPTER EIGHTEEN

A Season of Frustration
Gets Under Way

When it came to the specialized racing in the restrictor plate events at Daytona and Talladega, it was often said that Dale Earnhardt could literally see the air. As his crew chief, I came to believe it. He was incredible at those two tracks. After all the testing we did in January of 1997, when we finally got to Speedweeks, I couldn't wait to get up on top of the transporter to watch him. And Dale didn't disappoint me. He wasn't happy until he got his car at the front of the pack, leading every practice session.

In my first race at Daytona with Dale, the Budweiser Shootout, he finished third. Then we moved on to the 125-mile qualifying race. Dale powered past John Andretti on lap 19 and led the rest of the way. I'm sure glad they didn't tell me until afterward that Dale had won seven 125s in a row going into that race. I would have worried myself to death thinking I'd be the crew chief who broke the streak.

"If you can get a streak going like this, it's history, and it's history I don't know if anybody else can match or will match," Dale told the press.

We moved ahead to the Daytona 500. But on the morning of the race, I had to do one of the toughest things I've ever had to do as a crew chief. I had to take two guys off the team for violating team rules. I had always laid down the law when it came to after-hours social lives. I didn't have a curfew, but they had to use their heads. If they wanted to go to a bar and have a couple beers after dinner, fine. But the night before a race, I wanted them in bed by 10 or 11. They were athletes who were going out the next day to change tires and tighten lug nuts, and the driver depended upon the lug nuts being tight. The crew had to be sharp and fresh. Guys who say they can party the night away before a race and don't need a full night's sleep are full of it.

I was at the track at six o'clock on race morning. At about 7:45 or 8 a.m., I noticed that I hadn't seen two of the guys—a tire changer and a tire carrier. I asked Rich Burgess, a mechanic who was also our travel liaison, where they were. I could tell from the look on his face that he wasn't ready for me to ask that question.

He said, "You mean they aren't here?"

"No, they aren't here," I said. I asked him if he had knocked on their door. He told me they had just about knocked the door down. Finally, at about nine that morning, those two showed up as if nothing had happened. They told me they woke up late.

"Don't bullshit me," I said. "You guys weren't even back to your room when they were knocking early this morning." They insisted they were.

I could tell by their eyes they had been out all night partying. I told them my call was that they would not go across pit wall for the race. I said I'd talk to Richard, but that's what I was going to recommend. Richard looked at me with a raised eyebrow. He told me I was the crew chief and would have to make the decision. I knew all eyes would be watching me. All I could think about was how a month or so earlier Lou Holtz, the coach at Notre Dame, who I greatly respected, had left his star running back at home and out of the Sugar Bowl because the player had broken curfews. That's the way I viewed this. I made the call: they would not go across the wall. They begged and pleaded. I told them they knew the rules, so the consequences shouldn't surprise them.

We didn't have very good pit stops that day. We mixed and matched between Richard's two teams. Somehow ol' Earnhardt bailed us out. He was leading with 15 laps to go. I walked up to Richard and said, "What do you think?"

"Larry, I've been here too many times," he said. Richard had stood there in the pits for every one of Dale's long catalog of late-race misfortunes in the Daytona 500. Dale had nearly won it so many times, and had lost it every way you could imagine.

Three laps later, when the No. 3 car was upside down on the backstretch, I understood what Richard was talking about. I watched a replay of the wild wreck on the television monitor in our pit. The car had finally landed on its wheels and spun to a stop. Dale was out of the car, so I headed back toward the garage.

I was just about out of the pits when I noticed, out of the corner of my eye, a car go by on pit road. And it was that black No. 3 car! What the . . . ? Several crew guys were with me. We all turned and ran back to the pits. When we got there, poor Dale was sitting there almost alone. Richard was still there, as well as John Hester, a good friend of his. They were trying to duct tape that thing back together. NASCAR was raising hell because the roof flaps were torn up. But we got that car fixed, and we finished that race with a car that was the damnedest mess you've ever seen.

Just before the wreck, Dale's car had become loose again, as it had so many other times at the end of the Daytona 500. The only reason Dale was able to hang on so long was that he was a master at driving a loose car. This time, part of the problem was that, in order to maintain track position, we had given him only two tires on his final pit stop on lap 166.

By lap 189, Dale had slipped to second, with Jeff Gordon behind him. As the pack came off turn two, Jeff got right up under Dale's bumper. The No. 3 car skated and smacked the outside wall, then bounced off Jeff's car, turned sideways, and got into the air. It twirled around and flipped back over on all four wheels.

Before Dale got out, he told me on the radio that he was OK. Then he unbuckled, hopped out, and walked to the ambulance. Dale described what happened next: "I got in the ambulance, and I looked back at the car and I said, 'Man, the wheels is still on that thing.' I got out of the ambulance and asked the guy inside the car who was hooking it up, I said, 'See if it will crank.' And he cranked it up. I said, 'Get out of there. Give me my car back.' So I drove it back around over here, and we taped it up."

We didn't gain any positions, but we put six more laps on the car. Afterward, a guy came up to the side door of the hauler and asked me if we had any hats. I told him we didn't. He said, "I'm the guy who was over there trying to load up the three car after the wreck, and Earnhardt told me to get the hell out of it because he was getting back in."

I found him a hat.

We left Daytona with a 31st place finish. A good finish at Daytona or Talladega is always a crapshoot, so I wasn't discouraged. Dale and Richard had backed me on my discipline of the two crew members. We fired one later that week, and the other soon quit.

The next race was at Rockingham. Dale got around that track pretty well. In fact, he was the defending race champion. And I did well there, too. In my final Rockingham race with Robert, our cars had finished second and fourth. We were both looking forward to it. But we were terrible in practice. And we qualified poorly—27th. I'd always watched Dale run so well at the Rock. Now Dale and I couldn't get around the track together. I was much more discouraged than Dale. He was calm and patient about it.

But I was learning, too. It took me a few races to figure out there was definitely a big difference between the Chevy body and the Ford body. The bodies were aerodynamically different, the Chevrolet had a different balance than the Ford. It required an entirely different chassis setup.

I also quickly learned that Dale's driving style was much different than, say, Dale Jarrett's, in terms of the feel he was looking for in a race car. Dale Earnhardt loved to drive a car deep into the turn with the throttle, while Dale Jarrett likes to back off the throttle early but pick it up sooner coming out of the turn. It didn't take me long to see that my old notes from Robert Yates Racing were not going to work. I might as well toss them out and start a new book.

Dale finished 11th at Rockingham. He was the last driver on the lead lap. After the race, he didn't leave with his usual speediness but stuck around. "We just had a tight race car all day—an aero push," he said. "We adjusted all day, but we never could get the front end to do what we wanted it to do. We're still struggling a little bit. We had a change on the pit crew and we're still adjusting to that. But Larry and I work well together, and we'll get 'em at Richmond."

I dreaded going to Richmond. It's not that I hadn't run well there. I'd won at Richmond three times with two different drivers. I always had a pretty good package there. Dale probably wasn't as good at Richmond as some other tracks. But my dread came from how badly we had tested there in late January. We had the same car Dale drove there in 1996. It hadn't been good then, and it wasn't any better at the test. On the final day, we were still slower than Steve Grissom, who was not in a first-line Chevy.

When we returned for the race, we struggled in practice. But qualifying was rained out, so we started fourth. The starting lineup was based on 1996 owner points. If we'd had to qualify, I doubt we would have made the top 25.

On race day, we ran terribly and finished 25th, three laps down. Dale was so disgusted with the car, he told Ray Cooper, Chevy's PR representative: "We're probably going to take it out of rotation and make it a show car."

I rode back to Mooresville with Dale and Teresa on their jet. We just looked at each other, scratched our heads, and said, "Man, how could we miss it that bad?" I am not exaggerating to say that if we had purposely tried to set up the car as badly as possible, we couldn't have done a much worse job than the setup we used at Richmond.

Dale was always a terrible qualifier. When I started work at RCR, I had announced, "We're going to get this qualifying straightened out."

The whole team looked at me skeptically. "Yeah, right," someone said. "We've been trying for 15 years, and we *never* got it straightened out."

Dale was a rhythm racer. He couldn't just go out there and rip off a fast lap. But if Winston Cup qualifying had been Formula One–style— where the drivers go out and run as many laps as they wish for an hour and take their fastest lap—there's no telling how many poles Dale would have won. Many drivers win more poles than races. Dale won 76 races and only 22 poles. We didn't win any together, and he didn't win any after I left. Dale's last pole was at Watkins Glen in 1996. What was confusing was it didn't look like Dale was trying as hard as he could. Sometimes when my mind drifted, I wondered, "Does Dale care anymore?" But I'd tell myself, "No, no. It just can't be."

At a track like Bristol, for instance, most drivers would almost hold their breath during qualifying. They were so close to the edge they were afraid that breathing would throw off that delicate balance they'd achieved with the car, and they'd crash. Mike Skinner would be absolutely out of breath after qualifying at Bristol. I'd ask him how the lap was, and he'd say, "Hold on a minute. I'll tell you when I catch my breath." Mark Martin was the same way. I'd tell Dale, "These guys are so on the edge and so close to being out of control, they're out of breath after it's over."

"I don't know what they're doing," he'd say. "I don't care what they're doing. I'm not worried about that. That's just all I could do."

Time and time again in 1997, Dale came into the garage and saw me sitting by the car with my head in my hands. He'd reach down and lift my chin up and say, "Larry, you don't need to panic. You need to calm down. We're going to be OK."

Richard was as lost as I was. But I think Richard had an inkling about the source of some of the trouble. I think Richard knew deep down that Dale was not feeling 100 percent physically. I never had a clue and didn't find out about his physical problems until years later. I always thought it was the car when Dale said, "I just don't feel comfortable."

Another thing that caused us problems was NASCAR's new "five and five" rule for the 1997 season, which was announced at about the same time I joined RCR. NASCAR increased the gap between the front air dam and the ground to five inches. And they cut the rear spoilers down to five inches. Both moves were designed to make the race cars a little slower and a little less stable, which they hoped would promote better racing.

At first, Richard was thrilled with the new rules. He knew Dale was the master of driving a loose car. "When all of 'em start sliding those race cars around, Dale's going to love it," he said. "This is just giving him a license to steal."

But as it turned out, Dale loved sliding around when Goodyear was using bias-ply tires, which react much differently than the radial tires that Goodyear had been using since 1991. When you go into a corner and turn the wheel on a bias-ply tire, the car might start to push, but then you'd just turn the wheel a little more and the car would bite. And if you got loose on bias-ply tires, you'd turn the wheel back to the right a little bit until the tail end bit in and then you'd go on. In both cases, you could still stay on the gas.

But with the radial tire, the only way to correct the car if it pushes or if it's loose is to let off the gas and slow down. On radial tires, if you try to correct a tight or a loose car by steering it and staying on the gas, it will just get tighter or looser. The bias-ply tire is far more forgiving.

Dale had adapted well to the radial and won a ton of races on them. By the time the radial tires were introduced, the cars were a lot better aerodynamically and had good rear downforce, which was critical for Dale's style of driving deep into the corners while still on the throttle. But when that spoiler was cut down after 1996 and the air dam was raised, Dale just didn't like the feel of the car with that much less rear downforce. It's hard to drive deep into the corners with a lack of rear downforce. The car will slip suddenly. We both realized this, and soon Richard was saying, "You know, Larry, I was dead wrong about that. Dale don't like sliding around on those radials."

The season's fourth race was at Atlanta Motor Speedway. It was the last race run on the old one-and-a-half-mile true oval. In 1996, Dale had won the spring race. He'd won Rockingham and Atlanta back-to-back just one year earlier. And he'd finished second in the fall event at Atlanta. Dale Earnhardt owned Atlanta. But we were 25th fastest and struggling after the first practice. We made a gear change and a spring change before pole qualifying, and Dale was almost a half-second slower than he was in practice. The changes had made his car worse. It was a nightmare. He was 43rd fastest of 49 cars.

We ran terribly in the race, even though Dale managed to salvage an eighth-place finish on the lead lap. But he was no threat to the leaders. His car skated, pushed, and slid through the turns. He hated the way the car felt with that smaller spoiler and those radial tires. Still, we had the highest-finishing Chevrolet, and the fact that the Chevys had fared so poorly against the Fords was what Richard and Dale were angry about. We all felt that NASCAR had made too many rule concessions to the Ford camp.

"They . . . give, give, give to the Fords," Dale complained to the media. "I hadn't said much about it in awhile, but it's ridiculous right now." I agreed. But it was still personally frustrating. I knew how much Dale loved to run at Atlanta, and I couldn't even make him competitive, much less a winner.

Before the next race, at Darlington, NASCAR took away some of Ford's advantage by ordering that their spoilers be trimmed by a quarter inch and their front air dams be raised by .125 of an inch. It certainly wasn't enough to make up the disparity, but I respected NASCAR's policy of making incremental changes, erring on the side of caution and giving too little rather than too much.

On Monday, March 17, six days before the Darlington race, Ray Cooper called for my reaction to the NASCAR rule change. I told him it wasn't enough, but it was a start. Ray and I ended up talking not only about the rules, but about my struggle at Richard Childress Racing. We even talked about my moonlighting career as a racing broadcaster. I had just returned from Las Vegas, where I had covered the inaugural Busch series race at the new Las Vegas Motor Speedway. I had worked in the booth with Eli Gold and Buddy Baker and had enjoyed every minute of it.

I told Ray how much I liked broadcasting. "It's nice reporting on these people screwing up and making mistakes rather than being the guy who's doing it," I said.

Ray asked me about the timing of my career move in light of the current advantage enjoyed by Ford. "It's been an adjustment working on the Chevrolet," I admitted. "The chassis are a little bit different. The engines are a little bit different. The car is obviously different. It's like the only thing that's the same is it's got four wheels."

The front end of the Monte Carlo was much more sensitive to downforce than the Ford. We were always messing with the right front fender to get the front end to plant correctly in the turns. Getting it right was like trying to walk on the edge of a razor blade.

Despite those differences, Dale and Richard and I had agreed to use my notes for Darlington. We set up the car the way I'd set them up at Robert Yates Racing. "When we get to Darlington, the only thing different in the way Larry sets it up and the way he set up that 28 and 88 last year will be the Chevrolet Monte Carlo body with a Chevrolet engine," Dale told Cooper.

Darlington was the fifth race of the season, and that meant a change in the garage that was another small psychological blow. For the first four races, the transporters had been parked according to 1996 car owner points. So we had been parked fourth, near the front. Starting at Darlington, the transporters were to park according to current car owner points. We were 16th in points. And I remember thinking, "What in the world? I've never seen the three transporter parked this far down the line in my whole career!"

Darlington, where Dale had won nine times, was an even bigger disaster than Atlanta. In the first practice, we were 40th out of 46 cars. It was getting to the point where if Richard Childress had hired me and said, "You're job is to go to the racetrack every week and make Dale

Earnhardt as *bad* as possible," I'd be getting bonuses and raises for out-standing performance because I was doing that job to perfection.

After pole qualifying, we were still 40th fastest. The track was slower on Saturday, so we stood on our Friday time and ended up 39th, which meant we didn't qualify. Only the fastest 38 cars qualified. Dale took the provisional starting spot at Darlington, reserved for former Winston Cup champions, which meant we started the race 43rd and dead last.

But Dale was cool about it. He always had the attitude that we were going to find the solution, even though he was as lost as I was. He just didn't feel so threatened, and he certainly wasn't panicking over it like I was. I'd go crazy every weekend and finally, around Tuesday, would get over it.

The race itself at Darlington was no better for us than the rest of the weekend. Dale finished 15th, a lap down. "These guys have been working their guts out the last three or four weeks, and nothing has gone our way," Dale said afterward. "We need to turn this thing around, and hopefully we'll be able to do it in Texas."

Easter came before the inaugural Interstate Batteries 500 at Texas Motor Speedway, so I scheduled a test before the off weekend. The week before an off weekend is a good time to test. You can adequately pre-pare without the pressure of a race that weekend. But this was a violation of the rules of Dale Earnhardt. Richard told me, "Don't book any tests on the off weekends or during the days before or after an off weekend." Dale usually reserved the off weekends for the Bahamas, where he relaxed on his boat.

Actually, Dale had invited Linda and me down there to the Bahamas many times, but I just never found the time to do it. I probably should have. But with the way we were running, I always felt like I needed to be working on that race car rather than trying to relax in the Bahamas.

If we had been running good, it might have been a different story. Looking back, I wish I had taken a couple of days and gone down there with him.

Anyway, we got in a bind with the Texas test. I said, "Dale, I know your deal about testing. But Monday and Tuesday after the Easter off weekend is the only time we can get the racetrack at Texas." He wasn't very happy about it, but he agreed to fly in on Monday morning. The team flew in Sunday night. And when we got up Monday morning, it was monsoon outside. Dale arrived at 10 and was really irritated.

"Why didn't you call me and tell me it was raining?" he growled.

"Dale, you were *how* many miles away?" I said. "What difference would it have made? You still needed to come here. Did you want me to call you when the track dried and then you'd come?"

We finally got on the track early that afternoon. I had a good test program using two cars. I planned to work on the body and the aerodynamics of one car and the engine and chassis on the other. I always had a good methodical plan, trying A, B, C, D, and E to see what worked. Dale didn't have a lot of patience with that. He'd look at one combination and say, "What do you want to try *that* for? That's never worked."

"Dale, it's a different track, a different year, and a different car. We need to try it again."

Once he grabbed my list and went through his own checklist. "We tried that and it don't work," he said. "That one has never worked. I don't like that one. We tried that one before. And this one we ain't tried yet. We're almost done with this test."

I started to realize that the less-demanding work standards at RCR began with the driver. Dale had told me, "Now at three o'clock on Tuesday, I'm done. Because the little fly-in airport down in the Bahamas that I'm flying into don't have runway lights, so you can't land down there after dark."

By Tuesday, we were making headway. I was standing on top of the transporter and Dale was making runs. He made a few laps and came into the garage.

"Dale," I asked on the radio, "what did that feel like?"

No response.

"Dale, you got me? What did the car feel like that time?"

No response.

By the time I got down off of the truck, Dale was up in the lounge, changing clothes. My car chief, Jimmy Elledge, pointed to his watch. It was three o'clock. Dale hadn't answered me because he already had taken off his helmet and radio earpieces and was loosening his belts. He was just about out of the window as the car had come to a stop. He answered my questions with very few words as he hurriedly changed clothes. All he had on his mind was getting to the airport.

When we got back to Texas for the race weekend, we struggled again. Fortunately, and I do mean fortunately, qualifying was rained out. So we started by points, which meant we started 15th. During that rainy Friday morning on pole day, a reporter asked me if I'd ever guessed my debut at RCR could be this difficult.

"You couldn't have hit me between the eyes any harder with a clawhammer and caught me off guard or surprised me as much as I have been surprised with the first five races of the season," I said. "But I still see the light. It's not like we're looking at each other saying, 'What in the world should we do?' We know what we need to be working on. And we need to be working on a little bit of everything."

When the race started Sunday, Darrell Waltrip tried to go around the outside of everyone on this one-groove track. He spun and took about half the field with him. The next day, local newspapers had a picture of both of Richard Childress's cars crashing. It was almost like they were in sync, spinning the same way at the same time.

Dale went a lap down because of the accident. It really didn't hurt the car a whole lot. We got the car fixed and later got our lap back. We got better and better and ended up finishing sixth on the lead lap. As Dale said afterward, "Sixth place isn't what we're after, but it's better than where we've been."

It was hard to imagine I could feel so good about such a finish. I told the media, "We can reach it, touch it, and feel it now. We keep climbing the ladder. Now we just need to get this car over to victory lane where it belongs."

Both Dale and I couldn't wait to get to Bristol, because that was another track where he'd always run well. But once again, we were slow in practice and slow in qualifying. Dale started the race 29th. That put us in a pit on the backstretch.

The car was pushing horribly at the beginning of the race. The tires were chattering. Dale was slow. We got a lap down. That's when Dale showed why he was so good. At one point, we were about 10 car lengths behind the leader when a yellow flag came out. The track was halfway blocked in turn four. Dale drove down off the banking, onto the apron and almost into the infield to pass the leader and make his lap up. We stayed on the lead lap, made the car better, clawed up through the field, and finished sixth for the second race in a row. But it still wasn't even a top-five, much less a victory.

The next race was at Martinsville, where I had such a good record. Of course, Dale Earnhardt was always competitive at Martinsville, too. But again we were terrible. We looked like we didn't even know how to make a race car roll down a track. Dale qualified 25th, which meant another backstretch pit. I was starting to question everything—bodies, chassis, motors, crew, myself. When you do this, you usually start making wholesale changes. Before the race, you might change four springs, four shocks, the sway bar, and a gear and move some lead around in the frame rail for good measure. You'd change everything but the roof number. That's what we did at Martinsville and many other tracks in 1997. But 99 percent of the time, in my experience, you don't get good results.

We didn't do too awful at Martinsville, at least compared to how we'd been doing. We finished 12th, on the lead lap. But on the other hand, it wasn't even a top-10. For Dale Earnhardt, that was pathetic.

CHAPTER NINETEEN

At Least We Finished

I n the midst of our struggles, one thing I really wanted Dale to try
was the low-snout chassis that I had had so much success with at
Robert Yates Racing. Dale was not using one, and I knew it would
make him better at flat tracks like Martinsville and New Hampshire.
I wanted one built at RCR in time for Martinsville, but it didn't happen. We didn't even come close to getting it done for Martinsville. It
didn't happen because of the RCR system. In fact, it almost didn't happen for New Hampshire. Bobby Hutchins came to me in late June and
said, "Larry, I'm not sure we're going to get the car done." He pointed
out that Mike Skinner had been tearing up a lot of equipment and that
had put them behind. I wasn't buying that excuse. I finally had to put
my foot down. "One way or another, this low-snout car *will* be ready
for New Hampshire," I said.

It seemed as if the team members were dragging their feet as hard
as they could. They were not anti-Larry, but they were anti-change. So
many times I would hear, "This is how we did it last year." And I'd be

thinking, "I know you all won all those championships, but those flags on the wall are starting to turn yellow. Maybe you need to think about some changes."

But Dale's team was devoted to the RCR system, which was entirely different than what I was used to. If I wanted to cut off the front end of a car at the Yates shop, I'd shove it back to the fab shop, tell them where I wanted it cut, tell them where I wanted the new one put, and announce, "Guys, we've got to have it back in the race shop tomorrow at three." And the guys would swarm all over it. Nobody would ever question it.

At RCR, you had to go through a pecking order to get that done. I began to understand why Lou LaRosa had been able to thrive at RCR. It all made sense when I recalled how Lou had once had eight motors lined up and ready to go when he found some extra horsepower on the dyno with a ninth engine. You didn't even think about asking him to go back and redo the other eight. The ninth motor got the horsepower, and you had to use the others first.

At Yates, we'd all always operated as a team. We'd load the truck together before sending it to the racetrack. But at RCR, the people who loaded the truck were the ones who went to the racetrack. If we didn't get the truck loaded before quitting time at four, I had to make sure I had enough hands around to get it loaded. Time and time again, I'd tell a guy, "Look, we really need you to stay over tonight so we can get loaded by 8 p.m. and on the road." And it wouldn't be anything for them to say, "I've got dinner plans" or "I've got my dirt track car that I have to work on tonight."

I could see that the RCR system was a mountain I wasn't going to be able to move. It was the nature of the place. I think the team members liked me. I don't think they had anything against me personally. But when I started telling them that we needed to lighten the race cars, work on better aerodynamics, and get the motor shop working on finding more horsepower, it was too much for them.

You'd love to go in and do everything that felt right to the race team and have everyone rally around you, but as a crew chief, you can't get into a popularity contest. Then you start doing things that are not right for the team and the car. If I'd just gone with the flow at Richard Childress Racing—just followed the agenda they had before I arrived—everything would have been just fine as far as my relationship with the team. But I don't think our performance would have been good, and it might have been worse than it was. Richard hired me to go in and turn that program around.

For my part, I didn't do enough giving. I probably did a little too much taking. I should have done more to adhere to their system rather than trying to totally change their way of doing things. With some of the things we were doing, it probably didn't matter whether we did it my way or their way—it would have accomplished the same thing. I could have been more open-minded, especially now that I realize the RCR system is much better for providing a life outside racing. And the team could have done without my occasional sarcastic comments such as, "Maybe you guys need to realize why you all are not winning races anymore."

Some guys on the No. 3 team did support me wholeheartedly. Mike Moore would work there with me until three o'clock in the morning if need be. And Jimmy Elledge would act as a sort of intermediary between me and other team members. Jimmy was like my Raymond Fox at Yates. He would hang out and work late with me, too. He was always filling me in on RCR's way of doing things, telling me in a roundabout way, "You're trying to move a mountain that ain't gonna move. Internally, you've got people working harder against you than with you."

It wasn't too long before I had the feeling that even if we won 10 races in a row, the relationship between me and the team just wasn't there. I think Richard saw my point on a lot of issues, but he was kind of torn. He never looked at me and said, "Larry, I know you're the crew chief, but we're going to do things here the way we've always done them." But he also never told Bobby Hutchins, "Look, Larry is the crew chief now, and everyone is going to do things just the way he says."

At times I thought the only salvation was to clean house and start over. But that wasn't going to happen. Richard was very loyal to his employees, and there just weren't very many job-fearing people at his shop. Since no one had to worry about their job, they all began focusing on me as we struggled.

At Talladega, Dale finished second to Mark Martin in a race that was run without a yellow flag after two delays because of rain. I think the only reason we couldn't beat Mark was because of how aggressively they'd set up their shock absorbers to keep their car low to the ground. It gave Mark an extremely rough ride, but he won. Afterward I told Dale, "You might as well prepare yourself for a really rough ride when we come back here, because we're going to have to put some really aggressive shocks on this car."

"I know we got to run 'em," he replied. "But I don't like 'em. I'll be spitting up blood at the end of the day after running 'em."

After Talladega came Charlotte, where we qualified 33rd. I took some comfort in what one of Dale's former crew chiefs, Andy Petree, told me. "There's one day you will always struggle with Dale, and that's qualifying day at Charlotte," he said. In the race, we weren't great, but we weren't terrible. We finished seventh on the lead lap.

Before the Coca-Cola 600, Dale ran in the second round of the International Race of Champions at Charlotte. Dale had told Linda and me that if we wanted we could take the kids up to his condo in turn one and watch the race. So we did. Dale ran terribly in that race. He started ninth and finished eighth.

The veteran Dave Marcis, who did most of the testing of the IROC cars, said he had warned Dale that he couldn't use much brake with the IROC cars because they were sensitive. But as I watched Dale go underneath my vantage point in turn one, I could see that he had used so much brake that the wheel was as black as the tire from brake dust.

It was one of those times during 1997 when I thought, "Maybe it's *not* all me." I had nothing to do with the IROC cars. Dave had told Dale he couldn't use any brake, but still, Dale had used them so much you couldn't tell where the wheel ended and the tire began. After the race, he talked about how bad the car pushed. When you overuse the brakes on any race car, they're going to push.

Sometimes I felt like I was on a little island by myself. About the only person I had on my side was Linda. And she was trying to say the right things. She was trying to help, too. Everything she would suggest, I'd say, "Linda, I've tried that."

The season dragged on. We had to take another champion's provisional at Dover and started 43rd. We finished 16th, three laps down. My relationship with the fans had deteriorated, at least from their point of view. To get out of Dover, you walked underneath the grandstands. I was doused with beer as I walked out. These were the die-hard Chevy fans, and they were screaming, "Go back to Ford." They were accusing Ford of sending me over to screw up Dale.

At Pocono, we finally qualified decently. Dale started 12th. And it looked like we were on our way to our first top-five finish when we dropped a valve with three laps to go. It was really a miracle that we finished, but we crossed the line in 12th.

We finished seventh at Michigan, but the notable thing about that race was that Ernie Irvan won it in the 28 car. This third victory since his comeback, at the track where he nearly lost his life, was particularly satisfying for Ernie and all of his fans. I was really happy for him, too.

Then we headed west for our second inaugural Winston Cup race of the year—this one at the lavish new California Speedway, which was built by Roger Penske at the site of an old steel mill in Fontana, California. The speedways in Texas and California are great examples of the booming growth in NASCAR racing.

Since we came straight from Michigan to California, and the tracks appeared to be the same type of two-mile oval, I put the Michigan setup under the car at California. That was my first mistake. The turns at California are banked at 14 degrees, four degrees less than Michigan. That makes them two entirely different tracks.

NASCAR had given us an extra day of practice because it was a new track. Once again, I had a plan to make the most of that extra practice. I wanted to spend half the day working on our qualifying setup and half the day on the race setup. We went back and forth between the two, and Dale got frustrated. He said, "Damn it, you either have to put me in qualifying trim or put me in race trim. Make your mind up. I can't do both."

Everyone else seemed to be able to do it. But not Dale. That frustrated me to no end. But Andy Petree had warned me: "Larry, some days— usually race days—you'll love him to death. But there are going to be days when you absolutely want to take a ball bat to him. I can tell you from three years of experience that those days are going to be test days, practice days, and sometimes qualifying days."

Dale qualified 14th at California, but in the race we wound up 16th, one lap down. I didn't really figure out until race day how different California was from Michigan. But the race ended up as a fuel mileage race. That's one reason we finished so poorly. We had to pit near the end, and many cars didn't.

By the early summer of 1997, I had become so frustrated and had lost so much confidence that I seriously started thinking I needed a career change. Pam Miller was at our house for dinner one night. "Pam, if you guys had a TV opening that I could come in and take, and I could make close to what I'm making as a crew chief, I'm not so sure I wouldn't walk away from that deal tomorrow and start being a broadcaster for a living instead."

"We'd love to have you, Larry, but you don't need to quit being a crew chief," she said. "I can also tell you that TNN and TBS probably couldn't even pay you half of what you're making now."

A lot of things were stacking up against me. I was mostly frustrated by the inability to give Dale Earnhardt what he needed to run well, much less win. And that seemed to unearth the frustration I still felt over Davey getting killed in the helicopter and Ernie almost dying in the crash at Michigan. I was searching for that magic, that chemistry, that perfect combination of elements—driver, car, crew, owner, crew chief—that I had had with Davey and Ernie.

Richard Childress and I would sometimes talk. He was always telling me to be patient. Richard usually had Bobby Hutchins there when we talked. And they'd try to say things that would make me content and make me feel better about it. But I can't say I left a single one of those meetings feeling much better.

The Pepsi 400 at Daytona marked the halfway point of the Winston Cup season, and because it was a restrictor plate race, Dale didn't have trouble running well. He qualified second, next to our teammate, Mike Skinner. And we finished fourth.

As we headed north to New Hampshire International Speedway for the Jiffy Lube 300 on July 13, I had a real test on my hands. I had demanded that my low-snout car be ready for New Hampshire, and it was. But we didn't get to take it to the wind tunnel for aerodynamic tests, and we didn't get to test it. I went to New Hampshire knowing that, if we ran badly with my low-snout car, I was going to have to eat crow. As they were building the car, I could almost hear them saying, "Dale Earnhardt—he ain't gonna like that type of car. But we'll build it. We'll show Larry." And if Dale did do poorly, I knew I was going to hear, in many roundabout ways, "I told you so."

We qualified 26th, but I knew Dale qualified poorly and the low-snout car qualified poorly. It was hard to get it to stick to the track for the two laps of time trials, but the longer that race went, the better that car got. And that's exactly what happened. There were only two yellow flags, and the longer the race went, the better we got. We finally finished second, about five seconds behind winner Jeff Burton. But trust me, we needed that runner-up finish very badly. And Dale was happy with the low-snout car. He said it gave him the feel he liked and really turned well through the middle of the corners.

After New Hampshire, our season seemed to pick up just a little bit. We qualified fifth for the July race at Pocono. We finished 12th, but that was mostly because Dale tangled with another car early in the race and smashed in a fender. We worked on that car all afternoon, and he managed to stay on the lead lap.

Dale qualified fifth for the Brickyard 400. There were a few places where he had always qualified well, and Indy and Pocono were two of those places. We ran pretty well at Indy, but on lap 84, during a routine four-tire pit stop under a caution period, we had a bad stop. An air hose got caught and ripped, and we had to bring another one over the wall. More than half a minute passed before we got back out. Fifteen laps later we had to bring Dale back in. He had a vibration in the left front. Some of the lug nuts were loose—an after-effect of the air gun problem. We did a four-tire stop and lost more ground. Dale finished two laps down in 29th. It was our worst finish since Richmond in March.

With 13 laps to go at Indy, a yellow flag flew, and I had another one of those unsettling moments with Dale. I was trying to talk to Dale about the car. And Dale was on the radio with his turn three spotter, Mike Collier, who was also his pilot. Dale was telling Mike to get out of that spotter's stand right after the race and meet him at such-and-such a place so they could get out of there.

"Wait a minute, Dale!" I exploded. "You still got a race going on here! You're still racing people out there."

"Oh, calm down, Larry," he said. "Everything's going to be OK."

At Bristol in August, we got into a wreck that was bad enough to bring out the red flag. We didn't have a ton of damage, but we knew we had a busted radiator. And on this occasion, this team showed me how they could shine. Danny Lawrence, the engine tuner, formulated a plan to change that radiator when we went back under caution. (You can't work on your car during a red flag.) When that yellow flag came back out, we only lost three laps. They took no more than four minutes to change that radiator. We couldn't make up any of those laps, but finished 14th.

The next race was the Southern 500 at Darlington Raceway. It's NASCAR's oldest superspeedway race. It's lost a lot of its luster, but it's still one of those races every driver wants to win. Dale had won it three times. But what happened to Dale on that hot August day in 1997 will probably end up on television as an unsolved mystery or an episode of the supernatural. It was mind-boggling. And it was certainly one of the scariest times I've ever had at a racetrack.

Once again, we were terrible in practice. We were 37th fastest in qualifying. On race morning, we all noticed that Dale didn't seem to be his usual self. Richard thought he looked groggy. Danny Lawrence, who always did the window net after Dale buckled in, said, "It was like he was in a zone or something."

But it was Darlington and it was hot. You don't know what a driver is thinking sometimes, especially Dale. Don Hawk, Dale's business manager, noticed that he nodded off shortly before the race. Don thought nothing of it; Dale often did this. But Dale nodded off a second time just as the crew was telling him to start the engine.

Then, on the pace laps, Dale didn't respond to anything I was telling him or asking him. I asked him about his switches. I reminded him about pulling his belts tight. I tried to confirm the rpms for his pit road speed. He spoke only once during those three pace laps, and his voice was unclear. By now, we were pretty worried. Richard started trying to see if we could get another pace lap or somehow get Dale's attention and convince him to come in the pits. But it was too late. Starter Doyle Ford waved the green flag. As the field roared down the frontstretch, Dale lagged behind.

Then he reached the corner and drove right into the turn one wall. He came off the wall and drove up into the wall again in turn two. He missed the pit entrance and slowly drove by us. We were almost frantic. We called him: "Can you hear us, Dale?"

A weak voice answered, "Yeah." And a moment later, "I missed the pits."

Richard started screaming at him, "Dale, park the car! Stop the car now!" Dale made another slow lap around the track, but this time pulled onto pit road and came to the pits. Some of the crew helped him get out of the car and carried him back to the shade of the awning over the gas pumps. He was out of it, and he was limp as a dishrag. We called for an ambulance. When Richard talked to Dale in the infield care center, Dale said he was seeing double. But he didn't remember anything about starting the race, hitting the wall, or making those two laps.

Dale recalled later that he started having double vision while sitting in his car on pit road. "I shook it off and drove on down pit road, and at that time, everything was normal," he said. "From then on, I don't remember anything until about an hour and a half later."

Dale was taken to McLeod Regional Medical Center in Florence. He was held overnight and underwent a battery of tests. He felt fine Monday and went home, but headed up to Bowman-Gray School of Medicine in Winston-Salem, North Carolina, the next day for a series of circulatory, respiratory, body chemical, and neurological examinations. Dale was pretty nervous before those exams. He didn't know what they would find. The thought crossed his mind that he might never be able to race again. He racked his brain over what might have happened. He thought back over the previous weeks and months. Had he bumped his head? Had anything even remotely like this happened before? Had he had any different feelings, any headaches? He even went back over what he had eaten for several days before. But no one could really figure anything out.

"They dug and prodded and did everything they could do and didn't find anything," Dale said. "They didn't check to see if I was pregnant, but everything else they did. Swallowing the camera wasn't too easy."

Neurosurgeon Dr. Charles Branch of Bowman-Gray reported that he "could find no significant abnormality or identifiable problem." Branch explained that Dale had a "temporary dysfunction of his brain" that could have been caused by a couple of different things. He could have had a "migraine-like episode" where a blood vessel at the base of the brain went into spasms and restricted blood flow, causing the blackout. Or he might have had a "little short circuit in the brain because of an old injury," Branch said.

"It's an unexplained, momentary event," he said. "Most of the time, after fairly extensive testing, they're not going to have that problem again."

As they shipped Dale off to the hospital, we repaired his car and searched for a relief driver. We finally found one in Richard's son-in-law, Busch Series driver Mike Dillon, who had no Winston Cup experience. Mike got plenty that day. He completed 280 laps and moved the car from a potential 43rd-place finish to 30th. It kept Dale in sixth place in Winston Cup points and also kept alive our streak of no DNFs.

After the whole episode was beyond us, I felt pretty bad. I hadn't paid very much attention to Dale and his condition. In hindsight, I felt that my main concern should have been Dale. But it was the race car. I think I got too caught up in trying to fix that race car.

But I guess part of that was because I didn't have the same kind of relationship with Dale that I had had with Davey and Ernie. I think Richard and Dale had that kind of relationship, but not Dale and me. We never had a lot of personal conflict during our year and a half together. And we became even better friends after I began working with Mike Skinner. There were no hard feelings or grudges on either side. We just didn't get that close. But I cherish the times I did socialize with him, because Dale truly was one of a kind. Just eating with him was an experience. Dale was always in charge.

"Eat some of that right there, Larry!" he'd say. "Teresa, get him some more tea! You're eating too much of that, now, Larry. Eat some more of this!" Finally, he'd reach over, take your plate, and put it in the sink. "You're done eating now," he'd say.

When I'd get back to my motorcoach, I'd always have to take a rest—not from the food, but from Dale. I loved eating with him, but it made you tired. And you don't ever want to be with him in a car, especially leaving a racetrack. He'll drive across curbs and go through holes that aren't there to get out. It's almost like he's on another racetrack. If he drives, it's scary enough. If you drive, it's impossible. He'll tell you when to stop, when to go, how fast to go, and what lane to be in.

Michael Waltrip put it best one time when he told me what had he learned when he and Buffy would go to spend time with Dale and Teresa on their boat. He said the best thing to do was to take your brain out and park it on the dock, because Dale would do all the thinking for you. He'd tell you when to get up, when to eat, when to take a shower, when to go swimming, when to go shopping, when to go to bed. He'd make every move for you. That's just the way he was.

When relaxing, we rarely would talk about the race car. If the subject came up, I usually brought it up. He'd usually say, "Whatever you want to do, Larry. We'll be all right." I think Dale wanted to sit on every pole and win every race like every other driver, but by the late 1990s, the competition had become so tough that your car almost had to be perfect to win. In Dale's heyday, if he didn't qualify well, it was all right. He'd get 'em in the race. And usually he still had the first pit despite a poor qualifying effort because, back then, the Winston Cup champion had first choice of pits throughout the following season. Now the times had changed, but Dale hadn't changed with them. But when you've had so much success doing things one way, it's really hard to change.

When we were having a casual conversation, usually we'd talk about the Atlanta Braves, since we were both big Braves fans. We might talk about the Busch race or how Dale Jr. was running. If he got technical, it would usually be about the Winston Cup car he owned—the No. 1 Pennzoil Chevrolet driven by Steve Park. (Dale only fielded one car in 1997.) He might say, "Park and them put more sway bar in their car. What do you think about that? Want to try it?"

On the other hand, Dale had no use for Richard's other team, the No. 31 Chevy, or its driver, Mike Skinner. When I was with Dale, if the 31 car tried a set of shocks that made them better, we might as well not even waste our time bolting them on the No. 3 car if Dale found out where the idea came from. He'd say, "I don't want 'em, and I don't know how in hell Skinner can drive that thing with those shocks." Now if we could sneak around and just tell him, "It's something we wanted to try," Dale wouldn't mind.

But he was never a fan of that 31 car. And he would race Skinner harder than anyone on the track. I don't think Dale would have made a good teammate to anyone. I wish I knew why Dale felt that way about Mike and the 31 car. Maybe it was ego.

We had our next race at Richmond only six days after Dale's Darlington blackout. But all the tests had come back negative, and Dale felt fine, so he was given the go-ahead to race at Richmond. In the days before the Richmond race, I was preoccupied with family matters. Linda was pregnant with Kendall and due any day. I went to Richmond knowing I could be called back at any moment.

We had the low-snout car at Richmond, but we couldn't seem to get it hooked up there. Dale qualified 22nd. After qualifying, I got a call from Linda's mom that they were going to go ahead and induce labor. Richard put me on a plane and flew me home. The doctor was getting ready to perform a Caesarean section on Saturday morning, when Kendall decided she wanted to be born. She came naturally, and she came pretty quickly—just to help her dad out. Soon after she came, I was on my cell phone to Jimmy Elledge. Linda later told me, "I couldn't believe I was having that baby, and there you were, standing across the room talking on your cell phone about your race car!"

I held my little pride and joy number three, counted her little fingers and toes, hugged and kissed Linda and told her how beautiful she was, and flew back to Richmond. I got there right after Happy Hour was finished. I asked Dale, "How did practice go?"

"Not too bad," he said. "I think we're going to be OK."

I found Jimmy and asked him the same question.

Jimmy gave me a funny look. "What's the matter?" I asked.

"Well, we didn't practice very much," Jimmy said.

"Did you make a long run?" I asked. That was the only way to get a good read on the low-snout car.

"No, not really," Jimmy said. I looked at his practice sheet. They'd run a total of 20 laps.

"We're in trouble if you guys didn't run more than that," I told Jimmy.

"Well, that's what Dale wanted to do. He said he felt pretty good with everything."

That night we had another miserable run and finished 15th, two laps down. On the other hand, it was the last poor run we'd have for a while. We finished eighth at the second New Hampshire race, then had back-to-back second-place finishes at Dover and Martinsville. At Dover, we had a fourth- or fifth-place car, but played a good fuel mileage game and finished second. At Martinsville, Dale qualified 13th, which earned us a pit stall on the frontstretch. We couldn't catch the race winner, Jeff Burton, but at least that frontstretch pit allowed us to keep up with everyone else. Dale called me that evening.

"What did you think about today?" Dale asked.

"I'm pretty pleased with it," I said. "But let me ask you something, Dale. What do you think was the big difference today in us finishing second?"

"Well, the car worked good all day," he said.

"I'll buy that," I said. "But the big difference is where you started the race. You had a good starting position, and you didn't have to fight your way back through the pack all day long. You had a good pit stall, so we didn't have to fight a bad pit all day."

As I mentioned, one of the reasons Dale wasn't a good qualifier, I think, was because he got used to having the first pick of pit stalls as Winston Cup champion. During most of the early 1990s—1991, 1992, 1994, and 1995 to be exact—Dale always got the best pit and never had to worry about getting a pit on the backstretch at Bristol, Martinsville, Darlington, and Rockingham. I'm not sure Dale was buying what I was saying on the phone that evening, but I sure believed it.

With five races to go, my focus became winning a race, finishing in the top-five in points, and finishing the season with no DNFs. We had made vast improvements at tracks like Dover and Martinsville, where we were horrible in the first half of the season. Dale had bounced back from his blackout stronger than ever. We were gaining some momentum. I was beginning to feel a little bit better. We had three top-10 finishes in the final five races, including a third-place at Charlotte. We didn't win a race, but I think all of us on the No. 3 team, Dale included, ended the season feeling OK. We were disappointed that we didn't win. But the year was not that terrible.

We had finished fifth in points. And I was very proud that our car had finished every single race—all 32 of them. If nothing else, Dale still knew how to run consistently and how to finish races. As we looked forward to 1998, I was thinking, "OK, we've built something here. Now we can come back and improve on it."

CHAPTER TWENTY

Winning the 500 with Dale

As badly as the 1997 Winston Cup season had started, Dale had finished fifth in the Winston Cup championship, only one spot below his finish in 1996. This was because we didn't drop out of a single race. But the fact that we hadn't won a race still really hurt.

I was optimistic when we returned to Speedweeks at Daytona for the 1998 Daytona 500. It was Dale's 20th 500 in NASCAR's 50th year. It was also probably one of the easiest weeks I had ever experienced at Speedweeks, at least until the final practice.

We qualified fourth. The car was running well. Before the Twin 125s, I got busy preparing the car for racing. In every practice the car was good, and Dale was happy with it. My goal was to make the car stable in traffic and make it handle well in the lead, so Dale could get the lead and stay there. But on Wednesday, the day before the Twin 125s, Dale came down with a stomach virus and developed a fever. That just added to the tension. And the next day, he'd be racing for his ninth Twin 125 victory in a row. In 1997, I didn't know about Dale's Twin 125 win streak. Now I was all too aware of it.

But Dale was fine during the race, leading from the green flag to the checkered ahead of a flock of challengers who couldn't do anything with him. During that race and afterward, Dale began to show his usual confidence and cockiness. After the 125s, the schedule gave us two more Winston Cup practices on Friday and the final Happy Hour on Saturday. I knew Dale didn't feel that good, and I knew what he thought about practice. After we left victory lane, I said, "Hey Dale, how about we skip morning practice? We'll put our race motor in, and you can check it out Friday afternoon."

"You've got a deal," he said.

So we skipped Friday morning practice. Friday afternoon practice was rained out. That left only Happy Hour. No problem. Except when Dale went out in Happy Hour, there was a problem. "Damn it, something's wrong with this motor," he barked on the radio. "Won't run."

He came in. We pulled the spark plugs. They looked good, but we put new ones in and sent him back out. "Something is still wrong with this motor," he said. He came back in. Danny Lawrence pulled off the valve cover and found a broken rocker arm. We replaced it and sent him back out for the final minutes of practice. The car was OK, but it just didn't have that dominant look anymore. All of us were concerned that if the engine had broken one rocker arm, it might break another. We weren't sure we could rely on it. So after Happy Hour, we decided to replace it. We made the swap on race morning. We put in a motor we had not used at all during Speedweeks.

But that didn't bother Dale. He was still confident. We started fourth and Dale barged into the lead past Sterling Marlin on lap 17. Both Dale and Jeff Gordon had strong cars and led a lot of laps. It was one of those days when the car was good, the pit stops were good, the driver was great, and our performance had no blemishes. When Dale took the lead on lap 140, he planted himself solidly there. No one could do much with him when he was in front. A critical moment came during a caution period on lap 175 when the crew knocked out a flawless two-tire stop and kept Dale in the lead.

The final eight laps were some of the most exciting—even at Daytona. How would Dale lose this year? Could he finally, actually win it? Pole winner Bobby Labonte charged toward Dale with some breathtaking attacks in the high groove. But Bobby had to deal with Jeremy Mayfield and Jeff Gordon and the others who also wanted a run at Dale.

I got on the radio on lap 195 and said, "Remember what you told me a year ago. Don't let 'em get a run on you." But it was that classic scenario you love to see when you're leading. The guys behind Dale got to racing among themselves and left Dale alone. On lap 199, John Andretti and Lake Speed crashed on the backstretch. The race was to the yellow and white flags combined, and now Dale had the lapped car of Rick Mast as a cushion between him and the rest of the field.

"Yes! Yes! Yesssss!" Dale shouted on his radio as that black No. 3 car passed under the checkered flag. He pumped his fist out the window as we exploded onto pit road, jumping and hugging and slapping hands. "We won! We won! We won!" Dale shouted.

I broke in on the radio and told Dale, "There are about 150,000 people here who have been waiting 20 years to see that. Gotta give 'em a victory lap."

"Twenty years . . ." Dale said. He sounded like he was choking up.

Dale had led 107 of the 200 laps, including the final 61 circuits. And he gave his adoring fans more than a victory lap. During that slow trip around the speedway, he asked us, "You all think I ought to take a spin around the Daytona 500 infield?"

"Damn right," Richard said.

Bill France came on the radio to congratulate Dale—and to tell him it was "fine with us" if he spun a few donuts in the perfectly manicured grass of the tri-oval between pit road and the track. But before Dale could tear up the infield, he had to come down pit road. All along the asphalt stretch, dozens and dozens of crewmen—entire crews from some teams—came out to shake or slap his hand. I was standing out on the grass, and it was one of the most incredible sights I've ever seen.

Dale turned off onto the grass. When he spun his donuts, he somehow created a pattern in the grass that looked like the famous "3" on the side of his car. As Dale drove into victory lane, he said, "Richard, I tell you, it's unbelievable. Unbelievable!"

"This is the greatest sport in the world right here, buddy," Richard replied. "The greatest sport in the world."

After Dale finally made it to victory lane, fans began taking chunks of the sod dug up by Dale's tires. Others posed for pictures while standing next to the tire marks. After victory lane, Dale, Richard, and I headed up to the press box. Dale had a little white stuffed monkey. When he reached the interview platform in front of the sportswriters from around the nation, he threw the monkey to the ground and shouted, "I'm here! I'm here! I'm here! I'm here! And I finally got that [expletive] monkey off my back."

Far below us, several dozen Earnhardt fans were still gathered in the infield. They began cheering, so Dale turned and saluted them through the window. Dale noticed the design of his double-donut in the grass far below. "It's in the shape of a '3,'" he said. "Well, I'm pretty good at writing, ain't I?" When the fans clasped hands and formed themselves into a "3," all three of us turned and waved. They responded with their own cheers and waves.

I couldn't say enough about the crew and that final stop. "When the chips were down, they were the best in the business," I said. "We knew we had to be in the pits for about five or six seconds to get the fuel we needed. The guys had about an eight-and-a-half-second stop for two right-side tires."

The race that had eluded Dale for so many years and had dished out so much heartbreak finally was his. "So many people were saying . . . this is your year," Dale said. "I'm talking about people you wouldn't think would say that—everybody from the top to the bottom. From the owners down to the guys who work on the cars—people like Todd Parrott and Bill France. Race fans said it, over and over. I felt good about the week, but they were just so adamant about 'This is your year, this is your year.' Somebody knew something I didn't know, I reckon."

Dale had been so close to winning so many Daytona 500s without me as his crew chief, but it sure made me proud to be in that position when he finally did win. I was the fortunate guy who was there when all the parts and pieces fell into place—no flat tires, no loose car, no wrecks. But the thing that meant the most to me was being there in victory lane to see up close how special it was for Dale and Richard.

After victory lane and post-race inspections and the press box interview and more interviews down on pit road, I finally made it back to my motorcoach in the infield. It was late at night. I sat there in a chair, all by myself, and let it really sink in. I had won the Daytona 500 with Dale Earnhardt.

But that's about all the time I had to enjoy winning the race. Qualifying at Rockingham was in five days. And when we made that trip back to the sandhills of North Carolina, we were awful. It was a repeat of 1997. Dale was 15th fastest in the first practice, but we didn't get any faster. Everyone else did. We picked up a few tenths of a second per lap in qualifying, but the entire field made another big gain, and we were 38th fastest. We stood on our time and had to use a provisional starting spot to make the race.

The race wasn't much better. We finished a lap down in 17th. Part of the problem was that Ford had introduced its new model, the Taurus, and the Fords were whipping GM—except Jeff Gordon, who won the race in his DuPont Chevy.

"You can't say much when that 24 car wins the race," Dale said afterward. "He won and had six Fords behind him."

The next weekend was the inaugural Winston Cup race at Las Vegas Motor Speedway. Linda and I flew out with Kendall, who was only seven months old. We had intended to stay in our motorcoach, but we ended up in the Rio Hotel. The motorcoach had its roof peeled off in a windstorm—the whole outer shell. It was really beat up. The windshield was broken, and the awning was torn off. Mirrors were blown off. A bunch of coaches were caught up in it somewhere on the road in Utah. Our driver, Carl Larson, used dozens of rolls of duct tape to tape the top back down. He made it to Vegas, but then drove straight back to the factory in Indiana for repairs.

While Linda and I were at the Rio, Dale and Teresa came over to have dinner with Richard and Judy Childress. You couldn't help but love Dale and love being around him. We had Kendall with us in a stroller. We were strolling through the casino, and Dale saw us and hollered at us to come over. He was sitting with Teresa at a lounge in the middle of the casino, which sat on a raised floor a couple feet higher than the casino floor.

"We're just sittin' here waiting on Richard and Judy," Dale said. "Y'all come up here and have a drink with us."

As usual, we didn't have a choice. So we went to roll up the ramp and a waiter said, "I'm sorry, but you can't bring that baby in the lounge."

Dale, as usual, had a plan. Their table was along the edge of the lounge, next to a railing.

"Roll that stroller right over here," he said. "I can look down on her and make sure she's OK." So we put Kendall and her stroller on the casino floor on the other side of the railing, a couple feet below Dale. Linda was a bit nervous about the arrangement, but Dale had it covered. He was checking that baby about every 10 seconds and giving us reports. Kendall served another purpose, too. Dale used her to keep pesky fans at bay: "Get back, now! Can't you see we have a sleeping baby here? Quit leaning all over that baby! Y'all gonna have to give us some more room, now."

We qualified 26th for the race and finished a distant and struggling eighth—behind seven Fords. Dale drove the only Chevy on the lead lap. After the race, all the Chevrolet crew chiefs, owners, and drivers gathered at the back of the NASCAR trailer, waiting for Mike Helton and Gary Nelson to come back from the tower. When Gary got there he looked around and quipped, "Do all of you want to start screaming at once or do you have an appointed person to speak?" Gary knew the Chevy teams were at a strong disadvantage, and NASCAR soon began making its usual incremental changes.

Afterward, I flew home with Dale and Teresa on their jet. (Linda had already flown home with Kendall on race morning.) It was only two weeks after we had won the Daytona 500, so we still had a pretty good bounce in our steps. Dale was so eager to talk about his days as a kid with his dad, Ralph, who was a legendary NASCAR Sportsman driver. Ralph maintained his own team out of Kannapolis, North Carolina. Dale told a lot of stories and enjoyed it very much. I learned more about him than I'd ever known.

Unfortunately, our fortunes on the track were just as dismal as they had been in the first half of 1997. Whatever we gained in the second half of the year was lost. At Atlanta, we qualified 30th and finished 13th, a lap down, just behind Terry Labonte in the highest-finishing Chevy. At Darlington, we qualified 27th and finished 12th, a lap down.

Around this time, Pam Miller came by for dinner again. I was so frustrated I told her, "If you guys had an opportunity for me to become a full-time broadcaster, I'd probably jump all over it. Pam, I just can't figure this deal out with the three car. I don't know if racing has left me behind. But I'm starting to feel like I want to walk away from it. I just can't stand not giving Dale Earnhardt what he needs to win."

At Bristol, we had to use another provisional, which put us in a backstretch. Then we had pit problems, left some lug nuts loose, hurt the studs, and finished four laps down in 22nd. It was one of those days when you couldn't see the checkered flag soon enough.

Texas was no better. Even though NASCAR gave everyone an extra day of practice, it didn't help us. None of the changes we made to that race car worked. Dale didn't complain much about the car. He said, "It drives good. I don't know what's wrong."

The morning of qualifying day, we changed everything. We changed gears, shocks, sway bars—you name it, we changed it. But the car was no better. Dale said, "Damn it, I don't know what's wrong with it. Get Skinner to drive it!"

Mike had been running pretty good. He was a lot faster than we were. So we got him to drive the car. We didn't change a thing. Richard and I got up on top of the truck to watch. In turns three and four, just getting up to speed for a two-lap practice qualifying run, Mike was about four-tenths of a second faster than Dale's best speed. I said to Richard, "This is really good and really bad. It's really good because we know that car can run a fast lap. And it's really bad because it's a lot faster than Dale Earnhardt ever thought about going in this car."

Mike ran two laps, and he was faster than Dale on both—by a half-second per lap overall. This wasn't about proving Dale couldn't run fast in the car. But there were several times when Mike got in Dale's car and was substantially faster. It was just another one of those confusing, inexplicable things during my year and a half with Dale. When Dale got back in the car, he did run faster. But we never could get him comfortable running a fast lap. We qualified 34th.

We were involved in a big 14-car crash on the second lap of the race. We had to do some serious repair work and spent 75 to 100 laps in the garage. Dale was trying to help. We needed nine or 10 people to work on the car and two or three to keep Dale away from it. We did get back out there, but finished 35th.

We took the low-snout car back to Martinsville and qualified 31st. But it was a race with long green flag runs, and that low-snout car carried us back to fourth. Dale even led a bunch of laps. But at the next race, at Talladega, Dale got involved in the big wreck, and we had to drop out. It was my first DNF with the No. 3 car.

The month of May brought even more struggle. By now the problems were so serious, it was only a matter of time before something had to give. We managed to finish ninth at California Speedway after starting dead last in 43rd. But Dale crashed in the Coca-Cola 600 and we had another DNF.

When we returned to Dover, it was not like in September, when we finished second. It was like May of 1997, when we were horrible. The Dover garage is inside the first turn, and from there you can see much of what's going on with your car and others. I noticed how deep the cars were going into the corners before backing off. And it's easy to track how far because the track's big concrete squares are handy measuring devices.

After changing everything we could change on the car during practice and not gaining a bit of speed, I told Dale that Geoff Bodine had one of the fastest cars. He was picking the throttle up about four concrete blocks earlier in the middle of the corner than Dale. That made a big difference. We were probably three-quarters of a second slower per lap than the fast cars.

"What is this car doing that won't let you get back on the throttle sooner?" I asked.

"I don't know," Dale said impatiently. Then he had an idea. "I'll tell you what," he said. "You go down there and stand in the corner with your radio. When you think I need to get back on the throttle, you say, 'Now!'"

I looked at him like, "Are you serious?" I could tell he was. But I could hardly believe it. Here I was fixing to tell Dale Earnhardt where to get back into the throttle at a racetrack. It was unbelievable. So Dale went back out, and I stood in my usual spot with the radio. When Dale got to the point where Geoff had hit the throttle, I said, "Now!"

Dale hit the gas and that ol' No. 3 car came off the corner nice and straight. The lap was three-tenths faster than any we'd run. I told Dale, and he wanted to try it again. So he drove that thing down in the corner and I said, "Now!"

Dale picked up another tenth. In just two runs with me on the radio, we had picked up almost a half-second. We were only a few tenths off the leaders at this point.

"Car actually ran good," Dale said. "What did I run?"

I told him.

"No kidding!"

Bob Riley, who was working with us, just shook his head. He said to me, "Is this the same Dale Earnhardt who has won all these races here?" I told Bob I was just as confused as he was. When we got ready for qualifying, I asked Dale if he wanted to do it again. He said, "Damn right I want you to do it."

In qualifying, Dale drove into the first turn and I said, "Now!" But he didn't do it this time. He just kept rolling and rolling and rolling through the turn before finally hitting the gas. He was six- or seven-tenths slower than his fastest lap. We qualified 34th.

When he got back in and learned what he had run, he said, "Why is that?"

"Dale," I said, "when I told you to pick up the throttle, it was another two seconds before you did it! Why?"

"Ah, damn, I don't know. I just didn't do it. It just didn't feel comfortable."

We ran terribly in the race at Dover and finished 25th, five laps down.

Six days after the Dover race, we had the new night race at Richmond. By now, the situation was out of control. Team morale was at a new low. My morale was at a new low. We had won the Daytona 500, but from then on, our spirits had been like a snowball rolling downhill. Once again, we struggled in practice, failed to qualify, and had to start the race with a provisional. I went in the lounge after qualifying. Dale and Richard were sitting there. All of us were just so frustrated. I said, "Dale, what did the car feel like?"

"I don't know," he snapped. "I don't know what the car felt like! That car felt fine. I just didn't get back on the gas."

"Dale," I said, "you need to figure out what you want to do with the rest of your career, and I will figure out if I want to be part of it, because I am not going to race this way. I work too hard and the race team works too hard for this. We are in this deal together, but we have to work it out together."

I left that lounge and went to my motorcoach. Linda and the kids were there. I told Linda I had probably just screwed up. I'd told Dale he needed to figure out what to do with his career. Linda gave me a look like, "Man, what are you doing?"

"I'm tired of fighting," I said. "It's too hard. I put so much into it. He's sitting there in the transporter watching TV. He's not worried about using a provisional. Nobody's getting anywhere. We're only digging our hole deeper. I can't fight it anymore."

The next day, we actually had to share a pit. You know your team has bottomed out when you have to share a pit. There were 43 cars in the field and only about 40 pits. So the last few qualifiers had to share. When someone fell out, you got to move to their open pit. We started the race at one end of pit road and finished it at the other. And we ran about as bad as we had run in the first two races. We finished 21st, two laps down.

We spent the night at our motorcoach. The next morning, I ran into Mike Skinner in the coach lot. He was struggling just about as bad as we were.

"Man, I wish you and I could get hooked up together," he said.

"You know, that would be pretty cool," I said. "I know you can drive a race car. I love the way you go out and qualify."

About 15 minutes after we left the track, my cell phone rang. It was Richard. He asked me to stop by Welcome on our way home.

"We need to talk," he said. "I'm going to have Bobby Hutchins here and Kevin Hamlin [Mike's crew chief]. And I'm going to call Dale and Mike."

A few hours later, in Welcome, Richard said he'd decided to swap crew chiefs. Richard wanted me to take over the No. 31 car and Kevin Hamlin to take over the No. 3 car.

"I understand where you're coming from, but I left Robert Yates Racing to go to work for the black No. 3 and for Dale Earnhardt, not the 31 car," I said.

"Larry, I don't know but one way to put it," he said. "You have intimidated the Intimidator. Both of you guys are great. He is a great driver. You are a great crew chief. But you guys aren't on the same page, and you're not even in the same book."

I knew better than anybody that it wasn't working, so I agreed to do it. But I didn't sleep a wink that night. And I got up Monday and decided I couldn't do it. I went in and told Richard. "If this is what you want, I need to do something else," I said.

"Larry, just try it," he said. "Try it for five races. I want you to stay with RCR. But it's not working with Dale. You know it. I know it. Dale knows it. Everybody knows it. Just try it with the 31 car. If it doesn't work out, you can walk out that door."

I'm glad he talked me into it. It was a relief to get away from the pressures and the stress of dealing with the No. 3 team. Mike and I started clicking right away. Kevin and Dale started clicking right away. I think it worked out best for both programs.

More than a year later, in October 2000, I was waiting for my daughter, Brooke, to return from a school field trip to the U.S. Space Camp in Huntsville, Alabama. Taylor Earnhardt, Dale's daughter, who goes to the same school, also was on the trip. The bus was late. As I waited, I noticed Dale sitting there in his Chevy Tahoe, waiting for Taylor. I went over to talk with him. I sat in his car, and we talked for an hour before that bus finally showed up.

Dale's 2000 season was his best since 1996. After undergoing surgery during the off-season to repair a ruptured disk, Dale had won in Atlanta in March. He was coming off a second-place finish at Martinsville five days before and was second in the Winston Cup championship. We finally got around to why it had all gone so wrong with us.

"Larry, I could never get comfortable in that race car," Dale told me. "After I had that surgery, I felt so much better. I had been fighting it since that wreck in Talladega in 1996." That was the big crash when he got upside down and broke his sternum. "I guess you and I didn't really get a fair chance with each other," he concluded.

Today, I am so thankful we had that conversation. It made me feel a lot better about the year and a half I worked with him. I had heard it so often in 1997 and 1998: "I just don't feel comfortable." I had always thought it was a problem with the car. Now I realize a lot of the problem was that when Dale was driving, he was in a lot more pain than he let on, and he really *wasn't* comfortable in the car.

CHAPTER TWENTY-ONE

The Mike Skinner Years

The harsh reality of the difference between the No. 3 Goodwrench team and the No. 31 Lowe's team was obvious at the very next race at Michigan in June. The No. 3 team always flew on Richard's jet, which got to Michigan in about one hour. The No. 31 team flew on Richard's King Air prop plane, which got there in about two hours.

When we left Winston-Salem in the King Air, the jet was still sitting there and the guys from the No. 3 team were nowhere to be seen. When we landed in Michigan, the jet was already parked for the weekend with its engine covers on. The No. 3 team was long gone. I tried not to see the switch as a demotion, but that sure begged the question.

Of course, when I first started, we drove to all the tracks—Pocono, Michigan, even Riverside, California—and then drove home. Today, race teams complain because it takes the King Air three hours to get to Texas or Michigan. In 2001, before Dover in June, Richard finally had had enough of the complaining. He decided to show his teams what hard times were really like. He made those guys drive to Dover in a van. What impressed me was that Richard got in with everyone else and rode up there, too.

It took us a few races to get going, but at New Hampshire in July, Mike finished a career-best fifth. Two races later, in the Brickyard 400, he finished fourth. A week after that, at Watkins Glen, he was third. My arrival at the No. 31 team shop at the bottom of the hill behind the main RCR shop brought a breath of fresh air to the team and to me as well. Those guys were looking for the kind of leadership I could offer.

It was a newer group of guys who hadn't gotten totally into the RCR way of doing things, so I had much closer rapport with them. They were ready to give that extra effort. We were at the bottom of the hill by ourselves, so we got by with a little more. I could say, "Guys, we gotta stay past eight tonight to get this car done," and they'd stay. We could pretty much ignore the clock down there. Not only did Mike start finishing better, he started qualifying better. Mike gave it his all and was gasping for air after he won the outside pole for the Bristol race. It was refreshing.

We finished seventh, but it was a hard-fought seventh. It was a hot night, and we had been terrible when the race started. We nearly went a lap down. But we kept working and working. Mike and I cussed each other all night long, although I don't remember what we cussed about. Bristol just has a way of bringing it out.

After the race, Mike was trying to drive the car back to the truck. It was difficult because the little infield was so crowded with people, cars, and crewmen. Mike was stuck in this traffic, and he was just cussing and raising hell. David Smith, who's pretty religious, had listened to us cuss all through the race. "Mike, why don't you just park that car and get out and give that ol' filthy mouth of yours a rest," David said. The next day, Mike and I had an appearance at Topeka, Kansas. We flew on

Mike's plane. We laughed and laughed about how we had cussed each other and what David said.

In the final races of 1998, we had our best runs at the restrictor plate races. At Talladega, we qualified fifth and finished seventh. Mike led 74 laps—more than any other driver. We were in a position to win, but Mike couldn't capitalize. Mike understood the draft and did a good job at Daytona and Talladega. But it seemed like he sometimes made the wrong choices with a few laps to go, or on the last lap.

But we'd had a good race, and the biggest thing I was excited about was the car was not torn up. Just four days later we had to take the same car to Daytona for the Pepsi 400, which was rescheduled after the July race was postponed by the bad forest fires in Florida that summer. We finished third at Daytona, and Mike tied his career-best finish.

Another highlight of the season was winning the 76 Pit Crew Championship at Rockingham on Halloween. I knew that the team was capable, even though we were a new team without a lot of experience. No one picked us to win. But it's all about not making mistakes. I always hammered on my guys, "Don't make mistakes, don't make mistakes."

But if you try not to make mistakes, you'll have a slow stop. So you wing it and hope there are no loose lug nuts, no gas is spilled, and the driver doesn't stall the car. Our seven-man crew, led by team manager David Smith, changed four tires and added fuel in 20.322 seconds, beating Steve Park's crew, who did it in 20.537 seconds. About half the teams were penalized three seconds or more for various infractions.

Mike was proud of his guys. "These guys work out," he said. "They practice on their own time. They practice every chance they get. I even went over to the shop the other day and practiced coming in and out." I had won 23 Winston Cup races plus a number of awards over the course of 20 years, but the moment they placed that 76 Pit Crew Championship ring on my finger, well, that was a feeling that ranks right up there.

But the biggest highlight of the year, without question, was Mike's victory in the NASCAR exhibition race at the Motegi oval in Japan, in November of 1998, after the regular season ended. I wanted to win at Motegi as much as anywhere else, and I worked hard to do that. Nobody tested there, and I don't think many teams prepared a lot for it. I knew the Indy cars had run there, and I knew Rick Rinaman, a Penske Racing crew chief.

I asked Rick which racetrack that he ran on in the U.S. was similar to Motegi. "That's easy, Larry," Rick said. "It's Homestead." He also told me, "Larry, we shift gears there because the racetrack is not even close to symmetrical. Turns one and two are very tight, while three and four are sweeping. If I was you, I'd figure out how to shift."

So I figured out how to have Mike shift, and we won that race. But we almost bombed out. Since nobody tested there, Goodyear took a very hard tire. And it was cold in the first practice. I told Mike to be real careful, but he slapped the wall the first time on the track. We had to about rebuild the car. Mike wanted to help, but I was so mad at him I just wanted him to go somewhere else.

We tried to pull a fast one in qualifying by leaving a spark plug wire off. Mike had to come back in, of course, and we thought we'd get an extra lap to heat up the tires. NASCAR Winston Cup Director Gary Nelson saw what we were up to and made us requalify at the end of the line, which allowed our tires to cool back down. But we qualified third, and Mike drove to a pretty clean victory. For me, it was fun winning both the first race and the last race of the year.

In January of 1999, during the off-season, Linda threw me a surprise 40th birthday party. We had maybe 22 guys on the 31 team at that point, and all but one or two of them came.

We started the 1999 season with four straight top-10 finishes after Mike was fourth in the Daytona 500. We had the lead in Winston Cup points for a month. I doubt anyone outside our team thought it was a remote possibility that Mike could be leading the points at any time in the season.

Then we had a couple of bad races and had dropped to ninth in points before Bristol. The race there was almost like a rerun of my 1992 blowup on pit road. Mike had stayed on the lead lap all day long. NASCAR has a rule that when they signal one lap to go before a restart, the cars have to be in line by the time they get to turn three. This is sometimes hard to do at Bristol. Just before one restart, everybody was driving on top of each other. Mike was a little late, but got in line about the middle of turns three and four. The race resumed, and NASCAR promptly threw a black flag on us. We had to come in for a stop-and-go penalty. It cost us two laps.

I went nose-to-nose with the NASCAR official on pit road. The race was running, and it was so loud he probably couldn't even hear me, but I made a fool of myself again. I tried to grab his headset, so I could talk directly to NASCAR in the tower. Of course, that earned me another trip to the NASCAR transporter. Actually, Gary Nelson and I had a pretty civil conversation. We reviewed the penalty, and Gary even gave us back a few positions. We didn't get back all we had lost, but it was better than nothing and it totally shocked me.

The next week, at Martinsville, I was called back to the NASCAR transporter. This time, NASCAR President Bill France wanted to see me. He was sitting by himself. "Have a seat, Larry," he said. He wasn't smiling.

"Larry," he said, "You have a nice, big house up there on that lake in North Carolina they call Lake Norman, right?"

"Yes, sir."

There was a long pause before: "I bet you own a boat, too, don't you?"

"Yes, sir."

There was another long pause.

"Haven't I seen you with one of those motorcoaches out in that motor-coach lot?"

"Yes, sir."

"And I bet you've got somebody driving that motorcoach for you, don't you?"

"Yes, sir, Mr. France."

He paused again. Then he leaned forward, put his arms on his knees, stared straight at me, and said, "You see, things aren't so damn bad, now are they?"

"No, sir."

"Now, get out of here and quit showing your ass!"

Needless to say, I got his point. It was yet another variation of the typical NASCAR line, which was, "You need this sport more than this sport needs you." After more than two decades in NASCAR, I'd heard every version there was.

We qualified 12th at Talladega, but we had a good car and it didn't take Mike long to drive to the front and take the lead on lap 16. Then he fell back, but once again clawed his way back to the front. On the backstretch on lap 49, Mike decided he was going to pass Tony Stewart where there wasn't a racetrack. He was down on the grass. Mike got sideways and wrecked a bunch of race cars. Jeff Gordon was involved, and the next thing I knew, his crew chief, Ray Evernham, was in the back of our pits, raising hell with me.

I told him, "Ray, I wasn't driving the race car. Talk to Skinner when he gets in here."

I told Mike, "You better hope this race lasts a long time, because I'm pretty ill. That was a pretty stupid move, especially so early in the race with a car that could win."

The car was not really torn up that bad. It had four flat tires and a bit of fender damage. The real damage occurred when the wrecker picked up the car. Mike was still sitting in it as they pulled the car around to the pits.

"How much damage is there?" I asked Mike.

He started screaming, "They're killing it! This wrecker is beating up the front end!" When the wrecker pulled the car behind pit wall, I could see that it had really smashed up the front end. The driver jumped out and started going crazy trying to unhook the car. He jumped up on the duct work around the radiator. It caved in. Just as he was getting ready to step on the air cleaner, I grabbed him and pushed him away. Mike Hawkins, our engine tuner, also pushed him. The wrecker driver got back in his wrecker.

We got the car fixed again, but we had to do a whole lot more than we would have before the wrecker got to it. We about had to replace the front end. We went back out and rode around for another 100 laps or so and finished 36th. Before the end of the race, a NASCAR official told me, "NASCAR wants to see you and Mike Skinner in the transporter after the race."

The incident with the wrecker driver had been televised. To me, that was good and bad. The good news was that the guy couldn't exaggerate the story. The bad news is that I was on national television pulling this guy off the wrecker and then pushing him.

But there I was, back in the NASCAR woodshed again, back in hot water. First on Gary Nelson's agenda was my incident with the NASCAR official on Bristol. Gary was hot about it again because he'd finally found out that "you took his headset and yanked it down around his waist."

Then someone hit "play" on the VCR, and it was a huge shock when I saw myself with the wrecker driver on pit road. They lit into me about that. Finally, Mike Helton made it clear to me that he was tired of seeing me in the NASCAR trailer and it better not continue. I got the message. To make a long story short, I had to deal with this wrecker driver, Fred Moore, for the next two years. He said his back was injured. The case was finally settled out of court.

At Richmond in mid-May, we qualified seventh, but lost two laps early in the race when we blistered a right front tire. By lap 150, we had made up those two laps. And on lap 244, we took the lead. We led the next 56 circuits. With 55 to go, we were second on a restart. All we needed to do to win our first points race was be patient. But it wasn't meant to be. Rick Mast, in a lapped car, drove up into us and put us in the wall. We finished 30th. Mike later asked Rick, "What happened? Why did you wreck me?"

"I didn't wreck you," Rick said. "I got into you. You're the one who elected to spin and hit the wall."

That was Rick's sense of humor. But it was hard to laugh about it at the time.

At Michigan in June, we struggled and Mike qualified 33rd. Mike's biggest drawback was his attitude. He always saw the glass as being half empty, not half full. And as we worked our guts out to get better at Michigan, Mike got an attitude. He was negative about everything— the car, the track, the crew. About halfway through Saturday morning practice, I yanked out the right-side window, crawled in there with him, stuck my finger in front of his helmeted head, and said, "You can either work with us or work against us. But I promise you, if you work against us, it's only going to get worse!"

Mike nodded his helmet. He changed his attitude. But that's the kind of relationship we had. Sometimes I had to ride him.

At Pocono in July, we won our first pole position together. It was a bit of a surprise, since we were not the fastest car in practice. But if you've got your car close for qualifying, Mike is able to reach in the bottom of the barrel and scrape out a little bit more. He may screw up sometimes and end up 15th, but if you're fifth fastest in practice, he'll try to put you on the pole. We led a bunch of laps at Pocono, but faded to 10th.

By the summer of 1999, Ernie Irvan was into his second year driving the No. 36 M&Ms car. He had stayed with Robert Yates through the 1997 season and had won a race at Michigan—the same racetrack where he had nearly lost his life. The victory seemed to say to everyone that Ernie had come back all the way. But in August, Michigan bit him again. Ernie had planned to run in both the Winston Cup and Busch races, but during Busch practice, he hit the wall hard and suffered a concussion. Even before this crash, he'd been pretty banged up. He had already crashed at Talladega and Charlotte. Two weeks later, at Darlington, Ernie announced his retirement. It was a tough way to end a career. Robert Yates and I went to the press conference to support Ernie. Before that crash at Michigan in 1994, Ernie Irvan was one of the best race car drivers ever. Even after the wreck, he was still better than 80 or 90 percent of them, and still good enough to win. But he'd had one too many head injuries.

That fall, I thought we had a good shot of winning at Talladega. We lost an engine on the first day of qualifying, but led the second day of qualifying and started 26th. We led a few laps in the race. But at the end, Mike made the wrong moves, got out of line, and fell back. We finished a disappointing 13th. We finished eighth at Atlanta and ended the season 10th in the Winston Cup points championship.

In 2000, we got off to a slow start. We didn't have a top-10 finish for the first nine races. But we did have some strong runs. At Atlanta, we qualified 14th, but led the race eight different times for 191 laps—more than anyone else. With just 27 laps to go, a yellow came out. We had battled Bobby Labonte and Dale Earnhardt all day. Everyone pitted for four tires and fuel. We beat everybody off pit road.

The race restarted with 20 laps to go, and Mike just left everyone. We were pulling away by two-tenths of a second per lap. And we could have run harder if necessary. I thought, "Nothing can keep us from winning." Then a rod bolt broke in the engine, and it blew up. Dale won in a photo finish with Bobby. But what could you do? It was one of those days when everything was right. The car was good, the motor was good, Mike was focused, and pit stops were awesome. Everything fell into place—other than a bolt that cost less than five dollars. When I walked into that shop on Monday, however, everyone was pumped up. "This shows we have a strong race team," I thought. And at Talladega, Mike had a career-best finish of second, trailing only Jeff Gordon.

In late April 2000, I received a call from Bill Brown, senior vice president of production at FOX Sports. Bill's call had been preceded months earlier, in December 1999, by a call from FOX Sports President David Hill, who had told me they were interested in considering me for their upcoming NASCAR broadcasts. FOX and NBC had won the contract to broadcast NASCAR races beginning in 2001.

Bill asked me to audition for FOX at Charlotte in May. They had me come up to the Speedway Club overlooking the track, where I did some practice work with Darrell Waltrip, who had been hired months before. FOX was still searching for a second analyst and a play-by-play announcer. They auditioned a lot of people. We all did a mock broadcast of the Busch race from the Speedway Club that was fed back to FOX in Los Angeles. Different people did different segments of the race. Everyone worked with Darrell, but they used different people for the other two spots. I wasn't really that nervous. I was excited.

After the audition, however, I didn't hear a thing for almost two months. Bill finally called in July. He said they were very interested in hiring me to be an analyst on the broadcast team. Other than that call I received from Dana Williamson in 1980 to be part of Bob Rogers's racing team, I doubt I have ever been so excited about a phone call.

And on a Tuesday night in early August 2000, while I was at a Bandelero race with Brandon, my cell phone rang while I was in the Porta-John. That's where I finalized the deal. I hoped that wouldn't make a statement about my career as a broadcaster.

The 10th race of the season was at California Speedway at the end of April. We had a fast car, and Mike went out there early in qualifying and took over the top starting spot with a new track record. Then we all settled in the back of the transporter to watch the rest of qualifying on ESPN. Mike was there with his girlfriend and soon-to-be wife, Angie. Richard was there, along with David Smith and me.

I held my breath as car after car came up short. We knew somebody would beat us. With about five or six cars to go, Richard got up and said, "All right, I'm going to go over and check on the three."

"No, you're not," I said. "We've all sat here for the last 25 qualifiers. No one even changed the position of their legs. You're going to sit down, and we're all going to see this deal out together." Richard sat down, and we waited out the last few cars. Nobody beat Mike, and he won the pole.

We finished seventh in the race. We were really good the first two-thirds of the race. Then the racetrack just went away from us. The car started pushing terribly in the last 100 laps. We could qualify well, but Mike and I and the team never did a very good job of adjusting the car to keep up with changing track conditions. We'd adjust too much, or not enough. Had the races been shorter, we would have won eight or 10 of them.

We had another great car for my last race at Talladega in October 2000. When they dropped that green flag, once again we had a car to beat. NASCAR had instituted new aerodynamic rules, and we had a great race, with 49 lead changes among 21 drivers.

We were leading with two laps to go. Dale Earnhardt had been about 20th with maybe 15 to go, but he came charging through the field, passed us, and led the last two laps to win. Dale just knew what to do with a race car, where to put it and how to go about passing folks. It was Dale's last victory.

I was really bitter about it. I thought, "Son of a gun. How can they win the race and we finish sixth after how good we were all day long?" Of course, now I'm happy that he won that race.

The highlight of that weekend for me was "Larry McReynolds Night" at Birmingham International Raceway on the Saturday night before the Talladega event. They paid tribute to me, my family, and all of my friends who had a big impact on my career. Linda and the kids were there, of course, as well as my Aunt Noreen and Uncle Butch. Charles Finley was there. He had given me my first job at the salvage yard. Bobby Ray Jones was there, still fielding a race car. Richard Orton came, along with Dave Mader III, who was racing that night in the 100-lap feature.

Even my grandfather made it. Back in the 1960s, when he was in his 60s, he had taken me to my first race at BIR. Now he was 102. They gave me a plaque. It was really a nice night. It made me realize how special these people are and how special BIR was in my early career. It was a good way to cap off my last race at Talladega as a crew chief.

My final race as a crew chief came at Atlanta Motor Speedway on November 20, 2000. I had been on the pit box, in charge of a Winston Cup team, for 457 starts going back 15 years. I had won 23 races, posted 98 finishes in the top five and 174 top-10s. In those 457 starts, my driver and car owner had won more than $20.5 million in race purse winnings.

Before the race, I walked up to the front of the field and watched the drivers arrive at their cars. Then I walked back through the field and found every driver I had worked with. I saw Dale Jarrett, Brett Bodine, Ricky Rudd, Kenny Wallace, Dale Earnhardt. I even went to Darrell Waltrip's car. I wished him luck. I told him to be careful. He was already buckled in and had his helmet on. He took my hand and held it to the mouth area of his helmet. I knew right then Darrell and I would have a good relationship.

We weren't fast enough to win at Atlanta. We had used a provisional starting spot. But I had a lot of fun plotting a fuel mileage strategy. At one point I thought we could win. But a yellow flag with 20 laps to go ruined our chances. Still, we finished sixth—our best finish since Talladega. We were 12th in the Winston Cup championship.

After the race ended, it was hard for me to crawl off the pit box. I sat up there for two or three minutes, reflecting on my 20 years as a mechanic and crew chief. I was proud of what I had accomplished. The success that I had had on the track and especially with the people I'd worked with meant so much to me. (This was reinforced in a special way later when the 31 team had a nice luncheon in my honor, and gave me a big box of cigars and a plaque that said, "Thank you for being our leader for the past two and a half years.") I finally got down from the pit box and walked to the garage to gather up my stuff. I was thinking about the past, but very much looking forward to the future.

CHAPTER TWENTY-TWO

My First FOX Broadcast

flew to Daytona Beach on a commercial jet for the first time in 2001.
I had always come in a van or a car, or on the team plane, so it was
odd to be on a US Airways jet. I sat next to Jeff Hammond, another
former crew chief hired by FOX for the broadcast team. We just
looked at each other and said, "Wow, *this* is different. What have we
bitten off here?"

Soon after I arrived, I met Mike Joy, who had been hired as FOX's
play-by-play man in the booth. We decided to take a walk around the
garage. It was Wednesday, February 7—two days before the first
Winston Cup practice. The only transporter there was the NASCAR
trailer. All the other parking spots were empty, and the garages were still
vacant. But I knew this place would be a beehive of noise and activity
in 24 hours.

There'd be 50 crew chiefs at work, and all of them would have to deal
with the idiosyncrasies of this funky old garage at Daytona. For one
thing, it's a big, old, chopped-up mess. One garage is over here, one is

over there, and another one is over here. If you don't mind your Ps and Qs, you can get run over. Cars are going this way and that. Some turn left, some turn right, some go straight. The crew chief whose hauler was parked a long way from his garage would be walking his fool self to death for 10 days. I used to see how far our transporter was parked from our garage stall to decide how many cans of Gold Bond powder to buy for Speedweeks.

When they built the garage, teams didn't have all the electrically powered equipment they have today, such as cool-down machines for the radiator and heaters for the oil tanks and rear-end housings. So you're blowing circuits every five minutes. We'd almost have to designate a person to go to the circuit breaker box and flip the switch every time we popped the circuit. You might send a guy down there two dozen times a day. Sometimes I thought it would be best to just post a guy at the box all day long with a two-way radio.

Just outside the main gate of the Winston Cup garage, as Mike and I started walking toward the ARCA garage, we ran into Dale Earnhardt. He was the very first person we saw. Dale and I had never quit being friends, despite our troubles together. Dale just couldn't quit talking about the 24 Hours of Daytona, which he had run a few days earlier. His grayish blue eyes were full of excitement. Us stock-car folks rarely pay much attention to the sports car endurance race, which is the first event of Speedweeks. But more and more NASCAR drivers have been competing in recent years. In 2001, Dale had run with his son, Dale Jr., and sports car drivers Andy Pilgrim and Kelly Collins. They drove a yellow Corvette to fourth place overall and second in their class.

The race had been run on a miserable weekend—chilly, overcast, and rainy—but Dale was gleaming as he talked about how much fun it had been and how exciting it was to run with his son.

"I learned a lot," he said. "It was real easy to get used to. I really improved my road racing abilities of driving, braking, and turning in the corners. I can't wait to get to Sonoma [the first NASCAR road race of the season] in my Winston Cup car."

Every time Dale Jr. got in the car, the team lost ground, Dale said, laughing. Dale drove three shifts. He was in that car for almost five hours. He drove at night in the rain, reaching 170 mph on the high banks. And the only thing he was unhappy about was that he wasn't in that car longer. He kept saying, "They wouldn't let me get back in the car."

I couldn't imagine what it was like having Dale Earnhardt in the pits wanting to be back in that race car. He had to have been like a worm on a hot rock. In a Winston Cup race, when Dale was behind the wheel, he was the driver, the crew chief, the car owner, the race director, the track clean-up supervisor, and everything else. At least that's how he operated when I was with him. I'm sure he didn't treat those sports car guys any differently.

Mike and I chatted with Dale for about five minutes. As he walked away, I couldn't help but notice the look on his face, the confidence in his voice, the air about him—it looked like the whole package was in place. I told Mike, "Man, that guy is really pumped up."

I spoke with Dale briefly a couple more times during Speedweeks, but that was the last time I ever talked with him at any length. Looking back, it gives me a lot of peace of mind that I was able to talk with him like that before he died.

The next morning, Thursday, February 8, it was time to go to work. I was feeling just a little bit apprehensive. For 21 years, I had worked in the garage as a competitor. But now my role was different. When I walked into the garage that morning, I was wearing regular khaki slacks and a shirt with the FOX logo. For the first time, I was working as a full-time broadcaster.

It was a little awkward at first, but it didn't take long to feel comfortable. It's the people that make NASCAR racing such a great sport, and as soon as I began seeing all of those familiar faces, and no one raised an eyebrow, I was right back in my comfort zone.

Speedweeks 2001 was my 25th anniversary at Daytona. My first trip had been in 1976, when I was a junior in high school. My aunt and uncle and a good friend of ours, Ken Goodwin, who went to school with me, all pitched in money to buy gas and groceries. We rented one of those campers you set up in the back of a pickup truck, and we put it on Uncle Butch's truck. Off to Daytona we went.

We got to Daytona in the wee hours of Friday morning after driving all night. My uncle drove the whole way. Ken and I spent most of the time in the upper bunk of the camper—two kids looking out the window as we rolled toward Florida.

We didn't have a hotel room. All four of us were going to stay in that camper. We didn't have tickets to the race. After we arrived, we went nosing around to find out what we had to do to get into the Daytona 500. Of course, all the reserved grandstand seats were sold. But we learned that at five or six on Sunday morning the speedway would sell tickets for 4,000 to 5,000 unreserved seats down near turn one. And fans were already getting in line that Saturday afternoon.

"Heck, I'll get in that line," I said. I got in line after dinner. I had a lawn chair, a pillow, and a couple of blankets. I stayed all night. I was about the 200th person in line. People were building fires and having parties. It was chilly, but I actually slept quite a bit. The others came and checked on me periodically until they went to bed.

The next morning, right before the sun came up, they put those tickets on sale, and it wasn't long before I had four of them. Our seats were down in turn one, and they weren't very good. So we kept working our way closer to the start-finish line. Before I knew it, that race was half over, and we had finagled our way into seats that were almost right behind the start-finish line.

I was more excited about watching the guys in the pits than I was watching the cars on the track. Through my binoculars, I saw guys like Harry Hyde, Herb Nab, Junior Johnson, and Mario Rossi. They were the people who intrigued me.

Of course, until the last lap, I had no way of knowing we were watching a Daytona 500 that would go down as one of the most exciting in history. On that last lap, Richard Petty and David Pearson got together coming off that final turn. They spun a couple of times, and their cars slid into the tri-oval infield. Petty's car stopped, and I saw his crew run out there to push it. I was thinking, "Man, this would be an unbelievable deal to have your crew push you across the finish line to win the Daytona 500." Then I saw smoke coming out of Pearson's exhaust. Pearson got his car going and limped his way to the checkered flag. It was a pretty phenomenal Daytona 500, particularly for my first one.

Now, 25 years later, I was one of three people with the privilege of describing NASCAR's biggest race for 10 million television viewers back home. Along with Mike, we had Darrell Waltrip, the three-time Winston Cup champion, as my fellow color commentator. Darrell has the amazing ability to come up with comments and descriptions that are original, quick, and clever. Everyone knew he was perfect for broadcasting. I never felt any apprehension working with him. For one, we never viewed it as a competitive situation. And back in January, Darrell had called Mike and me and said, "Why don't you two guys come to Nashville, and we'll spend a day or so together just getting to know each other."

It was one of the best things we did in preparing for the season. Darrell had a suite in a hotel out by the airport, and we spent the day there talking. We talked about our wives, our kids, our feelings, things that upset us. We left there knowing so much more about each other.

I spent a good bit of time in the garage area on that Thursday, learning what was going on. What I learned was that the season hadn't even begun yet, and the teams were already tired. Crews used to come to Daytona all excited because it was a new season and everybody was starting equal. But the crew chiefs and crewmen I talked with were already beat up and rundown. Robin Pemberton, Rusty Wallace's crew chief, said, "Larry, I haven't had a day off since Christmas. I'm worn out." I saw a little bit of me coming out in Robin. I had beaten that bush for 20 years.

These guys had 38 events to run, with only three off weekends, and they were already used up. It was because of how hard they had worked during the off-season, and how close the competition is, and the pressure to please sponsors, and how tough it is to get any kind of competitive edge. And when they get to Daytona, they usually spend the first couple of days dancing to NASCAR's new tune. In 2001, many of the teams were working on the A posts of the cars—the side pieces that frame the windshield. "What's the deal with the A posts?" I asked. The answer was, well, a typical NASCAR deal.

For years, NASCAR had checked the A posts one way, so that's the way everyone built them. Well, wouldn't you know, in 2001, NASCAR was checking them in a different way. So everybody's numbers were off. And most of the teams had to reshape the A posts to get them to conform to the newest NASCAR standard.

Thankfully, I didn't have to work on A posts. But I did spend a lot of time in broadcast meetings. I had meetings and meetings and meetings—so many that I got to wondering if TV wasn't 90 percent meetings and 10 percent on the air. But the meetings were good because we all learned that much more about each other. And that was productive because good chemistry makes the difference between success and failure.

The next day, Friday, February 9, we were going into the booth for our first two hours of broadcasts. Beyond that, we had the Bud Shootout, the Gatorade 125s, the Busch Grand National Series race, and the Daytona 500 itself. But I wasn't as concerned about those as I was about the show right ahead of me, which was two hours of practice. And it was not going to be drafting practice. It was going to be single-car runs. The teams had to prepare for qualifying. So it was not exactly the most dramatic stuff you could put on TV.

But when the show started at 10 a.m., there was a moment that sent chills down my spine. I still get goose bumps when I think about it. Ken Squier, one of the deans of racing broadcasters, had come with FOX to be the host. Squier, who is a native of Vermont, had been broadcasting at Daytona since 1965, when he was a public address announcer. He called the 1976 race for Motor Racing Network and was the anchor on CBS for the first live, flag-to-flag coverage of the 500 in 1979.

And now Ken was set to bring a new network on the air in the world of NASCAR. There was no better guy to do it. I was in the broadcast booth, high above the start-finish line, 14 stories up. I could see Squier standing right in the middle of the tri-oval infield. He was a tiny speck in that big expanse of green grass. Then he started up.

"And a good, good morning. I'm Ken Squier in one of the most precious spots in all of sports. And where, for the past 36 years, I've had the opportunity to be part of the broadcast team for the Daytona 500. From the beaches to this modern superspeedway there have been many changes. But this year marks a special change.

"FOX Sports is proud to become the official broadcaster from Daytona. With respect for those who did so well in the past with this event, FOX looks forward to the opportunity to take televised motorsports to the next level. Get ready! The new era starts right now for the

Great American Race!" I've watched a lot of Ken Squier openings, but this one topped them all. He was awesome.

As the introductory footage rolled, Darrell and I instinctively kept our eyes on the track and even started timing some of the cars. Soon, we all turned our backs to the track to face the camera in our booth. Exactly five minutes into the first broadcast, the host, Chris Myers, sent it up to Mike. Chris and Jeff Hammond were in the "Hollywood Hotel," a studio behind the pits. It was dubbed "Hollywood Hotel" by Darrell because Jeff's flashiness had long ago earned him the nickname "Hollywood Hammond."

After Chris handed the broadcast to Mike Joy, Mike introduced Darrell, who said, "Man, we are ready to rock and roll."

Then Mike introduced me, and I said, "Well, I've been in the garage for 20 years, and hopefully over these next 21 weeks, things that I can do with the help of a lot of others, is explain things to the race fan, you know, maybe explain what that crew chief is thinking and why he's doing what he's doing—why he's telling that driver what he's tellin' him. And that's what our plan is—to tell the stories and take you guys places where you've maybe never been before and, mainly, talk about the race."

"We're going to have some fun," Mike said, finishing it off. "That's first and foremost on the agenda." Then he sent it back down to Chris, who quipped, "Good luck getting a word in with Darrell and Larry throughout the season."

We were on our way. We had 10 people on board for that first broadcast. In addition to us three in the booth, we had Chris and Jeff and Ken Squier. Out on pit road itself were Dick Berggren, Matt Yocum, Steve Byrnes, and Jeanne Zelasko.

It was a big relief when we wrapped up that first two-hour broadcast. After months of anticipation, stretching back to when I signed my contract in mid-August of 2000, we were finally on the air. Just before the show, as I stood in that booth high above the track and looked down on those race cars lined up on pit road, I had a funny feeling in the pit of my stomach. I had been down there so long, I still wasn't quite sure it was totally right to be up here in the booth. Once we got going, all of that went away. And I had more fun than I could have ever imagined. I realized I still had the same passion for the sport and didn't miss being a crew chief one bit.

And it all came together in the booth. It was as if Mike, Darrell, and I had been a team for a long time. When I walked into the trailer at the end of that first afternoon, Ed Goren, president of FOX sports, shook my hand, looked me right in the eye, and said, "Job well done." That was all I needed, because I know Ed tells it like it is.

Next up was qualifying on Saturday and the Bud Shootout on Sunday, both on the main FOX network. The Daytona 500 itself was still more than a week away. FOX was making its NASCAR debut in a big way, with 43 hours of Speedweeks telecasts on three channels—the main FOX network and the FOX Sports Net and FX cable channels.

For our second day on the air, on top of going on the main network for the first time, we faced a marathon—five hours of broadcasting. We started the day bright and early at 8:30 with a broadcast of a Winston Cup practice session on FOX Sports Net. And after three hours of qualifying on the main network, we finished the day with a telecast on FX of the Florida 200, a race for four-cylinder Goody's Dash cars.

Since we were on the main network, the brass came to town, including David Hill, chairman and chief executive officer of FOX Sports. Naturally, your nervousness increases in a situation like that. But I tried to take the attitude that it didn't make any difference if David was in New York, Los Angeles, or standing right by my side. As it turned out, it wasn't long before David *was* there, right by my side, and not at the best of moments. It happened in the middle of the longest, slowest broadcast I had ever known. Before the show started, Mike told us, "This is going to be the worst show of the year."

"Why?" asked Darrell and I at the same time.

"Trust me," Mike said. "What's happening today is that you're going to be watching one car at a time go around a two-and-a-half-mile track. You're going to have a lot of time to fill." So I tried to be prepared for that. We told a lot of stories. We tried to keep the enthusiasm up. But we didn't have a lot to work with. Watching one car at a time go around for two laps, hell, it's hard to hype that up.

Right in the middle of the broadcast, David came into the booth and he busted my bubble for the first time. David is from Australia and he doesn't hold back. He put his arms around Darrell and me and said he thought the audience was going to sleep. "You guys have got to pick up the pace. You guys have got to put forth some energy," he said.

I thought my energy level was topped out, to tell the truth. But I said, "OK, I'm with you." David told us afterward, "You guys didn't have a whole lot to work with." Sometimes, even the best in the business need re-energizing, he said. I knew we had to show energy, but David said we had to show it during pace laps and caution laps, too.

"Whew!" I thought. "Heaven help us all." But I knew that's what helps keep fans on the edge of their seats.

David told us that before one of FOX's biggest football playoff games, Terry Bradshaw, Howie Long, Cris Collinsworth, and J. B. Brown were doing a pregame show in the studio like they were on a home and garden show. He went in there and cussed 'em for everything they were worth.

"What am I paying you guys for?" he stormed. "If you're not going to do any better job than this, get out!"

That's just his style.

The big story in qualifying, and during much of Speedweeks, was the return of Dodge to NASCAR. Dodge had a rich NASCAR history. From 1953 to 1977, Dodges won 160 races. Legends like Bobby Allison, Buck Baker, Junior Johnson, David Pearson, and two generations of Pettys, Lee and Richard, had won for Dodge. Richard won 37 of his 200 races in a Dodge, including the 1973 and 1974 Daytona 500s. But in 1978 Petty had his first winless season in 18 years in the Dodge Magnum, and when he switched to a Chevrolet in midseason, Dodge all but disappeared from the Winston Cup series.

In 2001 Dodge was back in force, with 10 cars. The primary factory team, with two cars, was owned by Ray Evernham, who helped guide Jeff Gordon to his first three Winston Cup championships. Ray had been courted by Dodge in 2000. Ray decided to switch, but Gordon decided to stay with Chevy and inked a lifetime pact with car owner Rick Hendrick. One of the most successful partnerships in NASCAR history had ended suddenly one September day in 2000. And Evernham started creating his new empire.

I had watched the Dodges in practice for a day and a half. It looked like they were going to be just OK, no better. Ray looked like the most miserable human being walking the face of the earth on Friday and Saturday morning. But when it came time to go to the bottom of the bag, Ray and his group did it. Ray's primary driver, Bill Elliott, won the pole in a Dodge at a speed of 183.565 mph.

What a story. Less than two years earlier, in 1999, the return of Dodge to Winston Cup was nothing more than a thought. The manufacturer didn't get serious about it until the middle of 1999. One of the Dodge engine builders told me, "Larry, I didn't even have parts that I was comfortable with for Daytona until a month and a half ago."

What Dodge did was phenomenal. Not only was a Dodge on the pole, but it was an all-Dodge front row. And two more Dodges were among the 10 fastest. But the way the Dodges got the front row was pretty different. Jerry Nadeau had unofficially won the second starting spot in a Chevrolet. He hadn't made much noise Friday. It seemed like he was just laying in the weeds. And then, during qualifying, boom, he had a fast lap.

But when NASCAR put his car through inspection, it found some funny things with the rear jack bolt that controls the rear height of the car. Nadeau was disqualified. That meant that Stacy Compton, who was third fastest, moved to the front row. He was not only in a Dodge, he was driving for a single-car team—a real disadvantage in recent years.

Now that qualifying was over, all the teams began changing their cars from qualifying setups to race setups as they prepared for the Twin 125-mile qualifying races and the Daytona 500 itself. Basically, they change everything on the car—shocks, springs, sway bars, engine, transmission, gears. When I was a crew chief, my checklist had almost 30 items.

Even though pole qualifying was over, the starting field wasn't set. Under Daytona's unique way of qualifying, only the first row—the two fastest qualifiers—were in the race as of Saturday. The rest of the field was set after the Twin 125s.

But in the Winston Cup practice session Saturday morning before qualifying, there was trouble. With 52 Winston Cup cars down here, you would think that my old team would avoid being involved in the first controversy. But that's what happened.

During practice before qualifying, there was an accident during practice involving three cars, including Mike Skinner in the No. 31 Lowe's Chevrolet. There was no question Mike screwed up. We watched the replay more than once. During a break, Mike Joy looked at me and said, "Do you want to talk about it?"

I said, "This is my job. And one thing everybody has banged the gavel on the desk about is to tell it like it is. It's right there in front of us. The fans have seen it. If we don't tell it like it is, we're kidding ourselves if we say we're doing a good job."

As the pack was coming off turn two, Mike dropped down out of the pack to prepare to come into the pits. When he did that, he moved down on Jeff Burton, who had to check up. And Dale Earnhardt Jr. hit Burton from behind. They didn't wreck, but both Burton and Earnhardt Jr. had a little bit of damage to their fenders and quarter panels, which can make a big difference in aerodynamics. I felt like Mike didn't get out of the pack soon enough and wasn't really paying attention. And so I said it. I had to do that. I wondered if Mike would complain to me about it, but he never did.

Mike is a great friend. He and his wife have become close to Linda and myself. But when I was his crew chief, people came to me from time to time and asked me to settle him down. They told me he had a fast race car, but he was always all over the place. And up in that booth looking down, that is exactly what I saw.

We came back at the end of pole qualifying day and had a good show. It was that little ol' Goody's Dash race. The broadcast started out pretty rough. We knew very little about these cars and drivers, especially Darrell and me. We were calling them "the yellow car, the white car, the black car." But as the race went on, we learned the names of all the front-runners. And it was a good broadcast because it was a good race.

If I was disappointed with anything during those first two days, it was with some of the technical work. Something was always broken. The Telestrator wasn't working, or the scoring monitor wasn't working. With the Telestrator, you just stick your finger on the screen and draw a circle or square or whatever you want to use, to say, point out a hole in a tire or the amount of camber in a front tire. To reset the Telestrator, you touch the lower left-hand corner of the screen. Early in the season, I had trouble getting the thing cleared. I was making so many dots and circles on the screen it looked like a Dalmatian puppy. Finally I just said, "Darrell, will you clear that thing for me? I'm having no luck." I learned the secret is to go slower. It worked much better when I slowed down.

I knew we were rookies in the booth, at least Darrell and I, but one of the biggest surprises during the first two days was to discover that we also had a lot of rookies running our show. Many of them hadn't worked on NASCAR telecasts before. We needed better support behind us, but I also knew they had a tough job and they would probably get better really quickly.

Our Saturday marathon on the air did not relieve us from attending the meeting on Saturday night to discuss the day's shows. Right in the middle of the meeting, David Hill called. Well before we went off the air, David had left to fly to Miami. Ed Goren took the call. Ed always calls him "Dr. Hill." I heard Ed ask him, "Well, Dr. Hill, are there any last-minute instructions for these guys?"

Ed listened to David's response. Then he hung up. Ed turned to us and said, "Well, guys, he gave you his instructions in a few short words: *'Don't screw it up!'*"

The Bud Shootout is the traditional non-points race held on the Sunday before the Daytona 500. It started in 1979 as the Busch Clash, as a race primarily for the previous year's pole position winners. It's always been a short race—between 20 and 50 laps—but this year's version called for 70 laps. Eighteen cars were in the field. A race of that length forced all the cars to make at least one pit stop and provided a good test of the new rules that NASCAR instituted to try to improve the racing at the superspeedways.

After Daytona opened in 1959, door-to-door racing, last-lap "slingshot" passes, and close finishes became the norm. But when the cars began racing at over 200 mph and Bobby Allison about went into grandstands at Talladega in May of 1987, NASCAR began cutting speeds by order-ing the teams to use carburetor restrictor plates, which reduced the amount of air and fuel flowing to the engine and cut the horsepower.

In recent years, the size of the openings in the restrictor plate have become smaller and smaller. Horsepower has been cut from more than 700 to about 400. Potential speeds are cut from perhaps 225 mph to less than 185. Every driver can keep his foot to the floor all the way around, and the draft keeps everyone bunched together. But no one has the power to pass. Your foot is already on the floor, and as soon as you pull out to pass, if you don't have someone behind you, the wind resistance slows you down, and you end up losing two, three, five, or 10 positions or more before you can get back in line.

It all came to a head in the 2000 Daytona 500. No one could pass, and there was little action. Dale Jarrett won his third 500 after a measly nine lead changes among seven drivers, mostly during yellow flags. Afterward I said, "They need to go and replace all the seats here with cots, because with racing like this, nobody is going to want to watch. They'll all want to take naps."

I got called to the NASCAR trailer for that one. But I wasn't the only one complaining. *Everybody* was complaining. Dale Earnhardt told the press that "Big" Bill France, the late president of NASCAR who built the speedway, would "be turning over in his grave" if he knew racing had become that bad at Daytona.

Later in the 2000 season, NASCAR took steps to try to improve things at Daytona and Talladega. They added a lot of drag to the cars to slow them down aerodynamically. They ordered teams to raise their front air dams to increase the space between the track and the bottom of the body. They also put a roof strip across the roof to break the flow of air. And they increased the spoiler angle from 45 to 70 degrees and put a one-inch wicker bill, or 90-degree flange, across the top of the spoiler. All of these steps slowed the cars by something like 12 or 13 mph—from around 190 mph to the high 170s. Now NASCAR could give the teams a slightly larger restrictor plate, which adds about 25 horsepower and gives them back about half the speed they lost. Hopefully, the increase in horsepower would help give the drivers more throttle response, not only so they could pass easier, but also so they could recover easier if they had to back off.

The change was immediate and dramatic. In the Winston 500 at Talladega in October 2000, Dale Earnhardt won his 76th career victory after 49 lead changes among 21 drivers—one of the most competitive NASCAR races ever.

We had a terrific Bud Shootout as well. With three laps to go, Dale dove inside Tony Stewart going into turn three to take the lead. One lap later, Stewart returned the favor and then held off that black No. 3 car to win.

It was like the racing at Daytona used to be. There were 19 lead changes among seven drivers in only 70 laps. Afterward, Earnhardt mentioned the comment he'd made in 2000 about France turning over in his grave. "I'd say he'd be jumping around this year about this kind of racing," Dale said.

And we had a good show, too. One of our producers put it this way: "You know, after our qualifying show and the Goody's Dash race, that was such a long day I needed to get back to the hotel to find a fifth of vodka as fast as I could. But after the shows we had today, all I want to do is go back and sip some fine wine."

We were over a little hump. We had one broadcast a day on Monday, Tuesday, and Wednesday, all of them practice sessions. The next big deal came on Thursday with the Twin 125 qualifying races, which were to be shown live on FOX Sports Net. In the past, they had been taped and shown later.

Being a broadcaster is not as pressure-packed as being a crew chief. But it is still very intense. You have to be focused the entire time in the booth. It doesn't matter whether the broadcast is two hours or five hours. There is no letting up, even during commercial breaks, when you have to work on what you're going to do when you're on the air again.

During commercials, I usually scanned some of the team radio channels with my scanner to see if I could pick up on something that a team was concerned about. But I kept the scanner off when we were on the air. During a broadcast, you're trying to talk and you're listening to your fellow announcers, and you also have the producer's voice in your ear. He's often telling you something right while you're talking. With all of that going on, a scanner is one voice too many.

As the Speedweeks broadcasts continued, I had to work hard to keep eye contact with Darrell and Mike. If you don't keep eye contact, you tend to talk across each other. It doesn't sound very professional. The fans at home think, "Those guys, they just don't have their act together."

So I began working hard at stepping back and looking at Mike and Darrell with my peripheral vision. That helped me a bunch. The FOX technical people kept getting better too and ironed out the problems with the Telestrator, which I began using a lot. You can *show* the fans something with the Telestrator rather than *tell* them about it.

One of the big stories of the week was the fines and suspensions NASCAR handed out for breaking the rules. Eighteen different crew chiefs were fined a total of $40,750 for various rules violations. Most of them were $1,000 or less for minor violations, but NASCAR also suspended two crew chiefs for four weeks: Tony Furr, Jerry Nadeau's crew chief, and Kevin Cram, Jason Leffler's crew chief.

Furr was suspended for using improper rear jack bolts that lowered the car during qualifying. To go faster, race teams try to get their cars to run as low as possible to reduce drag. What Tony did was insert a metal piece about an inch and a half long between the jack screw and spring plate in the right rear part of the suspension. The metal piece did what it was supposed to do—it broke off during his qualifying run, which allowed the right rear corner of the car to drop about an inch and a half. Unfortunately for Tony, corner workers saw the piece of metal fall out.

Plus, if you are going to lower your car, make sure it comes back up. Tony's car would not come back up. The inspectors asked Tony how he had planned to bring his car back up to the proper height, since he obviously knew they would be checking the heights of the five or 10 fastest cars afterward. He wouldn't say anything.

But the talk was that the car was so slow before qualifying that Tony was just trying something to get the car among the top 15, never believing it would be fast enough to sit on the outside pole and be forced to go through post-qualifying inspection. Well, it was obviously fast enough. Tony was suspended for four races and was also slapped with a total of $12,750 in fines because he had two other violations as well. I could never imagine being at home with my car at the racetrack. I reckon I would be in line trying to buy a ticket just to get into the race.

Then there was Kevin Cram, a crew chief at Chip Ganassi Racing—a new team with a new sponsor and a new manufacturer. Kevin was fined $10,000 and suspended for four races for tampering with his fuel. Kevin's car, the No. 01 Dodge, hadn't been running well at all. But why would you mess with the fuel? Juiced-up fuel isn't going to fix a problem that big. When you're not even in the ballpark, why bother?

The team's former owner, Felix Sabates, who is still a minority owner, ran around afterward saying the fuel had been sabotaged. That's Felix. We love him. But sabotage? I don't think so.

I guess the biggest surprise was all of the small fines that were passed out by NASCAR for less serious violations such as using light A arms, lightweight fuel cells, oversized fuel cells, and other unapproved parts. In the past, NASCAR had simply confiscated parts like these. And the big violators were hit with big fines, but not suspensions. NASCAR was saying even more strongly that they were simply not going to play around with unapproved parts. They set a precedent with the hope that, as the season progressed, crew chiefs would remember the fines and suspensions at Daytona.

Another big story involved FOX. While we were announcing the starting lineup for the Bud Shootout, FOX and our graphics people did not show sponsor logos on 12 of the 18 graphic animations of the race cars that we used to announce the lineup. FOX did not block out sponsor logos when we were showing the actual cars on the track—only with a dozen of those little race car animations. The sponsor names that were omitted were companies that decided to not advertise on FOX during the race telecasts. As you can imagine, those sponsors weren't happy. And many viewers weren't happy, either.

I could see both sides. The sponsors paid big money to put their names on cars, not only because the fans in the grandstands would see them, but mostly because the millions watching TV would see them. But together FOX and NBC paid $2.6 billion for this TV package.

FOX sold a lot of advertising for the racing broadcasts, but it has never been more expensive to produce the shows. FOX tried to sell advertising to companies that sponsor race cars. The team sponsors that turned FOX down had their animations shown as plain cars, so FOX could put the spotlight on those that did advertise. But after getting bombarded by complaints, NASCAR called FOX executives in for a meeting on Monday. David Hill quickly reversed course and ordjered that all sponsor logos be shown. David told the press, "I figured the best thing to do was let sleeping sponsors lie."

CHAPTER TWENTY-THREE

Seven Seconds from Having a Great Day

The Monday after the Bud Shootout is usually a pretty slow day in the Winston Cup garage. But our broadcast of the practice session that day got pretty lively when Matt Yocum approached Dale Earnhardt for an interview.

During the Shootout, Darrell pointed out that Dale Earnhardt used an open-faced helmet. Darrell said he didn't think it was as safe as the full-face helmet that most drivers use.

Dale brushed off Matt's initial question and asked, "Is Darrell working today?" There was a little edge to his voice.

"Theoretically, yes," Matt said.

"He said something about my open-faced helmet during the race yesterday, and I didn't like that."

It caught Matt off guard. "Well, you know, uh . . . I could set up a meeting maybe. I could ... Do you want to talk to him?"

"As many years as he's been watching races . . . " Dale complained.

"Time out, time out. Hang on a second," Matt said. Then he put his own headphones over Dale's ears so Dale could talk to Darrell and hear him as well.

Darrell quickly steered the conversation away from the helmet: "Don't you think you might have made your move a little early yesterday, bud?"

"Well, Darrell, it was the only move I had," Dale said. "You know, it's sorta like when you see it, you gotta do it. And that was all I had. It may have been a little too soon, and I know it was too soon, matter of fact. And I knew it was wrong when I was doing it. But it was the only opportunity I had. So I had to go for it.

"Now the helmet deal," Dale continued, "you shouldn't be talking about the helmet. It's the safest helmet in Winston Cup racing today."

Darrell started joking about how Dale could supposedly see the wind at Daytona. Darrell said he'd tried Dale's helmet on.

"Maybe that's why my head is itching," Dale said.

I jumped into the conversation. "Hey, you two, wait a minute," I said. "Dale . . . Dale . . . "

"Yeah, Larry."

"This is your other nightmare."

"I won the Daytona 500 with you, buddy," Dale said.

"With an open-faced helmet and that seat you got in that thing, we won the Daytona 500," I said. (I was always trying to get Dale to consider something other than the low-back seat he's always used, which has been criticized for not offering enough protection to the driver.)

"On a serious note," I said. "This is the first time at Daytona in race conditions with the aero package. What are you seeing different than what we've had here before?"

"I like it," Dale said. "Honestly, the cars drive as good as they did before, but it does lend to drafting back up and keeping the cars side by side. I think it's a better race."

We talked some more, and joked some more, and then Dale said, "Look here, I gotta go. My car's ready, and I gotta go back out and practice." We kept the camera on Dale as he strapped himself into his car. Mike explained the difference between Dale's open-faced helmet and the full-face helmet, which comes all the way down to the neck front and back.

"There's pros and cons," Darrell said. "Dale is convinced that the chin guard at the bottom part of the closed-face helmet can actually act as a ratchet and cause your helmet to be pushed up. But I'm not so sure that I wouldn't rather have that happen than have my face bare like his is."

"Well," I said, "in the arguments him and I had about it, he just always said, 'Larry, I just can't see.'"

"He's not wrong," Darrell said. "He likes that open-faced helmet and those old bubble goggles that we've been wearing for 30 years. That's what he likes, and I can't argue with him. I did have to finally convince him to wear gloves, and he did come around to that way of thinking, anyway."

"Wait a minute," I said, "I worked with him a year and a half. He ain't never wrong."

"Have you ever ridden with him in a regular passenger car?" Darrell asked.

"Oh, yeah," I said.

"Oh my gosh," Darrell said. "What a nightmare."

The next day, during the next Winston Cup practice, we chatted with Dale again, this time when Jeanne Zelasko went up to him. "We're having more fun down here in the garage area, guys, since y'all aren't here,"

Dale said. I didn't agree, especially after being a part of great live television like that.

To prepare for the Twin 125 qualifying races on Thursday, February 15, I spent three hours in the garage area and talked to 28 different teams, crew chiefs, and drivers. Then those teams went out and gave us two great races. There were 21 lead changes in the two events. That was 20 more than in 2000.

In the first race, two-time Daytona 500 winner Sterling Marlin won after he passed Dale Earnhardt on the restart with one lap to go. It was Marlin's first visit to victory lane since he won a Twin 125 in 1998. And it was the first victory for Dodge and rookie car owner Chip Ganassi. On the last lap, Earnhardt broke out into a big lead. But that just left him a sitting duck for Marlin, who went from fourth to first to victory lane.

In the second race, my old driver, Mike Skinner, fought off Dale Earnhardt Jr. in a photo finish. They crossed the line side by side, with Skinner just a few inches ahead. We had to look at the replay to make sure. The official margin of victory was .004 second, the smallest ever. It was a great victory for a guy who really needed it. I was so happy for Mike and his crew chief, Royce McGee.

We did some cool things during the Twin 125s broadcast. And we introduced "Crank It Up," where the only sound broadcast is the roar of the cars. It became a trademark. FOX added a decibel meter at the bottom of the screen that measured the level of noise. I thought at first it was a little bit corny, but the fans loved it. Sometimes the simple and obvious thing really works well.

The fans had definitely liked our broadcasts during the first part of Speedweeks. FOX was ecstatic about the ratings, which were really good not only for the Bud Shootout, but for practice and qualifying, too. The rating for the Shootout was the highest in seven years, and 26 percent higher than in 2000. The actual rating was 4.8 with a 12 share.

Television ratings are based on the estimated number of television households in the United States, which in 2001 was 102,200,000 households. Each rating point represents 1 percent of those households, so a rating of one equals 1,022,000 households. So our 4.8 rating meant that 4,905,600 households were tuned in. The 12 share meant that 12 percent of all the operating television sets around the country were tuned to the race.

I was up at 5:30 a.m. on the morning of the 2001 Daytona 500. I showered and dressed in my motorcoach and then waited until a few minutes before seven before taking the short walk over to the garage. I could see the place was teeming with activity as I walked through the gate, and I thought, "Man, this place is awfully busy for being open only a couple of minutes."

Then I found out the garage had opened at six. NASCAR had changed the time. The day was just starting, and I suddenly felt behind. But I made my rounds and discovered that no less than 10 of the 43 teams were changing motors. Some were changing motors because of little problems they'd experienced during Happy Hour. Some teams just didn't feel right about their engines. Jeff Gordon's team was changing engines because Jeff had blown his engine during the final practice. All the crewmen looked the same as last week. Nobody was having fun. The pressure to perform had overwhelmed the enjoyment.

In the booth before the race, the most phenomenal sight, for a guy who spent the previous 20 years at track level, was all the people—more than 250,000 fans in the vast grandstands and infield. The only thing that interrupted the solid mass of cars and campers in the infield was Lake Lloyd, the huge, rectangular man-made lake that was created when soil was excavated to build the banked turns. The race cars look pretty small from the booth, but it's amazing how close they run together and how well you can see whether they're handling or not.

Our pre-race show started an hour before the race itself. One of the first shots on the telecast was Dale Earnhardt at the drivers' meeting. This was the first of a number of moments in this show that, in hindsight, seem eerie. Had nothing happened that day, no one would have given these coincidences a second thought.

Dale was the third driver we interviewed live. He was reclined in front of his motorcoach, with his feet resting on another chair, when Matt Yocum approached. The camera panned slowly from his black driver's shoes up his uniform to his face. His eyes were covered with those familiar sunglasses. It was our last interview with Dale Earnhardt.

"Well, got a good shot at it, got a good race car," Dale said. "Wasn't really excited about the car yesterday afternoon in the last practice, but the car come around. I think it'll be OK. Got a good engine." He took a breath. "A little wind today, a little exciting. I think it's going to be some exciting racing," he said. Then he paused for just a second, nodded his head up and down slightly and said, "Gonna see something you probably hadn't never seen on FOX."

Matt finished up, "The seven-time champion rolls off seventh today. Jeanne . . . "

Jeanne Zelasko took over and told the audience about the death of Adam Petty. Then she interviewed Adam's father, Kyle, about the emotions of coming to Daytona to drive the race car that Adam was supposed to drive.

Later in the show, we aired a segment that had been taped the night before when Dale gave Terry Bradshaw a Saturday night spin around the lighted speedway in a pace car at speeds up to 140 mph. Coming off the fourth turn banking, Dale told Terry, "What's bad about this is the racetrack falls out from under you right here, and if you don't hold it, you can go WHAM! into the wall." Dale jerked the steering wheel as he said "wham" to give Terry a thrill.

At the end of the segment, Terry said he would be in victory lane after the race.

"You gonna be here?" Dale asked excitedly. He gave Terry a big hug and added, "I'm awful lucky when you're around. You remember that?"

"You know it, don't you?" Terry said. Bradshaw had been at Daytona in 1998 when Dale won his only 500.

The only time I got sweaty palms was about five minutes before the race itself, as we started the final ceremonies before the call to start engines. For just a few moments, reality set in. I was about to start talking to an audience of 12 million or more. I got a little bit jittery. But I took heart in what Linda had told me as I left the motorcoach that morning. "Larry," she said, "just go up there and do what you've always done. Go up there and be yourself and the results will be just fine."

As we switched from the pre-race show to the actual telecast, Dale was again the first driver we showed, as he walked down pit road toward his car. Teresa was on one side, Taylor Nicole on the other. Michael Waltrip was also walking with them. Moments later, we had another shot of Dale, this time with one arm around his son and the other around Teresa. He leaned forward and spoke into Dale Jr.'s ear. Just before the drivers got into their cars, we showed Earnhardt again. He gave Teresa a kiss and a hug. Then I noticed he gave her a second kiss.

Once the race got under way, Mike, Darrell, and I had a fast pace going, but it was smooth. Early on, Darrell explained what it means when a car is "tight."

"It's oversteer," Darrell said. "You can't get it to turn."

I jumped in, "And the only thing you can do most of the time is back off the throttle."

"No, no, no!" Darrell shouted. "That's not the only thing you can do! You can call your crew chief and raise Cain!"

It was fun to be Darrell's straight man.

On lap 27, Dale Earnhardt dove onto the apron of the backstretch and almost into the grass as he passed leader Sterling Marlin and took the lead for the first time. Four others already had led, and soon Skinner would take the front as well as Jeff Burton.

"This year, they don't even need seats, because *nobody* is sitting down up here," I said.

The racing continued this way, lap after lap, as the drivers often went three wide to pass. D. W. said, "I feel that old clock tickin' boys, and it's getting louder."

With 35 laps to go, Michael Waltrip charged up the middle in a three-wide pack to challenge Marlin for the lead. It was his first appearance at the front during our telecast.

"A Waltrip leading the Daytona 500—all right!" said Darrell.

"Look at 'em, four wide off turn four!" I said moments later.

With 30 laps to go, Dale Earnhardt's entire three-car team was leading the big show, and the owner was sitting right behind them. Knowing Dale as I did, it had to be one of his proudest moments as a racer.

The inevitable "big one" happened on lap 174. Eighteen cars wrecked. Tony Stewart's No. 20 Home Depot Pontiac veered hard right into the outside wall, turned over, rode upside down across Gordon's car, and then tumbled down the track, shearing off Bobby Labonte's hood before sliding to a stop on all four wheels. So many cars were involved, I said, "I only see about seven or eight cars that do *not* have damage."

As the damaged cars that could still move limped back to the pits or the garage, I remembered seeing that black No. 3 car come around the track unscathed. I thought to myself, "That son-of-a-gun almost never gets involved in the big one." Ken Schrader also miraculously avoided the mayhem.

"Darrell," I said during a replay, "I gotta ask you. What is Tony Stewart feeling and what is he hearing while this is going on?" Darrell had taken his own tumble down the backstretch of Daytona during the 1991 Pepsi 400, flipping six and a half times.

"When it gets silent, that's when you know you're in big trouble," he replied. "It doesn't stay that way very long, but you know you've gone airborne. So you just hold on with all your might so that your arms don't go flying all over the place."

The race was brought to a halt with the red flag. During the delay, which was 16 minutes, 25 seconds, Jeff Hammond talked about some of the safety factors built into Winston Cup cars, using a show car model of Dale Earnhardt's famous black No. 3 Chevrolet on which half the body had been removed

The race resumed with 21 laps to go. Dale Jr. was in the lead as it started, but he had his father, Michael Waltrip, Bill Elliott, and Sterling Marlin pecking at him. Marlin had lost three-quarters of a lap earlier when one of his tires went down. But Sterling closed the gap during caution laps and took the lead from Dale Jr. on lap 182.

With 18 to go, Waltrip got a big head of steam coming through the tri-oval and made a great move from fourth position. He passed Bobby Hamilton, shot to the outside of Earnhardt, and passed him, too. Then he got by Marlin on the backstretch to take the lead on lap 184 after a side-by-side battle with Earnhardt to the line. Soon, two generations of Earnhardts were behind Michael.

Mike Joy asked Darrell what he would tell his brother to do in this position.

"I'd tell him to guard the inside," D. W. said. "Make 'em go around you on the outside."

Later, I learned that Dale Sr. was relaying the same instructions by radio to his drivers. "Tell 'em to run low," he said. "Tell 'em to stay low."

As I watched Dale run those last 10 laps, I saw something different in him. He was running to protect those two drivers at the front. You never saw that from Dale. For the first time, he wasn't driving offensively; he was driving defensively. He was doing it for those two drivers ahead of him—his drivers. I can only imagine how thrilled he felt right up to the moment of that terrible accident. Michael was more than just Dale's driver; he was one of his best friends. Michael and his wife, Buffy, did everything with Dale and Teresa—vacations, dinners, you name it. It was a really good friendship.

With two laps to go, Ken Schrader moved up in the outside line and pulled side by side with Earnhardt. That's as close as the outside line could get to Michael.

"The last lap!" Mike announced. D. W. took over. Our producer, Neil Goldberg, jumped in and said, "Let Darrell keep it." I did not say a word during that last lap.

"One to go, buddy," Darrell said. "Keep it low, Mikey. Keep it low. Don't let them under you. Make that back straightaway wide, buddy. Get all over the place. Don't let 'em run up on you. C'mon, man. C'mon, now. Watch the mirror. Watch him. He's going to make a run inside. Block him! Block him! Atta boy!"

"Three wide behind them," Mike said as the pack sped through turn three.

"You got him, Mikey!" D. W. shouted. "You got him, man! You got it! C'mon, man."

Suddenly, Dale's car turned hard right, hit Schrader, and then plowed almost head-on into the outside wall.

"Ohhhhhhh!" Darrell screamed.

"Big trouble!" shouted Mike. "Right behind them!"

I thought to myself, "Dale Earnhardt hit that wall awfully hard."

"To the flag," Mike continued.

"C'mon Mikey, you got it, man," D. W. said. "You got it! You got it! You got it!!!! Mikeeeeey all right! all Right!"

"Michael Waltrip wins!" Mike said.

"It's a television dream come true!" Darrell said. Then he paused and said, "How 'bout Dale? Is he OK?"

Mike said, "Schrader climbed out of his car. He and Earnhardt have crashed together in turns three and four."

"This is great," Darrell said quietly. He was spent. He had tears in his eyes. "I just hope Dale's OK. I guess he's all right, isn't he?"

But I was already plenty worried. After Dale's car slid into the infield, I grabbed my binoculars and started watching. I kept my eyes glued on the scene. I saw everything. Even after he hit the wall as hard as he did, I thought Dale was going to climb out and throw his helmet through the driver's-side window. Then he would start raising hell with some-body—maybe Marlin, maybe Schrader, or maybe just a poor ol' track worker.

But Dale didn't get out. When the rescue workers arrived at his car, pandemonium broke out. I saw a lot of people running around, pan-icking. One rescue worker got the "jaws of life" hydraulic cutting tool to cut the roof off. I started to feel that the worst had happened, but I hoped for the best. I told myself that it wasn't unusual to cut off a roof. Maybe Dale was complaining about his back. Maybe he had a broken leg or arm, or a bad contusion. I saw them get Dale out of the car, but I couldn't tell what was going on. There were too many people around him. Then I saw the worst sight ever at a race—any race. They covered up Dale's car.

We weren't talking about all this during the broadcast. All the atten-tion was centered on Michael in victory lane, and that's how it should have been. I watched as the ambulance with Dale drove away from the scene of the accident. It passed by the infield care center and headed straight toward the tunnel under turn four. Our cameras were on it by this point, and we were talking about it. We followed the ambulance out of the racetrack and down a near-empty International Speedway Boulevard toward Halifax Hospital a couple of blocks away. I couldn't help but notice the ambulance wasn't in a big hurry.

When the broadcast was over, all three of us grown men up in that booth simultaneously hugged each other. We did it out of relief that Speedweeks was finally over. We'd been in that booth for 43 hours, broadcasting everything from practices to qualifying to the Busch series race to Winston Cup races to events we didn't know a whole lot about. We also hugged because we felt we had done a good job. And we did it for Darrell, too. Not only had he watched his brother win the Daytona 500, Darrell had called that dramatic last lap on national television. Finally, we hugged each other because each of us knew in our hearts that one of our best friends and one of the best race car drivers to ever put on a helmet was in bad trouble.

I thought back to the beginning of the race, when FOX opened with live, quick hits on the drivers, and Dale had given his wife, Teresa, an extra kiss. I had noticed it and said to myself, "These guys could be giving their wives their last kiss and last hug." The thought lasted just a second. Then it went away.

After the broadcast, I walked from the track to the Daytona Beach airport to catch my commercial flight home. The airport is so close to the track that the easiest way to get there after the 500 is to walk. I worried as I walked.

At the airport, I was eating a hamburger and french fries and drinking a beer when my cell phone rang. Neil Goldberg was on the line. He asked me if I had heard anything. I said no, but I knew immediately what he was fixing to tell me. Neil said that Mike Helton, the president of NASCAR, was getting ready to make a statement. He was going to announce that Dale had passed away.

I sat there and finished eating, in a state of shock more than anything else. All I wanted to do right then was get on that airplane and get home. Later, as I walked back to my seat in coach, dressed in my coat and tie with a briefcase and a bag in one hand, my cell phone rang. Linda was on the line. She was hysterical. I couldn't understand a word from her. She and Dale had become good friends during my time at Richard Childress Racing. They were buddies. I reached my seat and sat down and talked with her, but she never calmed down. Finally I said, "Linda, I'll call you from Atlanta. They're telling us we have to cut off our cell phones." I was kind of glad we had to terminate the conversation.

I didn't really talk to anyone on the flight. It was full, of course. A couple of people recognized me and told me they were sorry, but thankfully nobody overwhelmed me. I was just numb. When I reached Atlanta, I called Linda. She had calmed down a little bit, but not a lot. I don't remember all of what I said, but I'm sure I told her that Dale had died doing what he loved to do. I finally got home about 11 p.m.

I didn't sleep very well that night. I knew one of the first things I wanted to do in the morning was call Dale's crew chief, Kevin Hamlin. I'd been through this. I wanted to sympathize with him. I wanted to tell him that I knew what he was going through and one day he'd feel better again.

We had been seven seconds away from one of the best Daytona 500s in a long, long time, and one of the best racing broadcasts ever. Even before the accident, the nation said it was one of the best by watching in record numbers. When the ratings were tallied, FOX had the most-watched Daytona 500 ever, with a 10.0 rating and a 24 share. We had about 32 million viewers watching in 10.22 million households.

The reviews were great, too. Three days after the telecast, *Racer Magazine*'s Bill King gave us an "A-plus" on the broadcast and said we had raised the bar for racing broadcasts. "Darrell Waltrip and Larry McReynolds made a huge difference in the booth," King wrote. The FOX executives were happy. The fan feedback was great. At the grocery store and at the hardware store I ran into people who loved the show. I received a lot of phone calls. I heard nothing negative. So I felt fulfilled over the job we did at Daytona, yet I felt so empty leaving there.

It was impossible to believe that Dale Earnhardt was gone. Not Dale Earnhardt. Not the greatest, most popular driver in the sport. Around 9 a.m., I called the RCR shop and asked for Kevin. He came on the line. I wasn't surprised he was there. Sometimes the best therapy is to be in your normal environment. I knew how he felt. I talked to Kevin for about 15 minutes. Kevin is not very emotional. He doesn't show a lot of feelings, but I could tell Dale's death was working on him pretty hard.

Before the 500, when each driver was introduced, there was a new twist. Each driver's crew chief had walked across the stage with him. "I thought that was so stupid," Kevin said as he broke down in tears. "But you know what? I wouldn't trade that moment for anything on Earth. I got to walk across that stage with Dale."

For some reason, Dale had always called Kevin "Frank." As they walked across the stage, they could hear, as usual, a lot of cheers and a lot of boos. And Dale turned to Kevin and said, "Frank, listen to 'em. They're booing you."

I told Kevin, "Every crew chief on the circuit can call you and tell you they are sorry and they know how you feel. Unfortunately, I can say that and mean it." I said even though Davey's death was different, it was the same. We had each lost a driver. The hardest day, I said, would be his first day back at the racetrack—at Rockingham in just four days. I told him he'd be going back to the track with all the same parts, all the same pieces, all the same people—everything. But one big piece would be missing—his driver. "When I went to Talladega with that 28 car but without Davey, it was hard to work without tears in my eyes," I said.

As with Davey and me, Kevin and Dale had become good friends. You lose a driver, but you also lose a good friend. There isn't an easy way to handle it. But if this sport laid down, if the teams quit racing, if the fans stopped coming, if Dale's team laid down, if Richard Childress Racing laid down, Dale would be one angry individual. We all know that. That man did not know what quitting was. He qualified his car at Indy a couple of years ago with a broken sternum. He drove cars with casts on his legs. I tried to say all the right things to Kevin, but I also tried to be a good listener. "If you need anything, or just someone to talk to, give me a call any time."

Then came Dale's memorial service on Thursday, February 22. The day before, Teresa and the family had said good-bye at a small, private funeral in Mooresville, where he was buried. The larger service was for Dale's friends and all of the racing fraternity. When Teresa walked in with the family, I couldn't help but think, "What a strong lady."

During the service, Randy Owens, of the group Alabama, sang two songs, and Motor Racing Outreach minister Dale Beaver gave a short sermon. I had stayed fairly strong since hearing the news at the airport Sunday evening, but when Randy sang his first song, "Good-bye," I developed a big lump in my throat.

I guess it's been too much fun
But we've shared and we've won
And, yes, the best is yet to come.
Good-bye, good-bye, till I see you again.
Good-bye, good-bye, I'll love and I'll miss you till then.

I thought the words were exactly what Dale would have told us if he had still been among us. When Randy sang his second song, "Angels Among Us," I lost it. I was thinking about losing Davey in 1993, and losing my dad in 1990, and my mom in 1995, and I just broke down sobbing. It did me good to let it all pour out.

As the service came to an end, Teresa walked up near the pulpit, put her hands out to the crowd, then put them in front of her heart and moved her lips to say a silent, "Thank you." What a beautiful way to end the service.

Friday dawned gray and cold at North Carolina Speedway at Rockingham. Media from around the country arrived early and filed into a huge white tent just outside the track, where NASCAR President Mike Helton dropped a bombshell. He said Dale's left lap seat belt had come apart. "We don't know why," Helton said. "We don't know how. We don't know when yet. All we know is that there was a broken belt at this point."

The press conference set off a firestorm of controversy that continues even today. Bill Simpson of Simpson Performance Products, Inc., which made the belt, said in a statement, "We have never seen a seat belt come apart in the manner that occurred. Our seat belts, when properly installed, won't fail." That put the spotlight on Richard Childress Racing. Richard angrily responded that Dale's belts were properly installed.

NASCAR conducted a formal investigation and announced in August that Dale had died from a basal skull fracture, which is basically a fatal whiplash injury. Did the failure of the belt, and the possibility that Dale's head hit the steering wheel, have anything to do with the fatal injury? That remained a question.

But one fact was clear: Dale died of the same injury that killed Adam Petty and Kenny Irwin. Their seat belts hadn't failed. I was not at the press conference, but watched a tape of it before qualifying. I think NASCAR should have had more facts before it made that announcement. It was as if NASCAR was covering its own butt. It was like NASCAR was saying, "Well, it's not the very close racing at Daytona that's the problem. It's not the concrete walls that are the problem. Dale Earnhardt had a seat belt problem."

As Dale's former crew chief, I was besieged by the media the minute I walked into the garage. The requests for interviews were relentless. It got to the point where I just wanted to call a press conference. The more interviews I did, the more frustrated and angry I got. Some of the reporters knew just enough about racing to get them in trouble.

Did I ever know of Dale loosening his seat belts? Did I ever know if Dale mounted the seat belts wrong? One reporter actually asked me if the boxes in which the seat belts are shipped to the teams were sealed, raising the possibility of sabotage.

"Get a life," I snapped. "You're way out of line here."

Would Dale have survived if he had worn a full-face helmet? Would he have survived if he hadn't used that low-back seat he used— the one we used to get on him about all the time? Would he have survived if he had used the HANS (a head and neck restraint) device, which is designed to prevent whiplash injuries?

I could have speculated—just about everyone else was. But this is how I feel: For whatever reason, it was God's will to take Dale Earnhardt at that particular hour on that particular day. That means nothing would have made a difference. That doesn't mean you can walk off the top of a 30-story building and, if it's not your time, expect to survive. You have to be smart. But God's will is God's will.

Brandon had come with me to Rockingham. We had dinner together. Everyone in my family was taking Dale's death hard, but Brandon was really struggling with it. Brandon, like Linda, felt that Dale was his buddy. Brandon had even gone to victory lane back in 1997 when Dale won a 125-mile qualifying race. Brandon is very compassionate and has a heart as good as gold. He had dozens of questions about the seat belts and Dale's car.

And when we went back to Bandolero racing in May of 2001, there was no question that Dale's death was still really working on Brandon. He didn't run well in May or June, and he was constantly asking about seat belts and hitting the wall. We turned the corner in early July, when I put him in a head and neck restraining device developed by Bobby Hutchins, ironically a team engineer at Richard Childress Racing.

At Rockingham, on the first lap of the race, Dale Earnhardt Jr. was hit by another driver and crashed. The whole place went silent for a few seconds. But we knew pretty quickly from the in-car camera shots that Dale Jr. was OK. He told reporters, "The lap belt was a little too tight, so I'm a little bruised up." That little bit of sarcasm showed what he thought of the speculation surrounding his father's death. One of the rumors was that Dale Sr. had loosened his belts before the crash.

We didn't get very far in that race before it was rained out. It was almost like Dale was teasing us by making us stay an extra day at Rockingham. But the next day, we had awesome weather, with temperatures in the 70s, and an awesome race. Jeff Gordon and Steve Park swapped the lead all day, but Park won in his Dale Earnhardt, Inc., Chevy. It was an emotional victory. Park took a backwards "Polish Victory Lap," holding his No. 3 Dale Earnhardt hat out his window. He also gave his teammate, Michael Waltrip, a high-five while both were still in their cars. Maybe Steve's victory was another little sign from Dale Earnhardt. Maybe he was letting us know that everything was OK.

I couldn't help but notice how my old team and Mike Skinner struggled. I had a sense of relief seeing this from a personal standpoint, because I didn't have to figure out what the problems were. I wasn't the crew chief anymore, so I didn't have to leave Rockingham worrying about it. I didn't have to take that drive home saying, "Why didn't we do this? Why did the car do that?"

CHAPTER TWENTY-FOUR

Life as a Broadcaster

As the 2001 season got underway in earnest, the controversy over Dale Earnhardt's death continued. Dale would have said, "Y'all just get back to racing." And Richard Childress did just that, fielding rookie Kevin Harvick in a white No. 29 Goodwrench Chevrolet. Richard said he would never run a black No. 3 Chevrolet again.

The fourth race of the season was at Atlanta. With 20 laps to go, five drivers had a chance to win. Harvick, making only his third Winston Cup start, was one of them. He came to the finish line side by side with Jeff Gordon. At the last second, Kevin edged ahead of Jeff by a few inches in one of the closest finishes in NASCAR history. After we went off the air, I couldn't wait to get to victory lane, congratulate Richard, and hug his neck. When I got to him, he was speechless.

But some unpleasant side effects of the tragedy lingered. The most negative thing was the fight over Dale's autopsy photos. Less than two weeks after the crash, his widow, Teresa, felt compelled to fly all the way to Las Vegas to hold a press conference during the race weekend there. A couple of Florida newspapers were trying to get ahold of the photographs taken of Dale's body. I couldn't understand why anyone would stoop that low. Teresa vowed to fight in court to keep the photos from being made public. She took no questions, but it still had to be tough. I felt so bad for Teresa. It's amazing how some people can be so morbid and sick when it comes to things like this.

The press conference, of course, meant more questions for me from the press. And I became shorter with reporters than I had ever been. On race morning in Las Vegas, a reporter approached who I didn't recognize. His first two questions about Dale were decent, and I answered them. But his third question was about Dale's seat belt.

"Get away from me," I said. "I'm not going there. I'm not talking about it. You people have worn out this issue. Enough is enough." Of course, a minute later, I second-guessed what I had done. But I had reached my breaking point. We didn't need to blame anybody. We just needed to find out what caused his death and what we could do to prevent something like that from happening in the future.

The most positive thing in the early part of the season, and for that matter throughout our broadcast season, was the ratings. We backed up our record-setting Daytona 500 with an astounding 8.2 rating at Rockingham for a broadcast that was washed out after only a few laps. It was only two-tenths of a point lower than the rating for the 2000 Daytona 500 on CBS. Obviously, the tragedy had a lot to do with it, but we blew away the previous Rockingham rating (5.2). And that was considered outstanding.

Both Linda and I usually go to Las Vegas, and on Wednesday afternoon before the race there, we were playing blackjack at the Mandalay Bay Resort casino. I was in the rest room when my cell phone rang. It was David Hill. The reception was terrible.

"Larry," he said in that Australian accent of his, "we thought you were going to do a good job for us or we wouldn't have hired you. But you've been the total surprise of this whole package. You are *awesome*. The ratings are terrific, and we're getting great feedback from the press and the fans. Just keep doing what you're doing."

What David said made me feel as good as anything anybody had said to me in a long, long time. My confidence soared. I was grinning from ear to ear as I told Linda. I sat back down at the blackjack table and went right back to losing. All the Vegas casinos should have signs saying, "Welcome, Larry McReynolds. We're glad you're here."

The FOX broadcast team is kind of like a race team. Mike, Darrell, and I are the drivers—the ones you see perform. We usually get the credit or blame. But behind us, making it all work, is a gigantic team of executives, producers, production assistants, camera operators, engineers, electricians, and helpers who make the whole thing work.

And usually this team is literally behind us, working out of a half-dozen semi-trailers parked behind the tower where the broadcast booth is located. Several of the trailers are crammed with monitors and broadcast equipment. It's hard to believe, but there's an entire trailer for instant replay, another trailer for in-car cameras, and a third trailer just for producing the wide variety of graphics that we use on the screen.

The main production trailer is a scene of controlled chaos during a telecast. Three short rows of seats face a huge wall of television monitors in a dimly lit room. Neil Goldberg, the producer in charge, sits in the front left seat. Artie Kempner, the director, sits in the middle. Richie Bascilli, the technical director, is next to Artie. Pam Miller, the pit producer, and other producers and directors sit in the second and third rows.

The wall of television monitors they face has more than 80 separate screens. It's a far cry from the first broadcasts of the Daytona 500 on ABC's Wide World of Sports. Back then, they had only three or four cameras, Bill Flemming in the booth, and Chris Economaki on pit road. Today, we have three cameras alone on pit road, and 30 different in-car cameras. We have about 45 cameras total. The nicknames of the camera operators—T-Bone, Chopper, Pony, Thumper, Stoli, Goat, Turtle, Cubbi—are affixed to some of the monitors.

The scene becomes almost frantic as Neil calls out which camera to use and Richie punches the buttons. You have to shout to be heard, so Pam might be shouting, "Matt's got a report," while Neil is talking to us while changing cameras while we're talking to the audience. When you see the craziness of a production booth, it's hard to believe a telecast could be smooth.

Up in the booth, we have to adjust to various facilities at each track. Sometimes we'll have a great booth with plenty of room. Sometimes the booth will be so small you're packed in there shoulder to shoulder.

We face three monitors. In the center is a scoring and statistical monitor. To our left is the monitor with the race broadcast. And on our right is the isolation, or "Iso," monitor. During the broadcast, if, say, we're doing a commercial, I can ask Neil to show me a replay on the Iso monitor. Or they can show us something they want us to see. We have a talk-back button that allows us to communicate off the air directly with Neil and the others in the production trailer.

One of the ongoing issues that Mike, Darrell, and I had during the 2001 and 2002 seasons was the amount of talking in our ears by Neil and those in the production booth. Sometimes it would get to be too much, and we'd have a meeting with Neil, and things would settle down for a few races. Then the issue would resurface. Sometimes there were just too many words coming into our ears while we were talking to the audience. All they needed to do was lead us in the direction they wanted us to go with a few brief words.

As time went on, I found it to be less of a problem. That's because I learned to live with it. When Neil talked in my ear, I just concentrated on what I had to say and tuned out what I needed to tune out. That seemed to work really well, and I still even caught what Neil was saying perhaps 70 percent of the time.

One of my weaknesses as a broadcaster, I'll admit, is my grammar. Pam Miller started working with me about it early in the 2001 season. "Larry, it's 'we were' and 'they were,' not 'we was' and 'they was,'" she said. "And you've got to get rid of 'done did.'" I knew that my grammar was one of the biggest areas where I could improve.

At first, I stuck sticky notes around the monitor in the broadcast booth listing some of my bad ones, such as "done gone," and "done got," and "we was." But I learned that wouldn't work after I lost my train of thought a couple of times during a broadcast because I was thinking about my grammar. If I tried to focus on my grammar during a broadcast, I started sounding like a robot. I needed to be spontaneous.

So I work on my grammar around the house, and in general conversation. And I've studied, too. Pam bought me a book, *Woe Is I,* by Patricia T. O'Connor, which has helped, but also has made me realize just how screwed up the English language is. I've never been much of a book reader, but she said my grammar would improve if I read more. I told Pam I didn't want to get rid of all of the bad grammar. I'm still going to throw in the occasional "ain't," because that's me.

Another mistake I made early in the 2001 season was to spend time on the Internet Web sites that are devoted to viewer critiques of race broadcasts. Praise and criticism seem to come in equal measure. Of course, the criticism always stands out. I spent about 20 or 30 minutes one day reading the comments, and it screwed me up big time. The way I look at it, if you don't have anything better to do than dwell on every detail of how we broadcast a race, you've got too much spare time on your hands. But we all know NASCAR fans can get pretty fanatical.

Our FOX team is not only good on the air, I doubt we can be beat when it comes to logistics. I've never seen a group of people put so much effort into getting out of a jam-packed racetrack after a race. I used to think Dale Earnhardt put more energy and effort into how he was going to get out of a racetrack than he did in actually running the race. But our production team is every bit as dedicated about this as Dale was.

At Las Vegas, which is famous for bad traffic, Pam and her assistant, Nelson Crozier, and others on the production team devised an escape route from the speedway unlike any I had ever seen. We drove over mountains and through valleys. We went down private roads, dirt roads, and roads that had big signs saying, "No trespassing! Violators will be prosecuted." For all I know, we went 100 miles out of our way. But they had a basic rule: "As long as we're moving, we're happy." And, by gosh, they got us back to our hotel near the strip in less than an hour. A lot of fans were still sitting in traffic at the track, and we were sitting down to dinner.

Texas Motor Speedway is another track with notoriously bad traffic. In 1998, Richard Childress and Dale Earnhardt carefully planned their escape. I was in on the deal. After the race, we were to catch a helicopter ride from the infield over to Alliance Airport, an awesome little airport just three miles from the track. We must have waited on that helicopter for three hours. We could have walked to the airport and got there quicker. The guy who lined up the chopper kept saying, "About 10 more minutes. About 10 more minutes." He did that for two hours. I'm sure that flight cost $150 or more per person. I told Richard we should have walked and saved the money.

After we broadcast the race at Texas in 2001, I was included in the FOX escape plan. A number of people on our broadcast team had booked flights that were scheduled to leave the Dallas–Fort Worth airport not long after the race. My flight was a little later, but I arranged with Artie Kempner to ride in his van. I had my motorcoach driver, Donald "Fat Boy" Epling, take my rental car back to the airport on Saturday night.

On race morning, I met with Artie to find out exactly where the van would be and what time I needed to be there. I was to meet them in the infield media center parking lot as soon as possible after the end of the broadcast. I felt comfortable with the arrangement. After the broadcast, I couldn't have gotten to that parking lot any quicker than I did.

When I got there, I saw no van. I had an uneasy feeling. After 10 minutes, the uneasy feeling turned into a bad feeling, a really bad feeling. Where were they? I knew they weren't going to screw around—they had early flights. After about 15 minutes, I called Artie's cell phone. I got his voice mail and left a message. I called Pam Miller. She answered. She said they were headed up the highway toward the airport. I asked her if she knew where Artie was. She told me that Artie's van had departed in front of her!

"Pam! He left me!" I cried.

"No way he would have left you," she said.

While I was talking to Pam, Nelson Crozier called Artie. This time, he answered. Yes, he'd left me behind. I lost it. I went off on Pam. Nelson told Pam that Artie said he'd come back and get me. "How in hell is he going to do that?" I said. "He's going to be going the wrong way against 90,000 cars leaving the racetrack!"

There I was, without a rental car and without a ride to the airport. What was I to do? Should I go find Fat Boy and tell him I was riding home with him in the motorcoach—a two-day trip? In the media center, I found a good friend of mine, Steve Rose, a racing photographer. He was carrying a suitcase. He had the look of a man headed to the airport. "Sure, Larry, I'll give you a ride," he said.

After we left the track, I was amazed at the lack of traffic. We drove to the airport as if there hadn't been a race within 100 miles of us. I actually got on an earlier flight. Artie called me while I was standing in the ticket line. He was very apologetic, but I still wasn't very happy and let him know it. I did everything but hang up on him. The incident became legendary among the FOX broadcast team. Artie is sometimes introduced as "the guy who left Larry behind at Texas."

One of my favorite events to cover has been the Food City 500 at Bristol Motor Speedway in April. The racing is so good there that, back in the late 1980s, before the night races in August, we'd try to hurry up and get our work done so we could get out of the infield before the Busch race on Friday. We'd pack up a big cooler full of beer and go sit on the hillside up in turn two and watch the race.

Back then, they could fit maybe 35,000 people in the grandstands along the front and back straights. They used to have seats at the very bottom of the grandstands that were actually below the surface of the track. The people sitting in those first few rows couldn't see the track at all. All they could see was the wall in front of them, the sky above them, and the grandstands around them. One day I asked a sheriff's deputy at the gate, "Why in the world would anybody ever think about purchasing a seat down there?"

"People stand in line for those seats," he said to me. "They call 'em 'pit people.' Yeah, you can't see any of the race, but down there they can smell those cars, they can hear 'em, and they can feel 'em. And besides, they drink so much beer down there and get so drunk, they don't know what world they're in anyway."

From the broadcast booth high above the track, Darrell said the race looked like a conveyor belt running wide open. At Bristol, before a competitor even goes inside the track, it's best for him to take his feelings out of his body and park them on the edge of Route 34 outside the speedway. Because if he didn't, those feelings were going to get hurt—and hurt more than once—during the course of the race weekend. By the time it's over, drivers are mad at drivers, crew chiefs are mad at drivers, drivers are mad at crew chiefs, everyone is mad at NASCAR, and a bunch of cars are torn up. And in 2001, Darrell and I had our first run-in with NASCAR as broadcasters.

I wasn't too worried about being politically correct with NASCAR. I didn't have to worry anymore about getting a car through inspection. But even as a crew chief, I had taken NASCAR to task many times. And I'd had my share of trips to the NASCAR transporter. As Darrell and I saw it, we had to answer only to FOX.

In the Busch race at Bristol, Kevin Harvick had been leading, but came out of the pits in second after a round of pit stops late in the race, trailing Randy LaJoie. A car on the tail end of the lead lap was in front of Randy. NASCAR has a rule that on restarts, when the green flag is displayed, you can only begin to pass the car in front of you, and only on the right, when you reach a designated point before the start-finish line—such as the end of the pit wall.

When the green flag came out, the lead car didn't go. Randy was boxed in, so he couldn't go. Kevin saw an opening to the outside, and he passed those boys on the right and took the lead. NASCAR black-flagged him for jumping the restart and made him come in for a stop-and-go penalty. Kevin finished seventh. The ruling may have cost him the race.

We had replays from a number of angles, but the best one was from turn one, looking down the frontstretch. It showed plain as day that the green flag was out and waving before Kevin ever made his move. We strongly challenged NASCAR. In fact, Darrell blurted out: "This is bull——!" It went out over the airwaves. He thought we were on break.

We weren't. Darrell was more worried about his wife, Stevie, coming down on him than anyone else.

NASCAR Control was several booths over. I looked over. Kevin Triplett, NASCAR's director of operations, was glaring at us and waving his hand in the air like, "What are you guys saying?" We came to discover that Kevin was the one who made the call. After a while, Mike Helton came in. In a nice way, he told Darrell and me: "You guys broadcast the race. Let us call the race."

And that's NASCAR's way. It will probably always be NASCAR's way. I respect NASCAR, but everyone knows it's like a dictatorship. And to some degree it needs to be. They saw their call like a balls-and-strikes call. Even if they're wrong, they're sticking to their call. The bottom line is Darrell and I knew they were wrong and called them on it.

The next morning, Kevin Harvick was still livid. Kevin said he went into the NASCAR trailer to review the matter. They looked at some of the replays. Kevin had seen the replay Darrell and I had focused on. "Let's look at that one," he said. And they immediately said, "No, that one doesn't have a good shot of it." NASCAR would not look at that replay because they knew it told the truth. Sometimes NASCAR isn't very good about admitting their mistakes. But as I said, it doesn't matter who you are, you need to leave your feelings out on the curb before you come in Bristol Motor Speedway.

I had been friends with Kevin Triplett for quite a while, but when I saw him in Texas the week after Bristol, he almost turned his nose up at me. Kevin's frostiness lasted a couple weeks, but soon we were on the best of terms again. NASCAR has a right to make mistakes. After all, NASCAR's people are human, too. But they need to be like the rest of us and admit it when they make a bad call.

Our broadcasts continued to be more popular than ever. Bristol was the sixth consecutive race where our TV rating was higher than a six.

In 2000, the only NASCAR Winston Cup race besides the Daytona 500 to get a rating as high as a six was the race in Texas, which scored a six. At Texas in 2001, we scored an even seven—one full point better than 2000. Our ratings continued strong throughout the rest of our broadcast season. We exceeded the 2001 ratings in every race but one, and most by more than a full point.

Our broadcast season ended after the road race at Sears Point at the halfway point of the Winston Cup season. NBC had the contract to broadcast the second half of the season and the 2002 Daytona 500. Then we took over again in 2002 at Rockingham and finished our season with the Pepsi 400 at Daytona.

I have to believe that our success at FOX was intimidating to some at NBC, particularly Benny Parsons, one of their color analysts. In the Michigan garage in June, Benny approached and lit right into me: "You need to straighten your language out, Larry," he said. "Your grammar is terrible. It's hurting our sport." He went on and on.

I was at a loss for words. But I'm glad he went on like he did, because it gave me a chance to cool down. "Benny, I sure appreciate that," I told him. "It's something I'm already working on." But he was way out of line. I doubt I'll ever have much respect for Benny Parsons again. I tried to be friendly to him at a celebrity golf tournament in 2002, but he was still as frosty as could be.

Perhaps it has something to do with the ratings. As it turned out, our average rating for 2001 NASCAR telecasts was almost a full point higher than NBC's. Mike Joy had told me after the encounter with Parsons, "Larry, they're worried to death they won't even come close to competing with us."

Our ratings certainly made our blunders easier to accept. During the Winston Cup broadcast at Talladega in April 2001, I had one of those moments any broadcaster fears. It's like shooting an air ball in basketball or hitting a shank in golf. I started to say something, and I totally forgot what I was going to say. I had my thought and was ready to say it, but someone else said something that distracted me and suddenly I was in a panic, thinking, "Oh God, what was I going to say?" I danced through it, and I am sure there were some keen listeners who picked up on it, but at least I didn't freeze.

At one point during the broadcast of the 2001 Busch race at Charlotte in May, I was listening to the producers, who were talking in my ear. At the same time, Darrell was directing a question at me, but I didn't realize it until after he asked it. I had no idea what his question was. All I knew was that he had been talking about one car's problem and said something about "Monday."

I responded, "Well, if I'm crew chief, what I'm going to do is have a big meeting on Monday. And I am going to try to figure out not who did it, but why it happened."

I didn't have a clue whether I'd answered his question. As it turned out, I more or less had. The question was: When you have something like a shock fall off, what do you do with your race team? I told Darrell we must be getting pretty good if he could ask me a question I didn't hear, and I could still manage to answer it.

In the hot weather, a common practice for broadcast cameramen is to find pretty women with the least amount of clothing. It was warm enough at Talladega in April, and during breaks that weekend, a producer would often speak in our ears, "Check your Iso monitor." Then we'd see women in bikinis, women in halter tops, women in short shorts. They even found one woman who decided she didn't want anything on top. We didn't do it much during the races—maybe a little during breaks—but the cameramen sure had fun with it during the qualifying and practice shows.

Along those same lines, before the race at California Speedway in April, I was invited with most of the FOX team to the Playboy Mansion. I declined the invitation. I know 95 percent of males in this country would not pass up an opportunity like this, but I wasn't really that interested, and I would have had to change my travel plans.

Besides, here I applied the same philosophy that Bobby Allison had. When Davey complained about someone getting into him, Bobby said, "If you stick your finger in a rattlesnake's mouth, you can't get mad when it bites you."

In my position, I don't need to put myself in any situation where there's even a potential of something embarrassing happening. I enjoy bars and nightclubs as much as anyone, but when I'm on the road you won't often find me in them. When Linda is with me, we go out and enjoy ourselves immensely. But I generally stay away from clubs when I'm out of town by myself. The last thing I want is even the appearance of a problem, because I love my wife more than anything on this earth. She has been my backbone, my supporter, my cheerleader—everything you could ask a wife to be. Now if Linda had come to California, both of us would have gone and had a great time.

To give you a personal example of how stuff gets started, several years ago Linda had her hair cut pretty short. Soon after that, she and I went to a nightclub during an off weekend. A little over a week later, a rumor got started at Brooke's dance studio. Someone told someone who told the lady at the dance studio that I was seen at a nightclub with another woman. Whoever saw us didn't recognize Linda with her new haircut. That was more confirmation that people like to talk about people— especially people in the limelight—and how you need to be really careful to avoid even the appearance of impropriety.

The history of NASCAR, of course, is filled with stories of partying and carousing, but I don't think there's anywhere near as much of it going on now as in the past. There are a multitude of reasons for that. Financially, a driver has a lot more to lose today than he used to. And the environment for the driver is a lot different now.

Twenty years ago, most wives didn't travel with their husbands, because you stayed in motels and traveled in cars and vans. Today, almost every driver has his own plane and his own motorcoach. The motorcoach is home for a driver and his family at the racetrack. It's a much more family-oriented atmosphere in the infield. So I think the opportunity for carousing is far rarer today than it was, say, 20 years ago. If any of my drivers fooled around or engaged in questionable behavior, I never witnessed it. If I had seen it, or strongly suspected it, I think I would have said something.

I feel just as much pressure being a broadcaster as a crew chief, but there's far less stress. My life these days is a lot more complicated. That's been the biggest surprise. During most of my years as a crew chief, I was focused on one thing—race car preparation. Now my life is all over the place. In addition to the FOX broadcasts, I'm doing work for the shows "Totally NASCAR," "NASCAR Tech," and "Trackside." I do radio interviews, write a column for the Crew Chief Club Web site, and I keep my own Web site (www.larrymcreynolds.com) and have various speaking engagements.

During the second half of the 2001 season, when we weren't on the air, I went to every race because I did consulting work for Petty Enterprises. But in 2002, my schedule was full of more broadcast work. On the Friday night before every race in the first half of the season, I did the live "Trackside" show with Steve Byrnes, Darrell, and Jeff Hammond on the Speed Channel, which is now owned by FOX. In the second half of 2002, I'm doing the same show from each race track with Jeff, Mike Joy, and Michael Waltrip.

These days it almost seems like my days are longer. Sometimes the only thing you can do is say "no" to people who want a piece of your time. By the time you read this, I'll probably have a business manager, so he can wear the black hat. I'm also recognized a lot more because of the exposure I get on television. Linda and I had the opportunity in 2001 to spend three May nights in Cancun, Mexico. Even there, I couldn't totally get away from it. Some of the other American tourists there knew about racing, of course. I signed a few autographs and chatted with the fans.

One of the greatest things about my broadcast career is that I've had more time for my family. After the race at Talladega in April 2001, I took time out during the week to do something I had wanted to do for a long, long time. I visited my grandfather, James Rogers, at his home in Panama City Beach, Florida. He was almost 102 years old then. I had lived with "Pa-Pa" and his late wife, Mary, while I was in elementary school.

I spent the better part of two days with him. He lived with his girlfriend, who was in her 80s. He still drove. He had the mind of a 60-year-old. He liked to show people his driver's license, because his birth year was listed as "99." He was born in 1899. He was pushing 100 when he moved to Florida, but he drove the car himself and towed a U-Haul trailer. It was good that I saw him when I did, because Pa-Pa had a heart attack a few months later. He survived, but moved back to Birmingham with my Aunt Noreen. He slowly went downhill and died in December 2001.

I also get to see my daughter Brooke's dance recitals, and I can work with my son, Brandon, on the Bandolero cars he races on the quarter-mile track in front of the main grandstand at Lowe's Motor Speedway. Sometimes, I find myself juggling my son's racing schedule against my work schedule. At Charlotte in May 2001 on Coca-Cola 600 qualifying day, I had to be in the booth around 6:30 p.m. to get ready for qualifying. Brandon was racing on the quarter-mile track. I was helping as much as I could, sweating up a storm in my good FOX clothes.

Fortunately, Matt Yocum, who wasn't doing the qualifying show, and Jimmy Fowler, a friend of ours, were helping out.

Brandon's motor started missing in practice. So we took the bonnet off and found a fouled spark plug. No matter how hard I try to be Dad, some of that crew chief in me keeps oozing out. No matter how hard I try to just make it a fun thing, sometimes that crew chief in me spills out and I'm focused once again on figuring out what to do to go faster and to win.

But I was looking at my watch as we changed the plug. Just about the time we finished, I said, "You guys are on your own. I've got to go to the booth." It's hard juggling helping your son and doing your job. But Neil Goldberg told me to take as much time as I needed. And our camera guys knew Brandon was racing down on the track, so they'd put his car on the Iso monitor for me. Darrell, of course, gave me a hard time about how rough the car was running.

The 2002 season was just as good a broadcast year for me as 2001. Some of our broadcasts, such as the ones at Talladega and California, rated higher than in 2001. At Talladega, we hit a seven rating—FOX's highest since 2001 Rockingham. And we dominated our main competition—the NBA Playoffs. Our broadcast on the FX cable network of the Martinsville race in April 2002 topped out at 4.5—the highest rated sports show ever broadcast on FX.

Personally, one of the most flattering things happened in early March, when FOX told me they had decided to exercise the final two "option" years on my four-year contract. They didn't have to do that until August, but they went ahead after only one race in 2002. So now I know what I'm going to be doing at least through 2004.

The real difference between being a crew chief and a broadcaster is that when I left the track as a crew chief on bad days, I realized that sometimes there was nothing I could have done that would have made a difference. The driver could have been in a bad mood, or the pit crew was off, or NASCAR's rules didn't give us a chance. There were so many things I simply couldn't control. But when I leave that broadcast booth, I know that whether the show was good or bad, the only person I could pin it on was the guy I see in my bathroom mirror every morning.

But the question that people ask me the most is "Do you miss being a crew chief?" I miss it on some days. I mostly miss the competition and the camaraderie and the challenge of making a car go fast. I often say that if I didn't miss it some, I'd feel as if I wasted almost 20 years of my working life. But when I look at the FOX team I work with, and the friends I've made, and how much fun I'm having, I have to say that I don't miss my old job all that much. I look forward to every broadcast. I even look forward to Tuesday's conference calls.

I always try to live and work by the Golden Rule, and treat people the way I would want to be treated myself. I never asked anyone on the race teams to do anything I wouldn't do, to work hours I wouldn't work. As a good crew chief I wanted to be the one who turned on all the lights in the morning and shut them off at night. I also believed in communicating with people and involving them in meetings and other decision-making processes so they'd feel that they were participating as much with their brains as with their hands. I listened to everybody's ideas and showed them respect for their contributions.

It's fulfilling to have seen a lot of the younger guys who worked under me go on to become successful crew chiefs, such as Ryan Pemberton and Jimmy Elledge. I may have put them through hell sometimes, but once they become crew chiefs, at some point they all seem to come back and say, "You know, Larry, I now understand why you sometimes were the way you were. Before, I never had a clue what it was like."

One of the things that makes me proudest is the loyalty that my approach has created among the crewmen I've worked with, from as far back as eight or nine years ago, and even the Kenny Bernstein days. Many times during the season, one of the guys will come up to me and say, "Larry, I'm still waiting. If you ever get that race team of your own or you ever go back to being a crew chief, I want to come be a part of that and work with you again."

I still love this sport as much as I did 20 years ago. Because of the love I have for broadcasting and the people we've assembled and the tools we've been given to work with, the pleasure wipes out most of the fantasies I might have about resuming a life as a top crew chief. But I'm smart enough to realize that nothing is forever. Will I still be a NASCAR broadcaster in 10 years? I can't answer that question. Would I be devastated if I wasn't? No, I don't think so.

I always tell myself that I have to take a step back and look at the big picture. And the big picture is that one day I may have to go back in that garage again as a crew chief or a team manager or a consultant. If I have to do that, I'll simply feel as if I've completed one big circle—one big lap—in my career in NASCAR stock-car racing, which is the best racing in the world.

INDEX

Index

A

A & S Auto Parts, 39
A posts, 340
ABC's Wide World of Sports, 375-376
AC Delco 500, 122-123
aerodynamics, 115, 116, 126, 137, 179, 215, 298, 349-350
air dams, 148, 284, 285, 349
air induction, 76
air pressure, 183
Alabama, 197
Alexander, Mike, 35-37, 40, 44-46, 80
Allison, Bobby
  Clifford Allison's death and, 160-161
  Davey Allison's death and, 195
  Neil Bonnett and, 209
  crashes, 73, 153
  Darlington and, 49
  Dodge and, 345
  Ernie Irvan and, 204
  Jimmy Morris Sportsmanship Award and, 33
  National 500 and, 47
  philosophy of, 385
  Raybestos Chevrolet and, 132
  relationship with Davey Allison, 129, 143, 187-189, 385
  on Darrell Waltrip, 158-159
  Winston Cup and, 19, 173
  Robert Yates and, 199, 201

Allison, Clifford, 155, 160-162, 199
Allison, Davey
  Clifford Allison's death and, 160-162, 199
  Atlanta and, 172-176
  brake problems, 136-137
  Bristol and, 104-105, 181-182
  Busch Clash and, 127-128
  Champion Spark Plug 400 and, 119-120
  Charlotte and, 185
  church attendance of, 68, 91
  Coca-Cola 600 and, 108-111, 139-143, 148

crashes, 100, 128, 133, 142-143, 153-156, 163-164, 176-177
  Darlington and, 148
  Daytona and, 178
  death of, 192-197, 225, 273, 298, 367-368, 369
  Dale Earnhardt and, 109-110, 131
  as helicopter pilot, 189-191
  injuries sustained by, 134-137, 143-162
  Ernie Irvan and, 128, 137, 166, 175-176, 187, 203
  Martinsville and, 106, 183-184
  Larry McReynolds and, 105-197
  New Hampshire and, 186-188
  North Carolina Motor Speedway and, 179
  North Wilkesboro and, 183-184
  pit stops and, 135
  Pocono and, 151-152, 176-177, 185
  relationship with Bobby Allison, 129, 143, 187-189, 385
  Richmond and, 179-181
  Sears Point and, 185
  Southern 500 and, 120
  Talladega and, 106-107, 156, 184-185
  victories of, 107-109, 111, 113-115
  Darrell Waltrip and, 103, 105, 150, 152, 154, 158
  Winston Cup ranking, 116-117, 125
Allison, Donnie, 40-41, 48-49, 51, 82, 115
Allison, Edmond J. "Pop," 131, 134
Allison, Elisa, 160
Allison, Judy, 115, 155, 195
Allison, Liz, 68, 138, 160, 192-193, 197
Allison, Pam, 115
Allison, Robby, 121
Allison, Tommy, 160
All-Pro/Grand American, 55-56
American Speed Association championship, 31
Andretti, John, 242, 266-267, 277, 310

"Angels Among Us," 369
antennas, 215
ARCA race, 78, 115, 155, 220-221
Armstrong, Ron, 80, 83, 86, 96
Arute, Jack, 89
Atlanta Motor Speedway, 68, 76, 79, 86, 92, 100, 103, 125, 172-176, 211-212, 235, 315, 330-331, 333-334
  true oval shape of, 284-285
  weather and, 180-181

B

backup cars, 86, 128, 146-147, 224-225, 266
backup motors, 109
Baker, Buck, 345
Baker, Buddy, 265, 286
Bandolero cars, 387
Bascilli, Richie, 375-376
Batson, Gary, 140-141
Beadle, Raymond, 52
Beam, Mike, 138
Beaty, Dick, 134, 148
Beaver, Dale, 368
Benson, Johnny, 242
Berggren, Dick, 342
Bernstein, Kenny
  Brett Bodine and, 92
  Dangler and, 77, 87
  engine design and, 82-84
  Hawkins's team purchase, 69-70
  Larry McReynolds and, 69-103, 245, 390
  North Wilkesboro win and, 95-96
  Ricky Rudd and, 79, 91-92, 99
  Joe Ruttman and, 75
  staff salaries and, 98
Beveridge, Gary, 215, 272
bias-ply tires, 284
Birmingham International Raceway (BIR)
  championship at, 31
  description of, 18-19
  Grand National, 19
  Jimmy Morris Sportsmanship Award and, 33
  Jones and, 29
  "Larry McReynolds Night" at, 333
  racing schedule at, 16